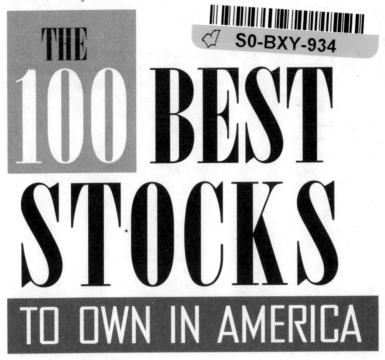

THE 100 BEST STOCKS

TO OWN IN AMERICA

SEVENTH EDITION

Gene Walden

Dearborn
Trade Publishing
A **Kaplan Professional** Company

This publication is designed to provide accurate and authoritative information in regard to the subject matter covered. It is sold with the understanding that the publisher is not engaged in rendering legal, accounting, or other professional service. If legal advice or other expert assistance is required, the services of a competent professional person should be sought.

Vice President and Publisher: Cynthia A. Zigmund
Editorial Director: Donald J. Hull
Senior Managing Editor: Jack Kiburz
Interior Design: Lucy Jenkins
Cover Design: design literate, inc.
Typesetting: the dotted i

Library of Congress Cataloging-in-Publication Data

Walden, Gene.
    The 100 best stocks to own in America / Gene Walden.—7th ed.
        p.   cm.
    Includes index.
    ISBN 0-7931-4436-1
    1. Stocks—United States.   I. Title.   II. Title: One hundred best stocks to own in America.
HG4963.W35   2001
332.63′22′0973—dc21

Dedication

To Laurie, Whit, and Ryan

Contents

Alphabetical Listing of the 100 Best Stocks

Abbott Laboratories (61)
ABM Industries (69)
AFLAC, Inc. (40)
Alliance Capital Management
   Holding (1)
Altera Corp. (82)
American International Group,
   Inc. (67)
Amgen, Inc. (50)
Anheuser-Busch Companies, Inc.
   (52)
AOL Time Warner, Inc. (85)
Automatic Data Processing, Inc.
   (46)
Avery Dennison Corp. (71)
BB&T Corp. (25)
Bed Bath & Beyond, Inc. (33)
Bemis Company (80)
Best Buy Company, Inc. (65)
Biogen, Inc. (79)
Biomet, Inc. (76)
Bristol-Myers Squibb Co. (38)
Cambrex Corp. (78)
Cardinal Health (30)
Chevron Corp. (87)
Cintas Corp. (21)
Cisco Systems (93)
Coca-Cola Co. (97)
Colgate-Palmolive Co. (39)
ConAgra Foods, Inc. (91)
Concord EFS, Inc. (32)
Danaher Corp. (49)
Dell Computer Corp. (57)
Dionex Corp. (95)
Donaldson Company, Inc. (44)
Ecolab, Inc. (43)

EMC Corp. (59)
Emerson Electric Co. (81)
Equifax, Inc. (96)
Fannie Mae (10)
Fastenal Co. (34)
Fifth Third Bancorp (4)
First Data Corp. (90)
Fiserv, Inc. (29)
Franklin Resources, Inc. (45)
Freddie Mac (12)
General Electric Co. (11)
Harley-Davidson, Inc. (13)
Hershey Foods Co. (94)
Home Depot, Inc. (19)
Household International, Inc. (23)
Intel Corp. (41)
Interpublic Group of Companies
   (47)
Jefferson-Pilot Corp. (42)
Johnson & Johnson (15)
Jones Apparel Group, Inc. (72)
Kohl's Corp. (26)
The Kroger Co. (66)
Legg Mason, Inc. (35)
Eli Lilly & Co. (73)
Linear Technology Corp. (48)
M&T Bank Corp. (24)
Maxim Integrated Products (54)
MBNA Corp. (20)
McDonald's Corp. (92)
Medtronic, Inc. (8)
Merck & Company, Inc. (9)
Microsoft Corp. (31)
Herman Miller (89)
Molex, Inc. (99)
Omnicom Group, Inc. (18)

Acknowledgments

With some 17,000 facts, figures, calculations, and computations, and more than 300 charts, graphs, and tables, this book has been a massive undertaking that required the efforts of several important contributors. Larry Nelson, who has helped with nearly every book I've written since 1990, worked from start to finish on the project, assisting with the research, fact gathering, and number crunching, as well as compiling many of the graphs, tables, and other key elements of the book.

I also want to thank Jack Kiburz, senior managing editor at Dearborn Trade, who has been the managing editor of 17 of my books dating back to 1987. Once again, Jack handled the editing and production coordination for this book. And I want to thank Don Hull, editorial director, Cynthia Zigmund, vice president and publisher, and Sandy Thomas, senior editorial assistant, who have all contributed along the way to help shape the book into an attractive, professional format.

Introduction

I'm easily satisfied with the very best.
                    —Winston Churchill

It might be the understatement of the decade to say that the stock market has endured some turbulent times in the two years since the last edition of *The 100 Best Stocks to Own in America* was published. Even before the World Trade Center attacks put an exclamation point on an already flagging economy, technology stocks had crashed and dozens of Internet companies had gone under. Sales and manufacturing across a wide range of industries had slowed dramatically, and layoffs had climbed to the highest level in years.

Yet through it all, an amazing thing happened: the 100 Best stocks went up—many dramatically. This underscores what investment experts have been saying for years: If you want to succeed in the stock market over the long term, nothing succeeds like success. Through seven editions of this book, I've picked the most obvious stock prospects in the market—the ones that had posted record earnings and revenue year in and year out for many years—and watched them outperform the overall market consistently. Certainly there are exceptions, but generally speaking, blue chip stocks with solid track histories have been the best bet for long-term investors.

In the 24-month period after the sixth edition of this book was published (September 1999 through September 2001), the 15 top-ranked stocks in the book rewarded shareholders with an average annual return of 33.7 percent. (See chart on page xiv.) During the same period, the Nasdaq plunged 34 percent, the Dow dipped 8 percent, and Standard & Poor's dropped 14 percent.

What accounts for that dramatic disparity? The secret is in the selection process. I've made a point over the years of ignoring short-term trends in favor of the long-term picture. That's not always the most popular approach. When the sixth edition was published in 1999, investors largely ignored that all-star list of blue chips in favor of the high-flying tech stocks with short histories and no earnings. And that was despite the fact that the top-ten stocks in the fifth edition had posted a 97 percent return over the previous two years. Investors were looking instead for speculative start-ups such as Exodus, Ask Jeeves, and Excite@Home—all of which are now trading for just pennies, along with dozens of other fallen Net darlings.

What is the lesson for the millions of investors who collectively lost more than $5 trillion in the Nasdaq meltdown? Think of every investment cliché you've ever heard, and that's the lesson: Diversify. Be patient. Don't get greedy. Don't follow the crowd. Buy low, sell high. Load your portfolio with stocks of companies with a proven track record. And, if an investment sector seems too good to be true, it probably is.

There is nothing wrong with buying technology stocks and promising young companies as part of a diversified portfolio. Over the years, small stocks and tech stocks have certainly enjoyed some strong gains. But if you want to avoid the type of volatility and financial pain many investors have endured with their portfolios in recent years, diversification is essential. Build a portfolio that includes blue chips from a wide range of industries, along with a selection of smaller stocks and technology companies. The purpose of this book is to help you identify the best-performing blue chip stocks of the past decade.

SIXTH EDITION PERFORMANCE

The following chart shows the two-year performance of the top-ranked stocks from the sixth edition of *The 100 Best Stocks to Own in America.* (The number two stock from that book, Firstar Financial, was acquired by US Bank shortly after publication, so Firstar was replaced by the 16th ranked stock to round out the top 15.)

Stock	Rank in book	Stock price ($) 9/1/1999	Stock price ($) 9/1/2001	2-year dividend ($)	Total return (%)
Medtronic	1	39.19	45.54	0.36	17.1
Firstar (acquired 11/00)	2	NA	NA	NA	NA
Home Depot	3	40.59	45.95	0.31	14.0
Alliance Capital	4	27.44	52.36	6.05	123.5
Paychex	5	19.44	37.07	0.55	93.5
Schering-Plough	6	52.63	38.13	1.10	−25.5
Fifth Third Bancorp	7	43.75	58.30	1.35	36.3
General Electric	8	37.25	40.98	1.28	13.4
Merck	9	69.19	65.10	2.52	−2.3
Procter & Gamble	10	99.25	74.15	2.68	−22.6
Fannie Mae	11	62.13	76.21	2.26	26.3
State Street Corp.	12	29.94	64.43	0.67	64.4
Franklin Resources	13	35.94	41.03	0.48	15.4
Johnson & Johnson	14	51.38	52.71	1.24	5.0
Synovus Financial	15	18.81	30.80	0.84	68.2
Harley-Davidson	16	27.25	48.59	0.21	79.1
Average return					**33.7%**

	24-month gain/loss
Nasdaq Composite	−34.1%
Dow Jones Industrial Average	−8.1
S&P 500 Index	−14.2
Best 100 (top 15)	+33.7%

For the period Sept. 1, 1999, through Sept. 20, 2001

WELCOME TO THE SEVENTH EDITION

As in past editions, this edition is loaded with industry leaders from a wide range of sectors. Among the leading sectors are medical companies, banks and financial services firms, retailers, food makers, and corporate services operations. There are also a number of technology companies, including software, telecommunications, biotechnology, and semiconductor manufacturers.

The number one ranked stock in this edition is Alliance Capital Management, an investment company that operates a large family of mutual funds and manages corporate pension plans for many of the nation's largest companies. Alliance has seen its stock price climb 32 percent per year for the past ten years, including a 120 percent gain over the past two years. And it pays a dividend that has averaged more than 7 percent over the past five years. The company has posted 12 consecutive years of record earnings and revenue.

Rounding out the top ten are Paychex, a payroll outsourcing operation; U.S. Bancorp, a Minneapolis-based bank holding company; Fifth Third Bancorp, a Cincinnati-based bank; Pfizer, a leading pharmaceutical maker; T. Rowe Price, an investment firm; SouthTrust Corp., a bank; Medtronic, the world's leading heart pacemaker manufacturer; Merck, a leading pharmaceutical maker; and Fannie Mae, the nation's leading provider of mortgage funding.

This edition features 67 stocks that were also in the sixth edition, and 33 that are new to the 100 Best list. Seven stocks that had been in all six previous editions were excluded from this edition due to slowing growth: Albertson's, RPM, Bank One, Genuine Parts, Walt Disney, Heinz, and American Home Products. There are now just 18 companies that have been in all seven editions: Abbott Laboratories, PepsiCo, Anheuser-Busch, Automatic Data Processing, Sara Lee, Bemis, Bristol-Myers Squibb, ConAgra, Sherwin-Williams, Fifth Third Bancorp, Valspar, Hershey, Wal-Mart, Walgreen, McDonald's, Merck, Pitney Bowes, and William Wrigley.

FUTURE PROSPECTS

This book makes no pretense of projecting the future performance of any stock. The rankings are based strictly on the past performance of the companies. But in previous editions, many of the stocks enjoyed exceptional performance.

I looked at several factors in selecting stocks for the list: Has the company had consistent earnings, revenue, and stock price growth for the past ten years (or longer)? Is the company well diversified? Is it a leader in its market sector? Has it had solid stock growth over the past ten years? Out of the more than 2,000 stocks I evaluated for this book, the companies listed here have all passed with flying colors. They are the 100 major, publicly traded U.S. corporations that have fared the best over the past decade and given their shareholders the most.

Although there is no assurance that any of these companies will outperform the market in the years to come, they do have a couple of strong points in their favor. For one, each company listed here has proven its ability to compete as a market leader in one or more areas. Their concepts are working. Their lines of products or services have made an impact in the marketplace and have been highly profitable over the past 10 to 15 years. Each of these companies has a management team that has also proven capable of turning a buck on a consistent basis. They've ridden the ups and downs of the economy over the past decade, survived the rash of mergers and acquisitions (and probably made a few of their own), weathered the downtimes, and have still come away with an outstanding record of earnings and stock price growth. Presumably, most of these companies will continue their success throughout this decade.

Although it is certainly possible that companies like Abbott Laboratories (30 consecutive years of record earnings) and Automatic Data Processing (51 consecutive years of double-digit growth in both earnings and revenues) could slip into a sudden free fall after decades of uninterrupted growth, the odds would seem to bode otherwise.

Traditionally, the type of top-quality stocks selected for the 100 Best tend to do very well compared with the overall market. For instance, a portfolio of the top-40 ranked stocks of the first edition of this book (published in 1989) would have grown 102 percent over the following five years—a record good enough to outperform 89 percent of all mutual funds for that period. The top-ten picks of the fifth edition were up 97 percent in the first two years after publication—a performance record that surpassed well over 90 percent of all mutual funds for the same period. And, as noted earlier, the stocks of the sixth edition also dramatically outperformed the overall market and would have topped 98 percent of all mutual funds.

THE CASE FOR STOCKS

Although an individual's first investment priority should be money in the bank—everyone needs a cash cushion to fall back on—stocks should be a key component of any well-balanced portfolio. Why buy stocks rather than collecting that safe, consistent flow of interest earnings a bank account would offer? Here are some numbers to reflect on.

On average, over the past 75 years—including the stock market crash of 1929, the crash of 1987, and the bear markets of 2000 and 2001—stocks have provided an average annual return of about 11 percent. That's roughly double the return of bonds and three times the return of money market funds. The difference is even more dramatic when put in real dollar terms. A dollar invested in U.S. government bonds in 1925 would have grown to about $37 by 2000. That same dollar invested in the broad stock market would have grown to nearly $1,800 during the same period. While stocks may have their ups and downs, if you can live with the volatility, you would be a far richer investor by keeping your money in the stock market.

Sometimes stock market investing requires great patience. Stock performance can vary dramatically from one ten-year period to another. An investor entering the market in 1965, for instance, would have experienced an agonizing 1.2 percent average annual return over the next ten years. But an investor in the market from 1949 to 1958 would have reaped a 20 percent average annual return.

STOCKS OR STOCK MUTUAL FUNDS?

The other issue for many investors is whether to buy individual stocks or stock mutual funds. The fact is, mutual funds probably should be the investment of choice for many investors—particularly those who haven't the time, expertise, or resources to invest in a well-diversified selection of stocks. But if you have an interest in the market, the time to spend researching it, and the money to diversify your portfolio, individual stocks can offer several advantages over mutual funds.

For one thing, stocks are just more fun than funds. Investing in the market can be challenging, stimulating, sometimes nerve-racking, but ultimately very fulfilling. You pit your wits against the market and against the millions of other unseen investors who are also scouring the market for a bargain. It is a test of your insight, your shrewdness. At times, it can also be a test of your endurance during downturns in the market, and a test of your courage as you hold fast to your position in anticipation of that next market rally.

When you pick a winner, the results can be exhilarating. You watch the price move up. You see the stock split two-for-one. Suddenly, your 500 shares become 1,000. Your investment grows to a multiple of your initial outlay. You've won at the age-old game of picking stocks. And the victory is a boon not only to your pocketbook but to your ego as well. It's that psychological reward of picking a winner that motivates so many investors to set aside mutual funds and test their hand in the stock market.

There's also another important, though less publicized, reason to choose stocks over mutual funds. As they say, money is power. But it's only power if you use it as power. That means controlling it yourself and deciding exactly where each dollar is put to work. Socially conscious individuals who wouldn't dream of investing in companies that pollute the environment, produce tobacco products, or build weapons of mass destruction unwittingly invest in all those types of companies when they invest in stock mutual funds. Most mutual funds pay little heed to social concerns.

There are, of course, mutual funds that take an ethical approach and avoid investing in companies with questionable ethical connections. The problem is, when you invest in those funds you're still letting someone else decide the fate of your money. After all, you may not necessarily agree with all the fund's ideals. You might, for instance, enjoy a beer on a hot afternoon and see no reason to avoid investing in alcoholic beverage producers. You may prefer not to invest in a weapons manufacturing company, but you may think nuclear power is the best thing since windmills. So, a mutual fund that invests according to all the popular ethical issues of our time may not be exactly the investment for you. Stocks give you the freedom to make those choices for yourself.

RATING THE COMPANIES

In selecting the 100 companies for this book, I looked at a wide range of financial factors, the most important of which was earnings performance. I wanted companies with a long history of annual increases in earnings per share, because if a company is able to raise its earnings year after year, the stock price will ultimately follow.

Other factors such as revenue growth, stock price performance, and dividend yield also played into the screening process, but none carried the same weight as earnings growth. I made my selections after reviewing the financial histories of more than 2,000 major U.S. companies.

After narrowing the list to the final 100, the next step was to rank them 1 to 100 based on a four-part rating system. Each category is worth up to 4 points for a maximum of 16 points. The categories are *earnings per share growth, stock growth, consistency,* and *dividend.*

I've also tried to bridge the long-term performance with the short-term performance. Stock growth was judged on ten-year performance, while earnings growth and dividend growth were rated based on the most recent five-year period. And, finally, the consistency category rated stocks based on year-to-year earnings gains over a ten-year period. That gives the rating system a blend of the long term and the short term. Accompanying each company profile, you will see a ratings chart similar to this:

Earnings Growth	★ ★ ★ ★
Stock Growth	★ ★ ★
Consistency	★ ★ ★
Dividend	★ ★ ★
Total	**13 Points**

Each star represents one rating point. This company scored the maximum four points for stock growth and somewhat less for the other categories. The last line gives the total score.

The following charts offer an exact breakdown of the point system for the earnings and stock growth categories:

Earnings per Share Growth

5-Year Growth Rate	Average Annual Rate	Points Awarded
50% to 79%	9% to 12%	★ (1 point)
80% to 114%	13% to 16%	★ ★
115% to 139%	17% to 19%	★ ★ ★
145% and above	20% and above	★ ★ ★ ★

Stock Growth

10-Year Growth Rate	Average Annual Rate	Points Awarded
155% to 249%	10% to 13%	★ (1 point)
250% to 399%	14% to 17%	★ ★
400% to 599%	18% to 21%	★ ★ ★
600% and above	22% and above	★ ★ ★ ★

Consistency

A company that has had a flawless run of increases in earnings per share over the past ten years would score four points. The consistency of the stock price growth is not taken into account here, because the volatility in a stock price can often be dictated by market factors beyond the control of the company. But if the company is strong and growing steadily, the stock price, over time, should reflect that. Here is the scoring breakdown:

- 4 points—A company that has posted increased earnings for at least ten consecutive years
- 3 points—A company that has had a nearly flawless run of earnings increases, with gains nine of the past ten years
- 2 points—A company that has had a fairly consistent growth record, with earnings increases eight of the past ten years
- 1 point—A company that has been somewhat inconsistent, with earnings increases seven of the past ten years
- 0 points—A company with a very volatile growth record would score no points here, although it is very unlikely that a company would make the top 100 list if it has had fewer than seven years of increased earnings out of the past ten years.

Dividend

In previous editions of the book, I had two categories for dividends—yield and growth—plus another category for "perks" that awarded two more points to companies with dividend reinvestment plans (DRIPs). DRIPs allow shareholders to have their dividends automatically reinvested in additional stock and to purchase shares commission-free directly from the company. For example, Coca-Cola shareholders may buy up to $125,000 a year in additional shares through the company plan, and McDonald's shareholders may make up to $250,000 a year in commission-free stock purchases. About 80 of the companies in this book offer DRIPs.

Under the scoring system in the past, a company with a great dividend that it raised every year and that offered a dividend reinvestment plan would have scored 10 points higher than a company with no dividend. Although I believe a dividend is a positive factor for many investors—especially with a company that increases its dividend year in and year out—it is certainly not worth an extra ten points. In this edition, I've attempted to minimize the advantage by reducing dividends to a single four-point category. But the scoring is a little more complicated. Here is how it works:

For a perfect four points, a stock must have:

- A dividend yield of at least 2 percent
- At least nine consecutive years of increased dividends
- At least 70 percent growth in the dividend payout over the past five years
- A dividend reinvestment and stock purchase plan for shareholders

One point is deducted for growth of less than 70 percent. One point is deducted for fewer than nine consecutive years of dividend increases. One point is also deducted for stocks with a dividend yield of under 2 percent; two points are deducted for a yield of under 1 percent; 3 points are deducted for a yield of under 0.5 percent. One point is deducted for companies that do not offer a dividend reinvestment plan. However, all companies that offer a dividend reinvestment plan—no matter how low the dividend or how slowly it has grown—would still receive a minimum of one point in this category. On the other hand, a company with no plan, a low yield, and slow growth could receive a zero in this category.

Breaking Ties

The 100 companies are ranked in order by points. The company with the most points is ranked first, and the company with the fewest points is ranked 100. To break ties between companies with identical point scores, I looked at several factors, including 10-year total return, earnings growth momentum, and earnings growth consistency over the past 10 to 20 years.

Performance Graphs

At the end of each profile, you will see a five-year financial "At a Glance" summary of the company's performance, including revenue, net income, earnings per share, dividend, dividend yield, and range of price-earnings ratio (PE).

Also included is a "high-low-close" stock growth chart similar to the one below.

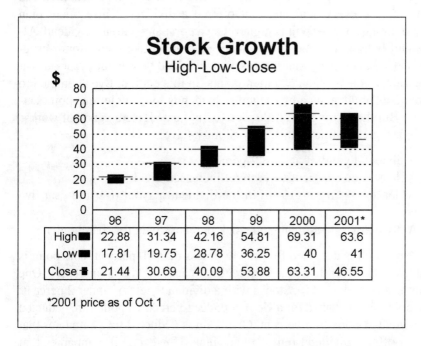

	96	97	98	99	2000	2001*
High ■	22.88	31.34	42.16	54.81	69.31	63.6
Low ■	17.81	19.75	28.78	36.25	40	41
Close ■	21.44	30.69	40.09	53.88	63.31	46.55

*2001 price as of Oct 1

This stock growth graph shows the yearly stock price range (all figures are adjusted for stock splits), including high price for the year, low price for the year, and closing price for the year. The graph shows the price range for 1996 through October 1, 2001.

Now you're ready to begin making this book work profitably for you.

How to Use This Book Profitably

Think of this book as a shopping catalog for investors. You can page through it, look over the merchandise, and make your selections.

Let's assume that you have $20,000 to invest in stocks. Here is the process I recommend that you use to select the best stocks for you based on the entries in this book.

Begin by reading through the 100 profiles and narrowing your choices to 10 to 12 stocks by asking these questions:

- Are they companies you like? Are they involved in business activities that you think have a strong future?
- Are they located in your part of the country? This is not essential, but it is easier to follow companies based close to home, because the local press tends to give those companies better coverage so you can stay better informed of your investment.
- Do they represent a diverse cross section of industries? Spread your choices around. You might select a financial institution, a computer maker, a medical products firm, a retailer, a food company, a consumer products maker, or a telecommunications operation. Choose no more than two or three companies from the same industrial segment. By selecting a broad portfolio, you can minimize your losses if one sector goes sour.

The next step is to narrow that list of 10 to 12 favorites to the 4 to 6 companies that you will ultimately invest in. (Investors with more assets may prefer to build a portfolio of 10 to 15 stocks.)

If you wish to use a stockbroker or financial advisor, call your advisor, read your list of choices, and ask if he or she has any current research on those stocks. If so, find out which ones the broker recommends and buy the stocks through your broker. If you are interested in enrolling in the dividend reinvestment plan, mention that to your broker. Most brokerage companies are happy to honor that request—even though it may cost them some brokerage commissions.

GOING IT ALONE

If you have no broker or wish to go it alone through a discount broker, here are some steps you can use to narrow your list to the 4 to 6 companies you will ultimately invest in:

- Write or call those 10 to 12 companies to request their annual reports and their 10-K reports (which are supplements to the annual reports)—or track down that information on the Internet—then skim through the reports. (The Web sites, phone numbers, and addresses of each of the 100 companies are listed in this book along with their corporate profiles.)
- Look up recent articles on those stocks on the Web or at the library. If it's a local company, there's a good chance your library will have an entire file on the firm. Make sure the company hasn't become involved in any major scandals or business problems. The library may also have two or three investment research books you can use to check up on your stock selections. Value Line Investment Survey and the Standard & Poor's report both offer up-to-date information and recommendations on hundreds of companies.
- Keep an eye on the stock prices of the companies you are interested in. Find out in what range each stock has been trading over the past few months. Then select the four or five stocks that appear at present to be the best values. Timing can be very important in your overall success. All stocks fluctuate greatly in price, tugged along by the current of the overall market. But some stocks vacillate more than others. For instance, you could have bought Walt Disney stock in 1973 for $27 a share and sold it for a mere $4 a share a year later. You could have reinvested in the stock in 1976 at $15 a share and sold out in disgust in 1984 at $11.50 a share. Or, on the other hand, you might have bought the stock for that same $11.50 a share in 1984 and sold out with a grin for more than ten times that price ($136 a share) in 1990. So timing can make a significant difference.

WHEN TO BUY

Volumes have been written on this topic. But the best advice may have come from Baron von Rothschild in the mid-1800s. He said: "Buy when the enemy is at the gate and sell when you hear your cavalry's bugle sounding charge."

Wall Street has a popular adage that reinforces that concept: "Pessimism is always most rampant just before the market hits bottom."

Two extraordinary buying opportunities have arisen in the past several years. The first came in 1987 following the October "Black Monday" crash. The crash frightened many investors out of the market, but those who bought when everyone else was selling got in on the bottom of a market that grew more than 50 percent over the next 18 months.

The second great opportunity came during Iraq's occupation of Kuwait, when oil prices were rising, and the world was transfixed by the Middle East crisis. The market dropped about 15 percent in the months after Iraq invaded Kuwait, then roared back more than 20 percent in a three-month span that began the day the Allies began the bombing.

But barring war or disaster, the best strategy for most investors is a steady, persistent, long-term investment program.

While investors may strive to buy stocks while they are well below their peak prices, market experts advise against buying a stock on its way down. Or as they say in the brokerage business: "Don't fight the tape." Wait until a falling stock has bottomed out and shown some upward momentum before buying.

Benefits of Dollar Cost Averaging

One of the easiest and most effective investment strategies is called dollar cost averaging, and it's as simple as this: Pick a number, any number—$100 for instance—and invest that amount every month (or every quarter or every year) in the same stock. Period. It's that simple. Elementary as it sounds, however, the dollar cost averaging method is also a very effective technique for beating the market. The reason? By sticking to a set sum each time you invest, you automatically buy fewer shares when the stock price is high and more shares when the price is low.

The table on the following page illustrates the advantages of dollar cost averaging. The table assumes that the stock price fluctuates somewhat each month (and lists the monthly price of the stock). The table compares the number of shares purchased through a dollar cost averaging strategy with the number of shares purchased through a method in which the investor buys a set number of shares each month.

As the table indicates, using the dollar cost averaging method, investor "A" would have purchased 3½ more shares than investor "B," who bought a set amount of shares each month, even though both spent a total of $1,200 during the year.

Tip: The dollar cost averaging method is most effective when you can make your purchases at no commission (or minimal commissions) through a company's dividend reinvestment and voluntary stock purchase plan. Such plans are ideal for dollar cost averaging, because they enable you to buy fractional shares and to make regular contributions (some companies offer stock purchase options once per month, others once per quarter). However, if the company you're interested in has no stock purchase

Example of Dollar Cost Averaging

(Investing a set dollar amount each month versus buying a set number of shares each month.)

	Jan	Feb	Mar	Apr	May	June	July	Aug	Sept	Oct	Nov	Dec	Totals
Stock Price[1]	$ 10	9	12	13	9	10	8	7	9	12	10	11	
Investor A Dollar Cost Averaging[2] Investment:	$100	100	100	100	100	100	100	100	100	100	100	100	$1,200
Shares	10	11.1	8.3	7.7	11	10	12.5	14.3	11	8.3	10	9.1	123.5
Investor B Set Quantity[3] Investment:	$100	90	120	130	90	100	80	70	80	120	100	110	$1,200
Shares	10	10	10	10	10	10	10	10	10	10	10	10	120

1. Indicates average stock price each month.
2. Assumes investor invests $100 a month in the stock.
3. Assumes investor buys 10 shares of the stock per month.

plan, the brokerage commissions you would have to pay to make regular investments in the company's stock would greatly diminish the advantages of a dollar cost averaging plan. Most of the 100 top performers in this book offer a dividend reinvestment and voluntary stock purchase plan.

PICKING WINNERS

There is no infallible system for predicting tomorrow's market winners— only ratios and theories and computer-generated formulas that seem fool-proof, but aren't. For investors who trade actively in stocks, the key to beating the market is not so much which stocks to buy, but when to buy them and when to sell them. And that's about as easy to predict as next week's weather.

Even Wall Street's finest can't consistently outfox the market. Stock mutual funds offer an interesting example. Despite being actively managed by some of the sharpest, most well-supported analysts in the investment industry, the average rate of return of stock mutual funds traditionally trails the overall market averages. Generally speaking, history has shown that you can do better just buying and holding a representative sample of stocks—without ever making a single trade—than most mutual fund managers do with their wealth of investment research, their finely honed trading strategies, and all their carefully calculated market maneuvers.

Nor do investment newsletters, on average, fare any better than mutual fund managers at timing their trade recommendations, according to Mark Hulbert, publisher of the *Hulbert Financial Digest* newsletter. "Most newsletters have not kept up with the Standard & Poor's 500," says Hulbert. In fact, in tracking the seven-year performance of a sampling of investment newsletters, Hulbert found that the ones that recommended the greatest number of buys and sells (switches) were the ones that did the worst.

"We've also conducted some studies that show that in the case of most newsletters, if you had bought and held the stocks they recommended at the first of the year, you would have done better than if you had followed all of their trading recommendations throughout the year," Hulbert adds.

The moral? For sustained, long-term growth, it's hard to beat a buy-and-hold strategy. Buy good companies with the intention of holding onto them for many years. But if the company shows little progress during a period when most of the rest of the market is moving up, it may be time to look for some more promising stocks.

The Strategy of Benign Neglect

Most of us know someone who bought a few shares of a stock many years ago, stashed the certificates in a drawer, and then discovered years later that the stock had grown to a multiple of the original cost. Benign neglect is often the smartest policy for stock market investors. Besides avoiding the difficulties of making timely buying and selling decisions, the buy-and-hold approach offers some other excellent advantages.

No commission costs. Let's assume that you turn over your stock portfolio just once a year. You sell out all the stocks you own and buy new stocks that you think have greater short-term potential. Typically, you would incur about a 2 percent commission to sell the old stocks and a 2 percent commission to buy new ones—total of 4 percent in round-trip commissions. That means, for instance, that a respectable 12 percent gain on your investments would suddenly shrink to 8 percent after you've paid off your broker. That commission may not seem like much at the time, but over the long term, it can add up to a significant amount. See the chart on page xxviii, which illustrates the hidden costs of a buy-and-sell approach. (Online brokers have cut those costs considerably. Ameritrade, for instance, offers trades for $8, regardless of how many shares you buy or sell.)

Tax-sheltered earnings. A buy-and-hold strategy is one of the best tax-advantaged investments available today. You pay no taxes on the price appreciation of your stocks until you sell them—no matter how long your keep them. (You are taxed, however, on any stock dividend income.)

However, every time you sell a stock, the federal government taxes you up to 33 percent on your gains (for most working professionals). And state taxes would very likely nibble away another 3 to 5 percent. That means each year Uncle Sam bites off more than a third of your investment profits. So you're looking at losing 36 percent of your gains, plus the brokerage house commission, every time you sell a stock at a profit. How does that translate into real dollars?

Let's assume that (1) you start with an investment of $10,000, (2) your stock portfolio appreciates at a rate of 12 percent per year, and (3) you sell your stocks, take the profit, and buy new stocks once a year. The following chart compares your performance with that of a buy-and-hold investor with an identical 12 percent compounded average annual appreciation rate.

The Hidden Costs of a Buy-and-Sell Approach

$10,000 investment @ 12% annual growth	Buy and hold (No commission and no taxes)	Buy-and-sell results[1]	
		With commission[2]	And with taxes[3]
After 1 year	$11,200	$10,800	$10,512
After 5 years	17,600	14,700	12,850
After 10 years	31,000	21,600	16,400
After 20 years	96,500	46,600	27,200
Total 20-year profit (minus initial $10,000)	$86,500	$36,600	$17,200

1. Assumes investor sells all stocks in portfolio one time per year (and reinvests in new stocks).
2. Assumes commission of 2% to buy and 2% to sell (an annual total of 4% of total portfolio price).
3. Assumes 32% federal and 4% state tax (an annual total of 36% of profits).

As you can see, over a 20-year period, the buy-and-hold portfolio could earn five times the profit of a buy-and-sell approach—even though both portfolios earn an average annual return of 12 percent.

Less emotional wear and tear. By adhering to a buy-and-hold strategy you also avoid the high anxiety of trying to buy and sell stocks actively— of watching the financial pages each day to see how your stocks have fared and of the inevitable disappointment as they rise and fall, then rise and fall again. Every stock goes through many ups and downs each year. There are no exceptions. The market moves like the tides of the ocean— it ebbs and flows—and every time it moves, it carries with it the broad market of individual stocks. Typically, about 70 percent of a stock's movement is attributable to the stock market itself. If the broad market is moving up, almost any stock you pick will also rise, but if the market is in a tailspin, almost any stock you pick—even those with record earnings— will fall with it. The remaining 30 percent of the movement of a stock is attributable to its industry group and to the performance of the company that issued the stock.

You skirt much of the emotional pressure the market inflicts if you invest with a buy-and-hold approach. You don't have to concern yourself with the inevitable daily ups and downs—or even the yearly ups and downs—of the market. Because over the long term, if you've bought stocks of good, solid, growing companies, the value of your portfolio will eventually reflect the strong performance of those companies. That's why it's crucial to select your stocks carefully. Because these are "one-decision stocks," that one decision takes on much greater importance.

WHEN NOT TO BUY

Assuming that you've selected 10 to 12 prospective stocks, you've researched the companies, and you're ready to buy, what financial factors should you look at to decide which 4 to 6 of those 10 to 12 stocks represent the best value at the time?

The easiest way to select your finalists might be through the process of elimination: weed out the stocks that appear to be overvalued and invest in the others.

To assist you with your elimination process, here are two of the most common "don'ts."

Don't buy when a stock is at an all-time high. Stocks constantly rise and fall. A noteworthy adage in the securities industry goes like this: "The market always gives you a second chance." In almost every case, when a stock reaches an all-time high, it will eventually drop back in price, bounce back up, then drop back again. Nothing goes in a straight line. If you see that a stock is at its all-time high, it's probably not a very good value at that time. Prior to the October 1987 crash, many stocks were at or near their all-time highs, which is one reason why many investment experts claimed—correctly—that there were few good values in the market.

Don't buy when the price-earnings ratio is unusually high. It sounds complicated, but the price-earnings ratio (PE) is actually a very simple formula that offers yet another barometer of a stock's relative value. And best of all, the PE is listed along with the company's stock price in the financial section of most newspapers, so you don't have to calculate it yourself. Specifically, the ratio is the current price of the stock divided by the company's earnings per share. For example:

ABC Corporation's stock price is $30.
Its earnings per share is $3.

$$\text{Stock price} \div \text{Earnings per share} = \text{PE ratio}$$
$$\$30.00 \quad \div \$3.00 \qquad = 10.0$$

PEs are like golf scores—the lower the better. Generally, the PEs of most established companies are in the 10 to 30 range. The real key, however, is not how the PE of one company compares to the PE of another, but how a company's current PE compares to its own previous PEs.

In this book, at the end of each company profile, you will see a financial summary "At a Glance" section that shows the PE range each year for the past six years. (The PEs in this book were calculated based on the earnings of the company's most recent four quarters, just as they are in the daily newspaper.) You might use that PE as a guidepost to provide a relative point of comparison.

If you find in comparing the company's current PE (as listed in your morning newspaper) with its past PE range (as listed in this book) that the PE is near or above the high end of its past range, that could be an indication that the stock is relatively overvalued.

WHEN TO SELL

The decision of when to sell is best made before you ever buy. Decide then how low you're willing to go, how long you'll wait for the stock to move, or how high you'll ride the stock before you sell out.

The most common mistake investors make in selling their stocks is that they tend to sell their winners to take a (fully taxable) profit and hold onto their losers in hopes that those stocks will someday rebound. That's an excellent way to assemble a portfolio full of losers. Prevailing wisdom in the investment business calls for just the opposite approach: "Cut your losses and let your profits run."

With that in mind, you might consider following a couple of basic strategies for selling stocks.

Sell when the company no longer meets your investment objectives. If you bought a stock because the company had enjoyed 40 consecutive years of record earnings, you should continue to hold the stock as long as the company continues to pile up record earnings. But if it hits a slump, and earnings stop growing, that company no longer meets your objectives. That's a time to sell. Weeding out your portfolio every two or three years can help make you a more successful investor.

Sell when news is grim. If a stock you own comes under legal siege or becomes involved in some type of disaster or health controversy, take your lumps and get out as fast as you can dial up your broker.

Sell when the stock price drops relative to the market. Barring disaster, you might also want to set up some other type of safety valve for your stocks. For instance, if the stock drops 10 to 20 percent while the market in general is moving up, it might be time to move on to something more promising. Some investors use a 10 percent/10 percent rule in which they sell a stock when it (1) drops 10 percent from its recent high and (2) drops 10 percent relative to the market. For example, if your stock drops 10 percent from $100 to $90, it meets the first criterion. But if the market has also gone down with it, then the stock still hasn't met the second criterion. If, on the other hand, the broad market has stayed the same or moved up while your stock dropped 10 percent, then it's time to sell—based on the 10 percent/10 percent rule.

More patient investors might lean toward a modified version of this: call it the 20 percent/20 percent rule. If your stock drops 20 percent and drops 20 percent relative to the market, sell it and move onto something more promising.

Sell when earnings drop. Investment professionals sometimes call it the "cockroach theory." When you see one disappointing earnings report, that may mean more bad periods loom around the corner—just as the sight of a single cockroach usually means that other bugs are in hiding under the sink or behind the cupboard. Money managers who follow the cockroach theory get out of a stock at the first sign of trouble—even if it means taking a small loss—to avoid taking a bigger loss later should the bad news continue.

Timing is a tricky business. As Mark Hulbert puts it: "You need to approach those decisions realizing that more than half the time you're inclined to sell you would be better off holding than selling. So you'd better make sure there's a preponderance of evidence in your favor before you sell."

That's why your buying decision is so important. This guide can help steer you to 100 of the best stocks of the past ten years.

Here's hoping you can cull from this collection some of the all-star stocks of the new millennium.

Alliance Capital
Management Holding LP

1345 Avenue of the Americas
New York, NY 10105
212-969-1000
NYSE: AC
www.alliancecapital.com

Chairman: Dave Williams
CEO: Bruce Calvert
President: John Carifa

Earnings Growth	★ ★ ★ ★
Stock Growth	★ ★ ★ ★
Consistency	★ ★ ★ ★
Dividend	★ ★ ★
Total	**15 Points**

Despite a stalled market that turned the fortunes of many investors upside down, Alliance Capital has hardly missed a beat. In the past two years the company has doubled its employees and raised its assets under management by more than 50 percent—from about $300 billion to about $465 billion.

It is the nation's largest publicly traded asset management investment firm. Alliance Capital manages about 120 mutual funds and provides investment management services to employee benefit plans for about one-third of the Fortune 100 companies.

The New York operation also manages public retirement funds in 34 states, plus accounts for hundreds of other corporations, unions, foundations, endowments, and financial institutions in the United States and overseas. It has 36 offices in 19 countries.

Alliance Capital markets its line of mutual funds through brokers, financial advisors, banks, and insurance agents. Its family of mutual funds includes a wide range of stock and bond funds, along with about 25 cash management funds, 15 closed-end funds traded on the New York Stock Exchange, a group of funds for foreign investors, and a variety of variable annuity policies.

In all, the company has about 7 million mutual fund clients and 1,800 institutional clients. The company's leading mutual fund segment is its equity and balanced funds, followed by taxable fixed-income funds, tax-exempt fixed-income funds, and closed-end funds.

Alliance Capital was founded in 1962 as the investment management department of Donaldson, Lufkin & Jenrette to specialize in pension fund management. In 1985, it was acquired by The Equitable Life Assurance Society, which took Alliance Capital public with an initial stock offering in 1988. The Equitable still holds about 57 percent of Alliance stock.

The company, which is technically a limited partnership, has about 4,400 employees and 1,700 shareholders (technically they are considered "unit" holders). Alliance Capital has a market capitalization of about $13 billion.

EARNINGS PER SHARE GROWTH ★ ★ ★ ★

Past 5 years: 232 percent (27 percent per year)
Past 10 years: 940 percent (26.5 percent per year)

STOCK GROWTH ★ ★ ★ ★

Past 10 years: 1,350 percent (32 percent per year)
Dollar growth: $10,000 over 10 years (including reinvested dividends) would have grown to $220,000.
Average annual compounded rate of return (including reinvested dividends): 38 percent

CONSISTENCY ★ ★ ★ ★

Increased earnings per share: 12 consecutive years
Increased sales: 12 consecutive years

DIVIDEND ★ ★ ★

Dividend yield: 5.7 percent
Increased dividend: Every year since 1988
Past 5-year increase: 249 percent (28 percent per year)
Alliance does not offer a dividend reinvestment and stock purchase plan.

ALLIANCE CAPITAL AT A GLANCE

Fiscal year ended: Dec. 31
Revenue and net income in $millions

	1995	1996	1997	1998	1999	2000	5-Year Growth Avg. Annual (%)	Total (%)
Revenue ($)	639	788	975	1,324	1,869	2,522	32	295
Net income ($)	155	193	250	293	462	712	36	359
Earnings/share ($)	0.94	1.13	1.44	1.66	2.53	3.12	27	232
Dividends/share ($)	0.91	1.10	1.40	1.60	2.49	3.18	28	249
Dividend yield (%)	9.5	8.8	8.0	6.3	6.9	7.1		
PE range	7–13	9–12	16–26	11–17	9–13	9–17		

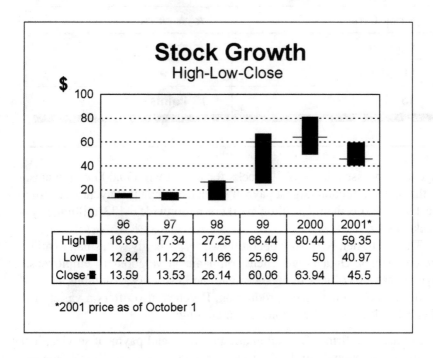

Stock Growth
High-Low-Close

	96	97	98	99	2000	2001*
High	16.63	17.34	27.25	66.44	80.44	59.35
Low	12.84	11.22	11.66	25.69	50	40.97
Close	13.59	13.53	26.14	60.06	63.94	45.5

*2001 price as of October 1

Paychex, Inc.

PAYCHEX®

911 Panorama Trail South
Rochester, NY 14625
716-385-6666
Nasdaq: PAYX
www.paychex.com

Chairman, President, and CEO:
B. Thomas Golisano

Earnings Growth	★ ★ ★ ★
Stock Growth	★ ★ ★ ★
Consistency	★ ★ ★ ★
Dividend	★ ★ ★
Total	**15 Points**

Paychex processes the payroll checks for more than 350,000 companies. As the nation's second largest payroll services company, Paychex cuts the checks for more than 4 million workers nationwide—133 million paychecks a year.

The Rochester, New York operation works primarily with small to midsize companies. On average, client companies have about 14 employees. Paychex has 110 offices in 36 states and the District of Columbia.

In addition to paycheck production, Paychex also offers a variety of other related services for employers, including:

- **Taxpay.** The firm offers automatic tax filing and payment service, including preparation and submission of federal, state, and local payroll tax returns, and the deposit of funds with tax authorities. About 75 percent of its payroll clients also use the Taxpay service.

- **Employee pay services.** The company can deposit payroll checks directly into an employee's bank account. The company also offers a Paychex Access Card, which is similar to an ATM debit card.
- **Check signing and inserting.** More than 35,000 firms use Paychex to apply authorized signatures to checks and insert them in envelopes for distribution.
- **Human resources services.** The company offers a wide range of services designed to assist companies in providing additional products and services for employees, including employee handbooks, personnel forms, compliance kits, insurance plans, and 401(k) plan recordkeeping.
- **Administrative services and professional employer organization services.** Paychex offers a bundled package that includes payroll, human resource administration, fringe benefit administration, and risk management. The firm also offers a professional employer plan that makes it easier to handle employment regulatory compliance, workers' compensation coverage, health care benefits, and other programs related to human resource management.

Paychex was founded in 1971, but took its present form in 1979 through the consolidation of 17 small companies in the payroll services business.

The company has about 6,000 employees and 4,000 shareholders. Paychex has a market capitalization of about $15 billion.

EARNINGS PER SHARE GROWTH ★ ★ ★ ★

Past 5 years: 353 percent (35 percent per year)
Past 10 years: 2,166 percent (37 percent per year)

STOCK GROWTH ★ ★ ★ ★

Past 10 years: 4,803 percent (47 percent per year)
Dollar growth: $10,000 over 10 years (including reinvested dividends) would have grown to $517,000.
Average annual compounded rate of return (including reinvested dividends): 47.5 percent

CONSISTENCY ★ ★ ★ ★

Increased earnings per share: 11 consecutive years
Increased sales: 11 consecutive years

DIVIDEND ★ ★ ★

Dividend yield: 1.0 percent
Increased dividend: 10 consecutive years
Past 5-year increase: 725 percent (52 percent per year)
Good dividend reinvestment and stock purchase plan; voluntary stock purchase plan allows contributions of $100 to $10,000 per quarter.

PAYCHEX AT A GLANCE

Fiscal year ended: May 31
Revenue and net income in $millions

	1996	1997	1998	1999	2000	2001	5-Year Growth Avg. Annual (%)	5-Year Growth Total (%)
Revenue ($)	333	400	494	597	728	870	22	161
Net income ($)	55	75	102	139	190	255	37	363
Earnings/share ($)	0.15	0.21	0.28	0.37	0.51	0.68	35	353
Dividends/share ($)	0.04	0.07	0.10	0.15	0.22	0.33	52	725
Dividend yield (%)	0.5	0.6	0.6	0.7	0.7	0.9		
PE range	39–83	37–75	48–88	42–80	47–120	40–80		

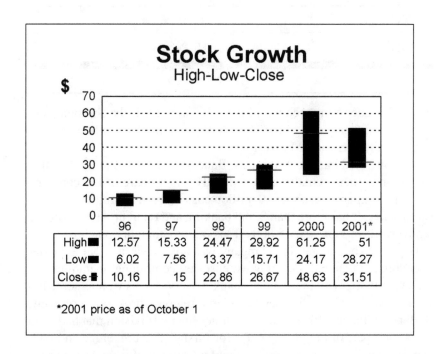

Stock Growth
High-Low-Close

	96	97	98	99	2000	2001*
High■	12.57	15.33	24.47	29.92	61.25	51
Low■	6.02	7.56	13.37	15.71	24.17	28.27
Close■	10.16	15	22.86	26.67	48.63	31.51

*2001 price as of October 1

U.S. Bancorp

601 Second Avenue South
Minneapolis, MN 55402
612-973-1111
NYSE: USB
www.usbancorp.com

Chairman and CEO: John Grundhofer
President: Jerry Grundhofer

Earnings Growth	★ ★ ★ ★
Stock Growth	★ ★ ★ ★
Consistency	★ ★ ★
Dividend	★ ★ ★ ★
Total	**15 Points**

When U.S. Bancorp merged with Firstar Bank in 2001, the combined operation was suddenly one of the biggest banks in the United States—particularly in the West and Midwest.

The combined bank kept the U.S. Bancorp name despite the fact that Firstar shareholders actually held a slightly larger share of the company stock. The company has about 10 million customers in 24 midwestern and western states. It has more than 2,300 banking and retail brokerage offices and a network of more than 5,000 ATMs (automatic teller machines).

As part of the merger, the company was able to slash about a quarter billion dollars in annual operating expenses by combining operations.

The bank offers all the standard banking services, as well as some additional related services. It operates a large regional brokerage company, U.S. Bancorp Piper Jaffray, and a consumer finance division that had been an important part of the profit center for Firstar. The brokerage and consumer finance divisions account for about 42 percent of the company's total income.

For consumers, the Minneapolis-based bank offers a broad range of products and services. In addition to checking and savings accounts, brokerage services, and certificates of deposit, U.S. Bancorp offers consumer loans and credit cards, auto loans, student loans, online banking, and life insurance.

It also offers a full complement of services for businesses, including business credit cards, employee banking programs and retirement plans, lending and leasing options, lines of credit, investment banking, venture capital, international banking, foreign exchange services, and a variety of merchant services.

The company offers corporate trust services, such as municipal trusteeships, business escrows, document custody services, international trust services, and money market instruments as well.

Prior to its merger with U.S. Bancorp, Firstar had been one of the nation's fastest growing banks. The Milwaukee-based operation had two megamergers before the U.S. Bancorp deal. It acquired Star Banc in 1998 and Mercantile Bancorporation in 1999.

The combined banking operation has about 53,000 employees and a market capitalization of about $20 billion.

EARNINGS PER SHARE GROWTH

Past 5 years: 204 percent (25 percent per year)
Past 10 years: 508 percent (20 percent per year)

STOCK GROWTH

Past 10 years: 733 percent (23.5 percent per year)
Dollar growth: $10,000 over 10 years (including reinvested dividends) would have grown to about $96,000.
Average annual compounded rate of return (including reinvested dividends): 26.5 percent

CONSISTENCY   ★ ★ ★

Increased earnings per share: 9 consecutive years

DIVIDEND   ★ ★ ★ ★

Dividend yield: 2.9 percent
Increased dividend: 29 consecutive years
Past 5-year increase: 261 percent (29 percent per year)
Good dividend reinvestment and stock purchase plan; voluntary stock purchase plan allows contributions of $50 to $25,000 per quarter.

U.S. BANCORP AT A GLANCE

Fiscal year ended: Dec. 31
Total assets and net income in $millions

	1995	1996	1997	1998	1999	2000	5-Year Growth Avg. Annual (%)	Total (%)
Total assets ($)	9,573	10,094	10,959	38,476	72,788	77,585	52	710
Net income ($)	137	158	195	604	1,253	1,475	61	976
Earnings/share ($)	0.50	0.60	0.73	0.91	1.25	1.52	25	204
Dividends/share ($)	0.18	0.21	0.27	0.33	0.46	0.65	29	261
Dividend yield (%)	3.3	2.6	1.8	1.5	1.7	2.9		
PE range	7–13	10–16	14–25	15–27	16–27	11–18		

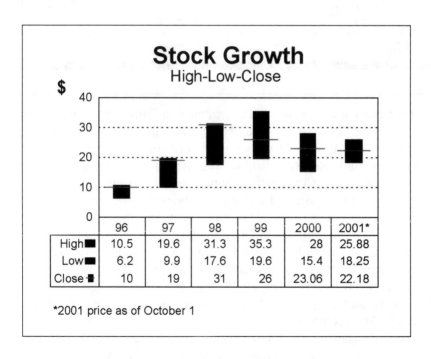

Stock Growth
High-Low-Close

$

	96	97	98	99	2000	2001*
High■	10.5	19.6	31.3	35.3	28	25.88
Low■	6.2	9.9	17.6	19.6	15.4	18.25
Close ■	10	19	31	26	23.06	22.18

*2001 price as of October 1

Fifth Third Bancorp

Fifth Third Center
38 Fountain Square Plaza
Cincinnati, OH 45263
513-579-5300
Nasdaq: FITB
www.53.com

President and CEO: George A. Schaefer, Jr.

Earnings Growth	★ ★ ★
Stock Growth	★ ★ ★ ★
Consistency	★ ★ ★ ★
Dividend	★ ★ ★
Total	**14 Points**

For more than a quarter century, an investment in Fifth Third Bancorp has been like money in the bank—only better. The Cincinnati-based banking organization has posted 27 consecutive years of record earnings and revenue—the most consistent banking organization in America.

The 143-year-old Cincinnati institution has thrived under strong management and steady, sustained growth of its branch network.

With its recent acquisition of Old Kent, Fifth Third has grown to about 1,000 branch offices throughout Ohio, Michigan, Kentucky, Indiana, Florida, and Arizona, including about 150 Bank Mart seven-day-a-week offices in supermarkets. It also operates about 2,000 Jeanie ATMs.

The company has grown rapidly the past few years through a series of acquisitions, including nearly 50 acquisitions of other financial institutions and related companies.

The Cincinnati-based institution has consistently ranked in the top 1 percent of all publicly traded companies based on dividend growth. Its growth has come through aggressive new product development, increasing market share in existing markets, and geographic expansion into new markets.

Fifth Third acquired its improbable-sounding name in the early part of the century through the merger of the Fifth National and Third National Banks of Ohio. Fifth Third has a reputation for quick response to credit problems, high credit standards, a strong sales culture, and strict cost control measures. The bank is also noted for eagerness to extend loans to businesses and consumers in the local markets it serves.

The company has won customers over the years through its mix of convenience and personal service delivered along with a comprehensive package of banking services. The bank also helped pioneer the use of automatic teller machines more than 20 years ago.

Fifth Third's loan portfolio breaks down this way: commercial loans, 25 percent; consumer loans, 23 percent; residential mortgages, 15 percent; commercial leases, 8 percent; commercial mortgages, 11 percent; consumer leases, 10 percent; and construction loans, 6 percent.

Fifth Third's Midwest Payment Systems subsidiary is the nation's largest third-party provider of electronic funds transfer services. The subsidiary processes Visa and MasterCard and other credit card transactions for more than 20,000 retail outlets throughout the country.

Fifth Third has about 12,000 employees and 38,000 shareholders. The company has a market capitalization of about $22 billion.

EARNINGS PER SHARE GROWTH   ★ ★ ★

Past 5 years: 119 percent (17 percent per year)
Past 10 years: 370 percent (17 percent per year)

STOCK GROWTH   ★ ★ ★ ★

Past 10 years: 1,331 percent (31 percent per year)
Dollar growth: $10,000 over 10 years (including reinvested dividends) would have grown to $170,000.
Average annual compounded rate of return (including reinvested dividends): 33 percent

CONSISTENCY   ★ ★ ★ ★

Increased earnings per share: 27 consecutive years

DIVIDEND   ★ ★ ★

Dividend yield: 1.3 percent
Increased dividend: 27 consecutive years
Past 5-year increase: 150 percent (20 percent per year)
Good dividend reinvestment and stock purchase plan; voluntary stock purchase plan allows contributions of $500 to $5,000 bimonthly.

FIFTH THIRD BANCORP AT A GLANCE

Fiscal year ended: Dec. 31
Total assets and net income in $millions

	1995	1996	1997	1998	1999	2000	5-Year Growth Avg. Annual (%)	Total (%)
Total assets ($)	17,053	20,549	21,375	28,922	41,589	45,857	22	169
Net income ($)	288	335	401	552	752	886	25	208
Earnings/share ($)	0.86	0.94	1.13	1.36	1.61	1.88	17	119
Dividends/share ($)	0.28	0.33	0.38	0.47	0.59	0.70	20	150
Dividend yield (%)	2.5	1.8	1.4	1.2	1.3	1.2		
PE range	11–18	13–23	15–31	26–41	26–35	16–33		

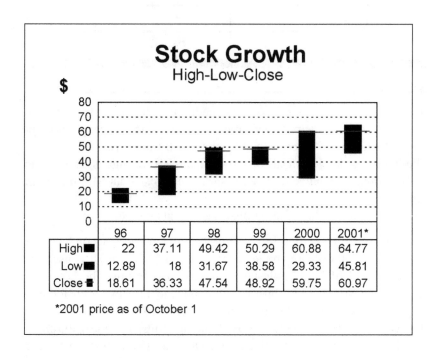

Stock Growth
High-Low-Close

$	96	97	98	99	2000	2001*
High■	22	37.11	49.42	50.29	60.88	64.77
Low■	12.89	18	31.67	38.58	29.33	45.81
Close▉	18.61	36.33	47.54	48.92	59.75	60.97

*2001 price as of October 1

5
Pfizer, Inc.

235 East 42nd Street
New York, NY 10017
212-573-2323
NYSE: PFE
www.pfizer.com

Chairman: William Steere
President and CEO: Henry McKinnell

Earnings Growth	★ ★ ★ ★
Stock Growth	★ ★ ★ ★
Consistency	★ ★ ★ ★
Dividend	★ ★
Total	**14 Points**

With five of the world's top 20 selling medicines, Pfizer has become one of the true leaders of the pharmaceutical industry. The company has eight different medicines that generate more than $1 billion a year in revenue.

Perhaps best known of all of the company's offerings is Viagra, the world's leading impotence remedy. Viagra generates about $1.3 billion in revenue.

The company's other leading pharmaceuticals include:

- **Cardiovascular medications.** Lipitor is the world's second largest selling medication with annual sales of about $5 billion. It is used for the treatment of high cholesterol and blood pressure. The company also makes Novasc ($3.4 billion in annual sales) for hypertension and angina, and Cardura ($795 million), an alpha blocker.
- **Infectious diseases medications.** Leading drugs include Zithromax ($1.4 billion), an oral antibiotic, and Diflucan ($1 billion), a fungus medication.

- **Central nervous system medications.** Pfizer makes Zoloft ($2.1 billion), a depression treatment, and Neurontin ($1.3 billion), the world's top-selling anticonvulsant medication.

Pfizer also has a line of animal health care products to treat livestock, poultry, and household pets. Pharmaceuticals account for about 81 percent of the company's $30 billion in annual revenue.

The New York operation is also the maker of a number of consumer products that account for the other 19 percent of revenue. Pfizer picked up a number of leading products when it acquired Warner-Lambert in 2000. Among the most familiar names are Listerine, Benadryl, Lubriderm, Neosporin, Sudafed, Schick, Visine eyedrops, Ben-Gay topical analgesics, Cortizone cream, RID antilice products, Unisom sleep aids, Desitin ointments, Plax prebrushing dental rinse, and Barbasol shaving cream.

Pfizer has sales in more than 150 countries. Foreign sales account for about 39 percent of total revenue.

Pfizer was founded in 1849 by two cousins who immigrated to the United States from Germany, Charles Pfizer and Charles Erhart.

The company has about 75,000 employees and 147,000 shareholders. It has a market capitalization of $260 billion.

EARNINGS PER SHARE GROWTH ★ ★ ★ ★

Past 5 years: 149 percent (20 percent per year)
Past 10 years: 410 percent (18 percent per year)

STOCK GROWTH ★ ★ ★ ★

Past 10 years: 1,239 percent (29 percent per year)
Dollar growth: $10,000 over 10 years (including reinvested dividends) would have grown to about $140,000.
Average annual compounded rate of return (including reinvested dividends): 31 percent

CONSISTENCY ★ ★ ★ ★

Increased earnings per share: 11 consecutive years
Increased sales: 51 consecutive years

DIVIDEND   ★ ★

Dividend yield: 1.1 percent
Increased dividend: 34 consecutive years
Past 5-year increase: 118 percent (16 percent per year)
Good dividend reinvestment and stock purchase plan; voluntary stock
purchase plan allows contributions of $50 to $120,000 per year.

PFIZER AT A GLANCE

Fiscal year ended: Dec. 31
Revenue and net income in $millions

	1995	1996	1997	1998	1999	2000	5-Year Growth Avg. Annual (%)	Total (%)
Revenue ($)	10,021	11,306	12,504	13,544	16,204	29,574	24	195
Net income ($)	1,554	1,929	2,213	2,634	3,393	6,495	32	318
Earnings/share ($)	0.41	0.50	0.57	0.67	0.87	1.02	20	149
Dividends/share ($)	0.17	0.20	0.23	0.25	0.31	0.36	16	118
Dividend yield (%)	2.1	1.4	1.1	0.6	0.9	0.8		
PE range	15–26	22–34	29–58	46–84	40–63	51–84		

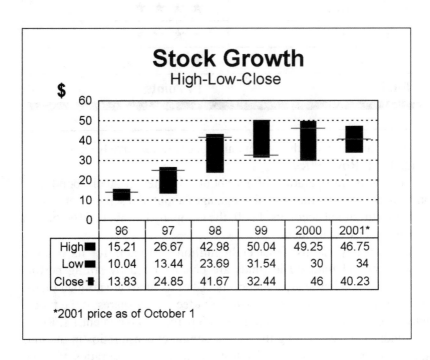

Stock Growth
High-Low-Close

	96	97	98	99	2000	2001*
High■	15.21	26.67	42.98	50.04	49.25	46.75
Low■	10.04	13.44	23.69	31.54	30	34
Close■	13.83	24.85	41.67	32.44	46	40.23

*2001 price as of October 1

6

T. Rowe Price Group, Inc.

100 East Pratt Street
Baltimore, MD 21202
410-345-2000
Nasdaq: TROW
www.troweprice.com

Chairman and President: George A. Roche

Earnings Growth	★ ★ ★ ★
Stock Growth	★ ★ ★ ★
Consistency	★ ★ ★ ★
Dividend	★ ★
Total	**14 Points**

No-load mutual funds with low annual expense ratios have been the stock-in-trade for T. Rowe Price.

The Baltimore operation offers about 75 different stock, bond, and money market mutual funds. It also manages about 450 separate and commingled institutional accounts. In all, the company has about $160 billion of assets under management.

The company claims about eight million customers for its popular family of mutual funds. The funds are characterized by strong performance ratings and low shareholder costs. All of its funds are no-load funds, which means that investors pay no up-front fee to buy shares of the funds. (Many other fund families charge fees of 3 percent to 8 percent.) T. Rowe Price funds also have among the lowest annual expense ratios in the mutual fund business. Many of its funds have annual expense ratios of about 1 percent or less. By comparison, many other funds have annual expense ratios of 1.5 percent to 2.5 percent.

The firm's three largest funds are the Equity Income Fund, the International Stock Fund, and the Science & Technology Fund. Combined, those funds account for 18 percent of the company's assets and 25 percent of its investment advisory fees.

T. Rowe Price was founded in 1937 by Thomas Rowe Price. Its oldest funds are the Growth Stock Fund, started in 1950 (with assets of $5.5 billion), and the New Horizons Fund, started in 1960 (with $6 billion in assets).

In addition to its mutual funds, the company manages about $60 billion in investment portfolios offered by other companies.

On the international front, the company acquired full control of Rowe Price-Fleming International in 2000. The London-based asset management and investment banking group manages about $27 billion in assets. Price had previously held a 50 percent stake in the company.

T. Rowe Price has about 4,000 employees and a market capitalization of about $5 billion.

EARNINGS PER SHARE GROWTH

Past 5 years: 230 percent (27 percent per year)
Past 10 years: 845 percent (25 percent per year)

STOCK GROWTH ★ ★ ★ ★

Past 10 years: 800 percent (24.5 percent per year)
Dollar growth: $10,000 over 10 years (including reinvested dividends) would have grown to about $100,000.
Average annual compounded rate of return (including reinvested dividends): 26 percent

CONSISTENCY ★ ★ ★ ★

Increased earnings per share: 10 consecutive years
Increased sales: 14 consecutive years

DIVIDEND

Dividend yield: 1.7 percent
Increased dividend: 14 consecutive years
Past 5-year increase: 200 percent (25 percent per year)
The company does not offer a dividend reinvestment and stock purchase plan.

T. ROWE PRICE GROUP AT A GLANCE

Fiscal year ended: Dec. 31
Revenue and net income in $millions

	1995	1996	1997	1998	1999	2000	5-Year Growth Avg. Annual (%)	Total (%)
Revenue ($)	439	586	755	866	1,036	1,212	22.5	176
Net income ($)	75	99	144	174	239	269	29	259
Earnings/share ($)	0.63	0.80	1.13	1.34	1.85	2.08	27	230
Dividends/share ($)	0.18	0.22	0.28	0.35	0.43	0.54	25	200
Dividend yield (%)	1.6	1.0	0.9	1.0	1.2	1.3		
PE range	11–19	13–28	16–32	15–32	13–23	14–24		

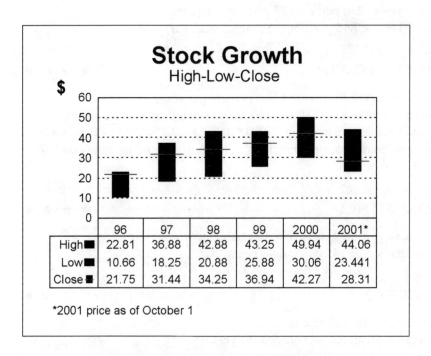

Stock Growth
High-Low-Close

	96	97	98	99	2000	2001*
High■	22.81	36.88	42.88	43.25	49.94	44.06
Low■	10.66	18.25	20.88	25.88	30.06	23.441
Close■	21.75	31.44	34.25	36.94	42.27	28.31

*2001 price as of October 1

SouthTrust Corporation

SouthTrust Corporation ≥

420 North 20th Street
Birmingham, AL 35203
205-254-5530
Nasdaq: SOTR
www.southtrust.com

Chairman, President, and CEO:
William D. Malone

Earnings Growth	★ ★
Stock Growth	★ ★ ★ ★
Consistency	★ ★ ★ ★
Dividend	★ ★ ★ ★
Total	**14 Points**

A prudent loan policy and a voracious appetite for acquisitions have helped make SouthTrust one of the fastest growing banking organizations in the country.

The Birmingham-based operation has more than 650 banking offices and several bank-related affiliates in Alabama, Florida, Georgia, Mississippi, North Carolina, South Carolina, Texas, and Tennessee.

It is one of the 20 largest banking organizations in the country, with a customer base of about 1.5 million households and more than 200,000 businesses. It has customers in all 50 states. The company has posted increased loan totals 14 straight years and increased earnings 10 consecutive years.

Commercial banking is the bread and butter of SouthTrust's business. Its banks offer a broad range of standard services such as checking and savings accounts, cash management, lending and credit services, discount brokerage accounts, corporate and trust accounts, and data processing services. The company also offers Visa and MasterCard merchant credit card processing services.

The company's loan portfolio consists of commercial loans (39 percent), construction loans (12 percent), commercial mortgages (22 percent), residential mortgages (17 percent), and consumer loans (10 percent).

The firm operates a number of bank-related subsidiaries, including SouthTrust Mortgage Corp., SouthTrust Data Services, SouthTrust Life Insurance Company, SouthTrust Insurance Agency, SouthTrust Securities, and SouthTrust Asset Management Company.

SouthTrust was among the first banks to offer corporate imaging technology for cash management customers. Using software provided by SouthTrust, customers can access check images online or on CD-ROM and electronically store those images, providing them with a permanent record of all of their canceled checks.

SouthTrust has grown quickly through internal expansion and acquisitions. It has acquired nearly 20 smaller banking organizations over the past three years.

The company has about 12,000 employees and 14,000 shareholders of record. It has a market capitalization of about $8 billion.

EARNINGS PER SHARE GROWTH   ★ ★

Past 5 years: 81 percent (13 percent per year)
Past 10 years: 276 percent (14 percent per year)

STOCK GROWTH   ★ ★ ★ ★

Past 10 years: 723 percent (23.5 percent per year)
Dollar growth: $10,000 over 10 years (including reinvested dividends) would have grown to about $109,000.
Average annual compounded rate of return (including reinvested dividends): 27 percent

CONSISTENCY   ★ ★ ★ ★

Increased earnings per share: 10 consecutive years
Increased sales: 14 consecutive years

DIVIDEND

Dividend yield: 2.5 percent
Increased dividend: 31 consecutive years
Past 5-year increase: 85 percent (13 percent per year)
Good dividend reinvestment and stock purchase plan; voluntary stock purchase plan allows contributions of $25 to $10,000 per quarter.

SOUTHTRUST AT A GLANCE

Fiscal year ended: Dec. 31
Total assets and net income in $millions

	1995	1996	1997	1998	1999	2000	5-Year Growth Avg. Annual (%)	Total (%)
Total assets ($)	20,787	26,223	30,906	38,134	43,263	45,147	17	117
Net income ($)	199	255	307	369	443	482	19.5	142
Earnings/share ($)	0.79	0.90	1.02	1.13	1.32	1.43	13	81
Dividends/share ($)	0.27	0.29	0.34	0.38	0.44	0.50	13	85
Dividend yield (%)	3.3	3.8	1.2	2.1	2.3	2.5		
PE range	7–12	6–8	7–21	11–20	12–16	7–14		

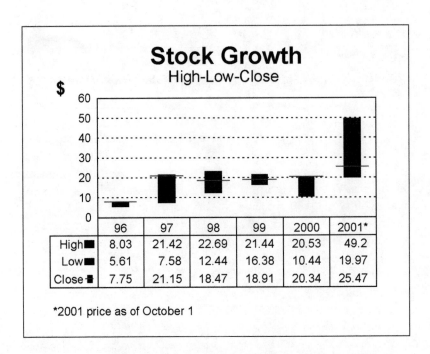

Stock Growth
High-Low-Close

$	96	97	98	99	2000	2001*
High■	8.03	21.42	22.69	21.44	20.53	49.2
Low■	5.61	7.58	12.44	16.38	10.44	19.97
Close■	7.75	21.15	18.47	18.91	20.34	25.47

*2001 price as of October 1

8
Medtronic, Inc.

710 Medtronic Parkway N.E.
Minneapolis, MN 55432
763-514-4000
NYSE: MDT
www.medtronic.com

Chairman and CEO: William W. George
President: Arthur D. Collins

Earnings Growth	★ ★ ★
Stock Growth	★ ★ ★ ★
Consistency	★ ★ ★ ★
Dividend	★ ★
Total	**13 Points**

When Vice President Dick Cheney needed to shore up his ailing heart, surgeons installed a special pacemaker made by Medtronic. The company is the world's leading manufacturer of heart pacemakers and other implantable biomedical devices. It markets its products in more than 120 countries. About 40 percent of its sales come from outside the United States.

Medtronic's products and therapies are used by nearly three million people a year. The company has grown rapidly, with 15 consecutive years of record sales, earnings, and book value per share. The Minneapolis-based operation designs and manufactures pacing devices for patients whose heartbeats are irregular or too slow, as well for patients whose hearts beat too rapidly. Medtronic's pacing devices can adjust electrical pulse intensity, duration, rate, and other characteristics.

Medtronic's pacemakers are small, coin-sized, implantable pulse generators with extended battery life. The implantable pacemaker is among a growing line of biomedical devices that Medtronic manufactures as part of its mission to "alleviate pain, restore health, and extend life."

The company's pacing business—its cardiac rhythm management division—accounts for about 50 percent of its $5 billion in annual sales.

Cardiovascular products such as blood pumps, heart valves, oxygenators, catheters, and other blood management systems contribute about 16 percent of the company's sales. In addition to its line of cardiovascular products, Medtronic provides such value-added services as physician education programs.

Cardiac surgery products, such as heart valves, perfusion systems, cannulae, and surgical accessories, account for about 9 percent of sales.

The company also makes neurological devices used for treating pain and controlling movement disorders. The company makes implantable neurostimulation devices used for spinal cord and brain stimulation to treat pain and tremors. It also makes drug delivery systems, neurosurgery products, and diagnostic systems. Neurological devices account for about 25 percent of total sales and represent the fastest-growing sector of the company's business.

Medtronic pioneered the pacemaker 42 years ago when Dr. C. Walton Lillehei of the University of Minnesota Medical School identified a medical need for young heart block patients. Working with Earl Bakken, an electrical engineer, Dr. Lillehei developed the first wearable, external, battery-generated pulse generator.

Founded in 1949 and incorporated in 1957, Medtronic has about 25,000 employees and 42,500 shareholders. The company has a market capitalization of about $55 billion.

EARNINGS PER SHARE GROWTH   ★ ★ ★

Past 5 years: 123 percent (17 percent per year)
Past 10 years: 600 percent (21.5 percent per year)

STOCK GROWTH   ★ ★ ★ ★

Past 10 years: 1,667 percent (33 percent per year)
Dollar growth: $10,000 over 10 years (including reinvested dividends) would have grown to $185,000.
Average annual compounded rate of return (including reinvested dividends): 33.5 percent

CONSISTENCY ★ ★ ★ ★

Increased earnings per share: 16 consecutive years
Increased sales: 16 consecutive years

DIVIDEND ★ ★

Dividend yield: 0.5 percent
Increased dividend: 14 consecutive years
Past 5-year increase: 171 percent (22 percent per year)
Good dividend reinvestment and stock purchase plan; voluntary stock purchase plan allows contributions of $25 to $4,000 per month.

MEDTRONIC AT A GLANCE

Fiscal year ended: Dec. 31
Revenue and net income in $millions

	1995	1996	1997	1998	1999	2000	5-Year Growth Avg. Annual (%)	Total (%)
Revenue ($)	2,438	3,010	3,423	4,232	5,015	5,552	18	128
Net income ($)	438	530	595	905	1,111	1,282	24	193
Earnings/share ($)	0.47	0.56	0.63	0.77	0.92	1.05	17	123
Dividends/share ($)	0.07	0.10	0.11	0.13	0.16	0.19	22	171
Dividend yield (%)	0.5	0.4	0.5	0.4	0.4	0.4		
PE range	22–29	25–39	28–52	44–75	77–115	36–69		

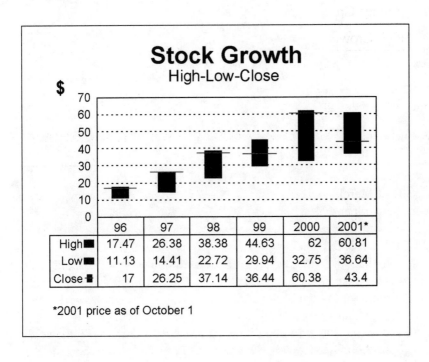

Stock Growth
High-Low-Close

$		96	97	98	99	2000	2001*
	High■	17.47	26.38	38.38	44.63	62	60.81
	Low■	11.13	14.41	22.72	29.94	32.75	36.64
	Close■	17	26.25	37.14	36.44	60.38	43.4

*2001 price as of October 1

Merck & Company, Inc.

P.O. Box 100
One Merck Drive
Whitehouse Station, NJ 08889
908-423-1000
NYSE: MRK
www.merck.com

Chairman, President, and CEO:
Raymond V. Gilmartin

Earnings Growth	★ ★ ★
Stock Growth	★ ★
Consistency	★ ★ ★ ★
Dividend	★ ★ ★ ★
Total	**13 Points**

As many of Merck's leading pharmaceutical products head for the generic ranks, the company is betting its future on a handful of new and recently released medications to keep its bottom line growing. Founded in 1881, Merck is the world's leading maker of pharmaceuticals.

By the end of 2002, the popular antiulcer medication, Pepcid, will lose its patent protection and be subject to competition from generic brands, as will Primaxim (an antibiotic), Prinivil (a heart medicine), Mevacor (a cholesterol medicine), and Vasotec (a heart medicine).

Merck is counting on some of its other newer products to fill the void, including the popular hair growth formula, Propecia, which became the first tablet approved by the U.S. Food and Drug Administration for the treatment of male pattern hair loss. About 400,000 American men began using the medicine in its first year on the market.

Other leading drugs offered by Merck include:

- **Zocor,** a cholesterol medication, which is the world's second-largest-selling medication with sales in excess of $5 billion a year
- **Vioxx,** an arthritis medication launched in 1999 that has already become Merck's second-largest-selling medicine with sales of nearly $2 billion a year
- **Cozaar,** an antihypertensive medication, which reached annual sales of $1 billion a year in its fourth year on the market
- **Maxalt,** which became the fastest-growing oral migraine medicine within weeks of its introduction in the U.S. market
- **Singulair,** which has become the top-selling asthma medicine in every country where it is sold

Merck's biggest selling segment is its cholesterol treatments (which the company categorizes as atherosclerosis medications), which accounts for about 14 percent of the company's $40 billion in annual sales. Cardiovascular medications, which are used to treat heart problems and hypertension, account for 11 percent.

Other leading segments include anti-inflammatory medications, 5 percent; vaccines and biologicals, 2 percent; respiratory, 2 percent; antiulcerants, 2 percent; osteoporosis, 3 percent; antibiotics, 2 percent; HIV medications, 2 percent; ophthalmologicals, 2 percent; and other products, 5 percent.

The company's other leading division is its Merck-Medco operation, which provides managed prescription drug services and managed patient health services. Its sales account for about 50 percent of Merck's total revenue (but a much smaller percentage of its profits).

Merck has operations in about 20 countries, with sales in more than 100 countries. Sales outside the United States account for about 36 percent of total human health sales.

The company has about 70,000 employees and 270,000 shareholders. It has a market capitalization of about $154 billion.

EARNINGS PER SHARE GROWTH

Past 5 years: 120 percent (17 percent per year)
Past 10 years: 281 percent (14 percent per year)

STOCK GROWTH ★ ★

Past 10 years: 389 percent (17 percent per year)
Dollar growth: $10,000 over 10 years (including reinvested dividends) would have grown to $57,000.
Average annual compounded rate of return (including reinvested dividends): 19 percent

CONSISTENCY ★ ★ ★ ★

Increased earnings per share: 10 consecutive years
Increased sales: 10 consecutive years

DIVIDEND ★ ★ ★ ★

Dividend yield: 2.1 percent
Increased dividend: 10 consecutive years
Past 5-year increase: 95 percent (14 percent per year)
Good dividend reinvestment and stock purchase plan; voluntary stock purchase plan allows contributions of $50 to $50,000 per year.

MERCK & COMPANY AT A GLANCE

Fiscal year ended: Dec. 31
Revenue and net income in $millions

	1995	1996	1997	1998	1999	2000	5-Year Growth Avg. Annual (%)	Total (%)
Revenue ($)	16,681	19,829	23,637	26,898	32,714	40,363	19	142
Net income ($)	3,335	3,881	4,614	5,248	5,891	6,822	15	104
Earnings/share ($)	1.32	1.56	1.87	2.15	2.45	2.90	17	120
Dividends/share ($)	0.62	0.71	0.85	0.95	1.10	1.21	14	95
Dividend yield (%)	2.5	2.1	1.6	1.3	1.6	1.4		
PE range	14–23	18–27	20–28	23–37	24–35	17–33		

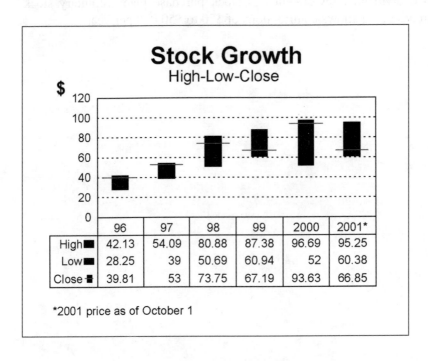

Stock Growth
High-Low-Close

$	96	97	98	99	2000	2001*
High	42.13	54.09	80.88	87.38	96.69	95.25
Low	28.25	39	50.69	60.94	52	60.38
Close	39.81	53	73.75	67.19	93.63	66.85

*2001 price as of October 1

3900 Wisconsin Avenue
Washington, DC 20016
202-752-7115
NYSE: FNM
www.fanniemae.com

Chairman and CEO: Franklin D. Raines

Earnings Growth	★ ★ ★
Stock Growth	★ ★ ★ ★
Consistency	★ ★ ★ ★
Dividend	★ ★
Total	**13 Points**

Fannie Mae (Federal National Mortgage Association) has helped more than 30 million American families put a permanent roof over their heads.

The Washington, D.C.–based operation is the nation's largest provider of residential mortgage funding. The company buys mortgages from lenders, such as banks, mortgage banks, and savings and loan associations, thereby replenishing their funds for additional lending. That leaves more money available for institutions to lend to other homebuyers.

Fannie Mae's primary business is buying mortgages that they fund by issuing debt securities on the global capital markets. Their profit comes on the spread between the yield on the mortgages and the cost of the debt. The company holds a mortgage portfolio of more than $600 billion—and growing.

The company is also active in the mortgage-backed securities business. It guarantees the timely payment of principal and interest on securities backed by pools of mortgages, earning a guaranty fee on the amount of mortgage-backed securities outstanding.

Fannie Mae also offers a variety of services to lenders and related operations for a fee. Services include issuing certain types of mortgage-backed securities and providing technology services in support of originating and underwriting mortgage loans.

Fannie Mae was created by Congress in 1938 as a U.S. government agency to supplement the mortgage market in order to help low-, moderate-, and middle-income American families buy new homes. It also lends stability to the market by buying, selling, and guaranteeing mortgages.

Since its founding, Fannie Mae has issued about $3 trillion in mortgage financing.

Fannie Mae became a shareholder-owned company in 1968 but is still subject to explicit federal regulation. In fact, 5 members of its 18-member board are appointed by the U.S. president. In terms of total assets, Fannie Mae is the nation's largest company with assets of about $675 billion. It is also the largest investor in home mortgage loans in the United States.

The company has posted 14 consecutive years of record earnings.

Fannie Mae has about 3,200 employees and 240,000 stockholders. It has a market capitalization of about $80 billion.

EARNINGS PER SHARE GROWTH ★ ★ ★

Past 5 years: 119 percent (17 percent per year)
Past 10 years: 282 percent (14 percent per year)

STOCK GROWTH ★ ★ ★ ★

Past 10 years: 780 percent (24 percent per year)
Dollar growth: $10,000 over 10 years (including reinvested dividends) would have grown to $100,000.
Average annual compounded rate of return (including reinvested dividends): 26 percent

CONSISTENCY

Increased earnings per share: 15 consecutive years
Increased sales: 10 consecutive years

DIVIDEND   ★ ★

Dividend yield: 1.5 percent
Increased dividend: 15 consecutive years
Past 5-year increase: 65 percent (10.5 percent per year)
Good dividend reinvestment and stock purchase plan; a voluntary stock purchase plan allows contributions of $25 up to $250,000 per year after an initial investment of at least $250.

FANNIE MAE AT A GLANCE

Fiscal year ended: Dec. 31
Mortgage loans and net income in $millions

	1995	1996	1997	1998	1999	2000	5-Year Growth Avg. Annual (%)	Total (%)
Mortgage loans ($)	253,511	287,052	316,678	415,218	522,780	607,399	29	140
Net income ($)	2,144	2,725	3,086	3,418	3,911	4,448	16	107
Earnings/share ($)	1.95	2.48	2.84	3.23	3.72	4.28	17	119
Dividends/share ($)	0.68	0.76	0.84	0.96	1.08	1.12	10.5	65
Dividend yield (%)	2.9	2.3	1.9	1.7	1.7	1.3		
PE range	9–16	11–16	12–20	15–23	15–20	11–20		

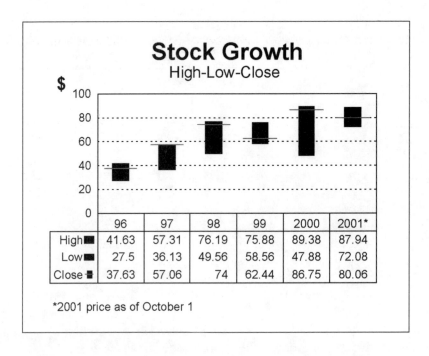

Stock Growth
High-Low-Close

	96	97	98	99	2000	2001*
High	41.63	57.31	76.19	75.88	89.38	87.94
Low	27.5	36.13	49.56	58.56	47.88	72.08
Close	37.63	57.06	74	62.44	86.75	80.06

*2001 price as of October 1

General Electric Company

3135 Easton Turnpike
Fairfield, CT 06431
203-373-2211
NYSE: GE
www.ge.com

Chairman and CEO: Jeffrey Immelt

Earnings Growth	★ ★
Stock Growth	★ ★ ★ ★
Consistency	★ ★ ★ ★
Dividend	★ ★ ★
Total	**13 Points**

This is the house that Jack built—long after Thomas A. Edison laid the foundation.

Jack Welch, who retired in late 2001 as chairman and CEO of General Electric, spent his two decades at the helm of GE turning it into the nation's largest capitalization company. Welch is considered perhaps the best CEO in modern corporate America, wringing consistent annual earnings growth of 15 percent or more from a company most considered far too big to grow at a rate normally reserved for emerging growth stocks. The company has posted record earnings for 25 consecutive years. Part of GE's growth has been through acquiring more than 100 companies a year for the past five years.

Whether GE can continue that type of growth in Welch's absence remains to be seen, but his successor certainly faces a challenge. Just the same, this company is built to last. It traces its roots to the Edison Electric Company, founded in 1878 by the great Thomas Edison.

The Fairfield, Connecticut operation breaks its business into several key segments. About 50 percent of its revenue comes from GECS (formerly GE Capital Services). GECS operates a number of financial, leasing, and insurance subsidiaries, including GE Capital, a financing institution that specializes in revolving credit, credit cards, and inventory financing for retail merchants.

GE breaks its manufacturing operations into seven key divisions, including:

- **Industrial products and systems** (10 percent of total revenue). The company manufactures factory automation products, motors, electrical equipment, transportation systems (including locomotives and transit propulsion equipment), light bulbs, and other types of lighting products.
- **Power systems** (11 percent). The company builds power generators (primarily steam-turbine generators) and transmitters for worldwide utility, industrial, and government customers.
- **Aircraft engines** (8 percent). It is a leading manufacturer of jet engines and engine parts for short, medium, intermediate, and long-range commercial aircraft and military aircraft and helicopters.
- **Broadcasting** (5 percent). GE owns the National Broadcasting Company (NBC), which serves more than 200 affiliated stations throughout the United States. NBC also owns the cable channel CNBC and television stations in Chicago, Philadelphia, Los Angeles, Miami, New York, and Washington, D.C.
- **Appliances** (4 percent). The company is known for its GE, Hotpoint and Monogram appliances, including refrigerators, ranges, microwaves, freezers, dishwashers, clothes washers and dryers and room air conditioners.
- **Materials** (6 percent). The company makes high-performance plastics for such uses as automobile bumpers, computer casings, and other office equipment. It also produces silicones, superabrasives, and laminates.
- **Technical products and services** (6 percent). The company manufactures a variety of medical instruments, including scanners, X rays, nuclear imaging, ultrasound, and other diagnostic equipment. It also manufactures communications systems.

Foreign sales account for about half of the company's total revenue.

GE has about 290,000 employees and 530,000 shareholders. It has a market capitalization of about $450 billion.

EARNINGS PER SHARE GROWTH   ★ ★

Past 5 years: 95 percent (14 percent per year)
Past 10 years: 217 percent (12 percent per year)

STOCK GROWTH

Past 10 years: 662 percent (22.5 percent per year)
Dollar growth: $10,000 over 10 years (including reinvested dividends) would have grown to about $90,000.
Average annual compounded rate of return (including reinvested dividends): 24.5 percent

CONSISTENCY

Increased earnings per share: 25 consecutive years
Increased sales: 7 of the past 10 years

DIVIDEND   ★ ★ ★

Dividend yield: 1.5 percent
Increased dividend: 25 consecutive years
Past 5-year increase: 103 percent (15 percent per year)
Good dividend reinvestment and stock purchase plan; GE's Stock Direct Plan allows weekly contributions from $10 to $10,000, following an initial investment of $250.

GENERAL ELECTRIC AT A GLANCE

Fiscal year ended: Dec. 31
Revenue and net income in $millions

	1995	1996	1997	1998	1999	2000	5-Year Growth Avg. Annual (%)	Total (%)
Revenue ($)	43,013	45,341	48,032	51,459	55,882	63,788	8	48
Net income ($)	6,573	7,280	8,203	9,296	10,717	12,735	14	94
Earnings/share ($)	0.65	0.73	0.83	0.93	1.07	1.27	14	95
Dividends/share ($)	0.28	0.32	0.36	0.42	0.49	0.57	15	103
Dividend yield (%)	2.8	2.0	1.6	1.2	1.1	1.2		
PE range	13–19	13–19	19–31	24–37	29–49	32–47		

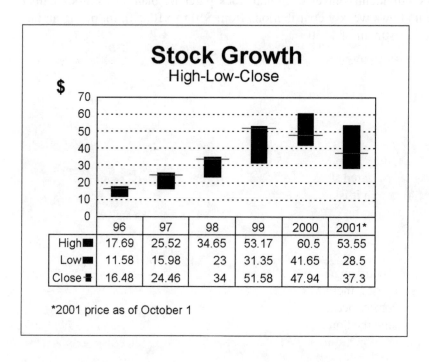

Stock Growth
High-Low-Close

	96	97	98	99	2000	2001*
High	17.69	25.52	34.65	53.17	60.5	53.55
Low	11.58	15.98	23	31.35	41.65	28.5
Close	16.48	24.46	34	51.58	47.94	37.3

*2001 price as of October 1

Freddie Mac

Freddie Mac

We Open Doors®

8200 Jones Branch Drive
McLean, VA 22102
703-903-3725
NYSE: FRE
www.freddiemac.com

Chairman and CEO: Leland C. Brendsel
President: David W. Glenn

Earnings Growth	★ ★ ★
Stock Growth	★ ★ ★ ★
Consistency	★ ★ ★ ★
Dividend	★ ★
Total	**13 Points**

Over the past 31 years, Freddie Mac (the Federal Home Loan Mortgage Corporation) has financed the purchase of one of every six homes in America. Established by Congress in 1970, Freddie Mac provides a continuous flow of funds for residential mortgages by buying mortgage loans and mortgage-related securities in the secondary market.

Although it is a publicly traded company now, Freddie Mac was originally created by Congress to fulfill four specific mandates:

- To provide stability in the secondary market for residential mortgages
- To respond appropriately to the private capital market
- To provide ongoing assistance to the secondary market for residential mortgages, including low- and moderate-income families
- To promote access to mortgage credit throughout the United States by increasing the liquidity of mortgage investments and improving the distribution of investment capital available for residential mortgage financing

Freddie Mac purchases residential mortgages and mortgage-related securities from lenders, other mortgage sellers, and securities dealers. To finance its activities, the company sells mortgage-related securities and debt and equity securities.

The McLean, Virginia operation has been very profitable, posting a return on equity in excess of 20 percent for the past 19 consecutive years. In all, Freddie Mac has financed homes for nearly 30 million families.

Through its activities, Freddie Mac helps facilitate home purchases by less affluent buyers. The company offers special mortgages designed to help homebuyers who need assistance with down payments and closing costs. It also sets underwriting guidelines to help lenders work with government agencies, nonprofit organizations, and other housing finance agencies to create secondary financing programs for potential borrowers. Freddie Mac tries to establish public-private relationships designed to increase access to mortgage credit for low- to moderate-income and minority households.

Freddie Mac has about 3,200 employees and a market capitalization of about $45 billion.

EARNINGS PER SHARE GROWTH   ★ ★ ★

Past 5 years: 139 percent (19 percent per year)
Past 10 years: 486 percent (19.5 percent per year)

STOCK GROWTH   ★ ★ ★ ★

Past 10 years: 1,257 percent (30 percent per year)
Dollar growth: $10,000 over 10 years (including reinvested dividends) would have grown to $142,000.
Average annual compounded rate of return (including reinvested dividends): 31 percent

CONSISTENCY   ★ ★ ★ ★

Increased earnings per share: 12 consecutive years
Increased sales: 10 consecutive years

DIVIDEND   ★ ★

Dividend yield: 1.2 percent
Increased dividend: 11 consecutive years
Past 5-year increase: 127 percent (18 percent per year)
Freddie Mac does not offer a dividend reinvestment plan.

FREDDIE MAC AT A GLANCE

Fiscal year ended: Dec. 31
Mortgage loans and net income in $millions

	1995	1996	1997	1998	1999	2000	5-Year Growth Avg. Annual (%)	Total (%)
Mortgage loans ($)	566,469	610,820	640,406	733,360	862,326	961,794	11	70
Net income ($)	1,091	1,243	1,395	1,700	2,223	2,547	18.5	133
Earnings/share ($)	1.42	1.67	1.90	2.32	2.96	3.40	19	139
Dividends/share ($)	0.30	0.35	0.40	0.48	0.60	0.68	18	127
Dividend yield (%)	1.8	1.5	1.2	0.9	0.7	0.1		
PE range	10–14	11–17	14–23	16–28	15–22	10–20		

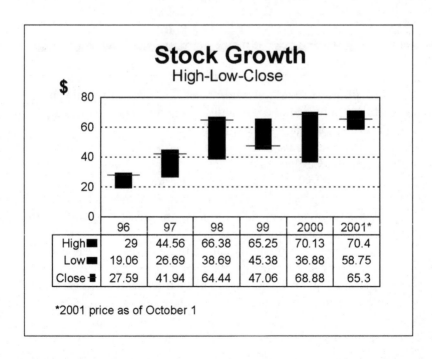

Stock Growth
High-Low-Close

	96	97	98	99	2000	2001*
High■	29	44.56	66.38	65.25	70.13	70.4
Low■	19.06	26.69	38.69	45.38	36.88	58.75
Close-■	27.59	41.94	64.44	47.06	68.88	65.3

*2001 price as of October 1

13

Harley-Davidson, Inc.

3700 West Juneau Avenue
Milwaukee, WI 53208
414-342-4680
NYSE: HDI
www.harley-davidson.com

Chairman and CEO: Jeffrey Bleustein

Earnings Growth	★ ★ ★ ★
Stock Growth	★ ★ ★ ★
Consistency	★ ★ ★ ★
Dividend	★
Total	**13 Points**

The hogs keep rolling and Harley-Davidson keeps growing. The Milwaukee-based operation continues to be the hottest thing on wheels, with 15 consecutive years of record earnings and revenue.

Although consumers have faced long delays on some Harley models—and many Asian and European consumers are simply unable to get their hands on a Harley no matter what the wait—Harley has refused to accelerate its manufacturing process simply to meet demand. It has opened some new plants, but management will not compromise the quality of its bikes to crank up the quantity.

The company sells 24 models of touring and custom heavyweight motorcycles, with suggested retail prices ranging from $5,000 to $20,000. Its touring bikes are equipped for long-distance travel with fairings, windshields, saddlebags, and Harley Tour Paks. The custom bikes have distinctive styling, with customized trim and accessories. The company manufactures all of its chassis and engines itself. The bikes are based on four chassis variations and are powered by one of three air-cooled, twin-cylinder engines of "V" configurations, with engine displacements of 883cc, 1200cc, 1450cc, and 1550cc.

The typical Harley buyer is not necessarily the young and restless biker you might expect. The company says its customers tend to be men in their early to mid-40s, with a household income of about $80,000. Only 9 percent of Harley buyers are women. About a third of Harley riders are college graduates. Harley buyers are also extremely loyal. The company's riders club, The Harley Owners Group (HOG), has about 300,000 members worldwide.

The company also manufactures the Buell line of sport and performance motorcycles.

Harley-Davidson, in its present incarnation, was incorporated in 1981 by a private investment group, which purchased Harley-Davidson Motorcycle from AMF and took it public in 1986. The reputation of the bikes—and the profits of the company—have been rising ever since. From a net profit of $4.5 million in 1986, the company's profits soared to about $350 million in 2000.

Overseas sales are also on the rise. Foreign sales account for about 20 percent of Harley's $2.9 billion in annual revenue. The motorcycles enjoy their greatest popularity in Germany, Japan, Canada, and Australia, which account for about 60 percent of export sales.

Founded in 1903, Harley-Davidson has about 7,500 employees and 35,000 shareholders. It has a market capitalization of about $15 billion.

EARNINGS PER SHARE GROWTH   ★ ★ ★ ★

Past 5 years: 205 percent (25 percent per year)
Past 10 years: 653 percent (22 percent per year)

STOCK GROWTH   ★ ★ ★ ★

Past 10 years: 3,072 percent (41 percent per year)
Dollar growth: $10,000 over 10 years (including reinvested dividends) would have grown to about $310,000.
Average annual compounded rate of return (including reinvested dividends): 41 percent

CONSISTENCY   ★ ★ ★ ★

Increased earnings per share: 10 consecutive years
Increased sales: 10 consecutive years

DIVIDEND ★

Dividend yield: 0.2 percent
Increased dividend: 8 consecutive years, since dividend inception in 1993
Past 5-year increase: 100 percent (15 percent per year)
Good dividend reinvestment and stock purchase plan; voluntary stock purchase plan allows contributions of $30 to $5,000 per quarter.

HARLEY-DAVIDSON AT A GLANCE

Fiscal year ended: Dec. 31
Revenue and net income in $millions

	1995	1996	1997	1998	1999	2000	5-Year Growth Avg. Annual (%)	Total (%)
Revenue ($)	1,351	1,531	1,762	2,064	2,453	2,906	16.5	115
Net income ($)	111	143	174	213	267	348	25.5	214
Earnings/share ($)	0.37	0.48	0.57	0.69	0.87	1.13	25	205
Dividends/share ($)	0.05	0.06	0.07	0.08	0.09	0.10	15	100
Dividend yield (%)	0.7	0.5	0.6	0.4	0.3	0.25		
PE range	12–25	14–26	14–27	18–34	24–37	26–44		

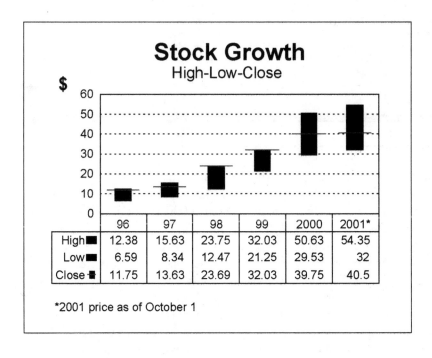

Stock Growth
High-Low-Close

	96	97	98	99	2000	2001*
High■	12.38	15.63	23.75	32.03	50.63	54.35
Low■	6.59	8.34	12.47	21.25	29.53	32
Close■	11.75	13.63	23.69	32.03	39.75	40.5

*2001 price as of October 1

Walgreen Company

Walgreens

200 Wilmot Road
Deerfield, IL 60015
847-940-2500
NYSE: WAG
www.walgreens.com

Chairman and CEO: L. Daniel Jorndt
President: David Bernauer

Earnings Growth	★ ★ ★
Stock Growth	★ ★ ★ ★
Consistency	★ ★ ★ ★
Dividend	★ ★
Total	**13 Points**

Charles Walgreen, Sr., opened the first Walgreens pharmacy a century ago in 1901. Since then, the Chicago-based retailer has become the nation's largest pharmacy chain, with more than 3,000 stores in 43 states and Puerto Rico.

Walgreens serves about 3 million customers a day and fills about 300 million prescriptions per year—nearly 10 percent of all retail prescriptions filled in the United States. And the company is continuing to expand aggressively, with nearly 500 new store openings per year.

The company's popularity with consumers is the result in large part of its focus on service and selection. Its nationwide computer database allows customers to refill their prescriptions at any Walgreens store across the country. And to make it even easier, the company has added drive-through windows at more than 1,500 stores that allow customers to pick up prescriptions without leaving their cars.

The company has also been pulling its stores out of the big shopping malls—where parking and access can be difficult—and relocating them at freestanding locations that provide quicker, easier access for busy consumers.

Walgreens stores average about 10,000 square feet per store and carry a wide range of merchandise, including clocks, calculators, jewelry, artwork, lunch buckets, wastebaskets, coffeemakers, mixers, telephones, tape decks, and TV sets, along with the usual line of cosmetics, toiletries, and tobacco. Many Walgreens also carry dairy products, frozen foods, and a large selection of other grocery items.

The company's newest stores are more than 13,000 square feet and often include pharmacy waiting areas, consultation windows, fragrance bars, and one-hour photo finishing services.

Prescription drugs account for 55 percent of the company's $21 billion in annual revenue. Nonprescription drugs account for 11 percent; cosmetics and toiletries, 8 percent; and general merchandise, 26 percent.

The greatest concentration of Walgreens stores is around its Chicago home base, with 398 stores in Illinois, 136 in Wisconsin, and 116 in Indiana. Other leading areas are Florida, with 494 stores; Arizona, 154; California, 234; Texas, 333; Massachusetts, 80; Minnesota, 72; Missouri, 112; and Tennessee, 111.

All of the company's stores are linked by satellite dish to Walgreen's home office, enabling the company to track inventory, monitor sales levels, and provide prescription histories for Walgreens customers.

Walgreen Company has 115,000 employees and 90,000 shareholders. It has a market capitalization of $36 billion.

EARNINGS PER SHARE GROWTH ★ ★ ★

Past 5 years: 130 percent (18 percent per year)
Past 10 years: 311 percent (15 percent per year)

STOCK GROWTH ★ ★ ★ ★

Past 10 years: 775 percent (24 percent per year)
Dollar growth: $10,000 over 10 years (including reinvested dividends) would have grown to about $93,000.
Average annual compounded rate of return (including reinvested dividends): 25 percent

CONSISTENCY ★ ★ ★ ★

Increased earnings per share: 26 consecutive years
Increased sales: 26 consecutive years

DIVIDEND ★ ★

Dividend yield: 0.5 percent
Increased dividend: 24 consecutive years
Past 5-year increase: 40 percent (7 percent per year)
The company has a direct purchase plan with a minimum $50 initial purchase (and a $10 new account fee). Dividend reinvestment and stock purchase plan allows voluntary contributions of $50 to $60,000 per year.

WALGREEN COMPANY AT A GLANCE

Fiscal year ended: August 31
Revenue and net income in $millions

	1995	1996	1997	1998	1999	2000	5-Year Growth Avg. Annual (%)	5-Year Growth Total (%)
Revenue ($)	10,395	11,778	13,363	15,307	17,839	21,207	15	104
Net income ($)	321	372	436	511	624	777	19	142
Earnings/share ($)	0.33	0.38	0.44	0.51	0.62	0.76	18	130
Dividends/share ($)	0.10	0.11	0.12	0.13	0.13	0.14	7	40
Dividend yield (%)	1.7	1.1	1.0	0.5	0.5	0.4		
PE range	11–22	19–29	21–38	27–56	36–55	28–60		

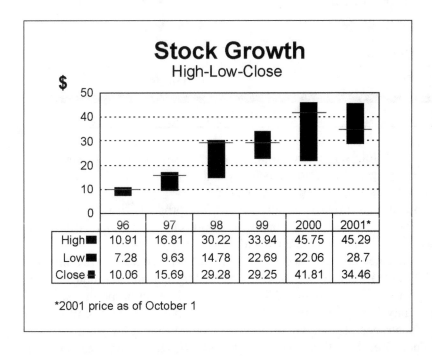

Stock Growth
High-Low-Close

$						
	96	97	98	99	2000	2001*
High■	10.91	16.81	30.22	33.94	45.75	45.29
Low■	7.28	9.63	14.78	22.69	22.06	28.7
Close■	10.06	15.69	29.28	29.25	41.81	34.46

*2001 price as of October 1

Johnson & Johnson

Johnson & Johnson

One Johnson & Johnson Plaza
New Brunswick, NJ 08933
732-524-0400
NYSE: JNJ
www.jnj.com

Chairman and CEO: Ralph Larsen

Earnings Growth	★ ★
Stock Growth	★ ★ ★ ★
Consistency	★ ★ ★ ★
Dividend	★ ★ ★
Total	**13 Points**

Johnson & Johnson is one corporation that most of us got to know at a very early age. The company is renowned worldwide for its line of baby care powders, oils, and related products.

But it also produces a number of other products that have become household names here and around the world, such as Band-Aids, Tylenol, Imodium A-D, and Mylanta antacid.

Consumer products account for about 24 percent of the company's $29 billion in annual revenue. Other leading consumer products from Johnson & Johnson include Nicotrol smoking cessation products, Carefree Panty Shields, Clean & Clear skin care products, Monistat, Pepcid AC, Neutrogena skin and hair products, Sundown and Piz Buin sun care products, Reach toothbrushes, Act Fluoride Rinse, and Stayfree and Sure & Natural sanitary protection products.

In addition to its consumer products, the company has two other key divisions:

- **Pharmaceuticals** (41 percent of total revenue). The company turns out a wide range of pharmaceuticals, including contraceptives, antifungal ointments, central nervous system medications, allergy and asthma medications, gastrointestinal treatments, and skin care formulas.
- **Professional** (35 percent). Johnson & Johnson produces a number of products for doctors and medical professionals, such as sutures, mechanical wound closure products, endoscopic products, dental products, diagnostic products, medical equipment and devices, ophthalmic products, surgical instruments, and medical supplies used by physicians, dentists, therapists, hospitals, and clinics.

The New Brunswick, New Jersey operation has subsidiaries in 50 foreign countries, with sales in about 175 countries. International sales make up about 42 percent of total revenue. The firm spends about $3 billion a year on research and development.

Founded in 1887, Johnson & Johnson has about 100,000 employees and 170,000 shareholders. The company has a market capitalization of about $135 billion.

EARNINGS PER SHARE GROWTH ★ ★

Past 5 years: 83 percent (13 percent per year)
Past 10 years: 254 percent (13 percent per year)

STOCK GROWTH ★ ★ ★ ★

Past 10 years: 609 percent (21.5 percent per year)
Dollar growth: $10,000 over 10 years (including reinvested dividends) would have grown to about $80,000.
Average annual compounded rate of return (including reinvested dividends): 23 percent

CONSISTENCY

Increased earnings per share: 14 consecutive years
Increased sales: 25 consecutive years

DIVIDEND

Dividend yield: 1.2 percent
Increased dividend: 35 consecutive years
Past 5-year increase: 94 percent (14 percent per year)
Good dividend reinvestment and stock purchase plan allows contributions of up to $50,000 per year.

JOHNSON & JOHNSON AT A GLANCE

Fiscal year ended: Dec. 31
Revenue and net income in $millions

	1995	1996	1997	1998	1999	2000	5-Year Growth Avg. Annual (%)	5-Year Growth Total (%)
Revenue ($)	18,921	21,755	22,830	23,995	27,471	29,139	9	54
Net income ($)	2,367	2,882	3,311	3,003	4,167	4,800	15	103
Earnings/share ($)	0.93	1.09	1.21	1.34	1.49	1.70	13	83
Dividends/share ($)	0.32	0.37	0.43	0.49	0.55	0.62	14	94
Dividend yield (%)	1.9	1.5	1.3	1.3	1.2	1.3		
PE range	14–25	12–16	24–33	24–32	37–52	23–37		

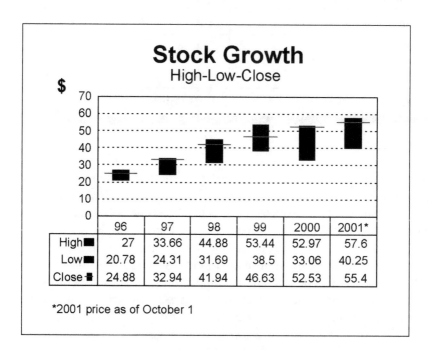

Stock Growth
High-Low-Close

	96	97	98	99	2000	2001*
High ■	27	33.66	44.88	53.44	52.97	57.6
Low ■	20.78	24.31	31.69	38.5	33.06	40.25
Close ■	24.88	32.94	41.94	46.63	52.53	55.4

*2001 price as of October 1

State Street Corporation

STATE STREET.
Serving Institutional Investors Worldwide

225 Franklin Street
Boston, MA 02110
617-786-3000
NYSE: STT
www.statestreet.com

Chairman, President, and CEO:
David A. Spina

Earnings Growth	★ ★ ★
Stock Growth	★ ★ ★ ★
Consistency	★ ★ ★ ★
Dividend	★ ★
Total	**13 Points**

When Merrill Lynch needed a company to do the daily pricing of its 227 mutual funds, it hired State Street for the job. When the Bank of Ireland and the Mitsui Trust in Japan each decided to offer index mutual funds in their markets, they hired State Street to help set up the funds. State Street is the largest mutual fund custodian and accounting agent in the United States, with nearly $3 trillion of mutual fund assets under custody.

Its customers include investment companies, mutual funds, corporate pension plans, corporations, investment managers, nonprofit organizations, endowments, foundations, unions, and other financial companies. State Street offers its institutional investors a wide range of services, including accounting, custody, daily pricing, and information services for investment portfolios.

Its mutual fund custodial services include safekeeping portfolio assets, settling trades, collecting and accounting for income, monitoring corporate actions, and reporting investable cash. The company also offers services for offshore funds and local funds in locations outside the United States, as well as foreign exchange services, cash management, securities lending, fund administration, recordkeeping, banking services, and deposit and short-term investment options. Investment services accounts for about 79 percent of the company's total revenue.

The other 21 percent of revenues comes from its investment management arm. State Street manages a family of mutual funds and offers investment management services for corporations, public funds, and other institutional investors. State Street was a pioneer in the development of domestic and international index funds.

The company has offices in more than 20 countries and does business in nearly 100 countries.

State Street traces its roots back more than two centuries to the Union Bank, which opened shortly after the American Revolution in 1792. State Street sold its small banking operation in 1999.

The company has about 17,600 employees and 6,500 shareholders. It has a market capitalization of about $18 billion.

EARNINGS PER SHARE GROWTH ★ ★ ★

Past 5 years: 143 percent (19.5 percent per year)
Past 10 years: 367 percent (16.5 percent per year)

STOCK GROWTH ★ ★ ★ ★

Past 10 years: 1,019 percent (27 percent per year)
Dollar growth: $10,000 over 10 years (including reinvested dividends) would have grown to about $122,000.
Average annual compounded rate of return (including reinvested dividends): 28.5 percent

CONSISTENCY ★ ★ ★ ★

Increased earnings per share: 24 consecutive years

DIVIDEND   ★ ★

Dividend yield: 0.8 percent
Increased dividend: 22 consecutive years
Past 5-year increase: 106 percent (15.5 percent per year)
Good dividend reinvestment and stock purchase plan; voluntary stock purchase plan allows contributions of $100 to $1,000 per quarter.

STATE STREET AT A GLANCE

Fiscal year ended: Dec. 31
Total assets and net income in $millions

	1995	1996	1997	1998	1999	2000	5-Year Growth Avg. Annual (%)	5-Year Growth Total (%)
Total assets ($)	25,785	31,524	37,975	47,082	60,896	69,298	22	169
Net income ($)	247	293	380	436	489	595	19	141
Earnings/share ($)	0.75	0.89	1.16	1.33	1.50	1.82	19.5	143
Dividends/share ($)	0.17	0.19	0.22	0.25	0.30	0.35	15.5	106
Dividend yield (%)	1.9	1.4	0.9	0.8	0.8	0.7		
PE range	10–15	11–19	13–27	18–27	14–25	17–37		

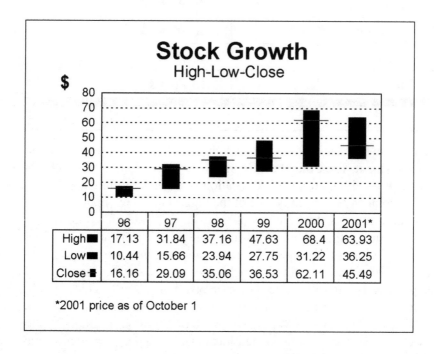

Stock Growth
High-Low-Close

	96	97	98	99	2000	2001*
High	17.13	31.84	37.16	47.63	68.4	63.93
Low	10.44	15.66	23.94	27.75	31.22	36.25
Close	16.16	29.09	35.06	36.53	62.11	45.49

*2001 price as of October 1

Synovus Financial Corporation

901 Front Avenue, Suite 120
P.O. Box 120
Columbus, GA 31902
706-649-2311
NYSE: SNV
www.synovus.com

Chairman and CEO: James Blanchard
President: James Yancey

Earnings Growth	★ ★
Stock Growth	★ ★ ★ ★
Consistency	★ ★ ★ ★
Dividend	★ ★ ★
Total	**13 Points**

If you live in the South, you may be a Synovus Financial customer without even knowing it. The Columbus, Georgia banking institution owns 39 separate banks—with more than 200 locations—all under different names.

The company has become one of the biggest banking organizations in the South through a steady series of acquisitions. But unlike most major banks that merge their acquisitions into a single operating unit with a single name, Synvous retains both the same name and the same management and board of directors. Only the back office duties, such as auditing and data processing, are rolled into the home office operations to cut costs.

So banks such as Bank of North Georgia, Citizens Bank of Cochran, The Citizens Bank of Fort Valley, The Bank of Tuscaloosa, and the Tallahassee State Bank can maintain their local identity and management while still becoming part of the Synovus banking organization. Twenty-six of its 39 banks are located in Georgia.

The company's unique hands-off management strategy has worked well. Synovus has posted 18 consecutive years of record earnings and was recently selected by *Fortune* magazine as the "Best Company to Work for in America."

In addition to the standard banking services of checking, savings, and money market accounts, Synovus also offers trust services and a full-service stock brokerage. Synovus also operates the Synovus Mortgage Corp., which offers mortgage services throughout the Southeast; ProCard, a software company that specializes in commercial card management; and TSYS Total Debt Management, which provides debt collection and bankruptcy management services.

Banking services account for about 70 percent of the company's $1.4 billion in annual revenue.

The rest of its revenue comes from its credit card processing subsidiary, Total System Services (of which Synovus holds an 81 percent share). Total System Services is one of the world's largest credit, debit, and private-label card processing companies. It provides a variety of bankcard and private-label credit card data processing services, including card production, international and domestic electronic clearing, cardholder statement preparation, customer service support, merchant accounting, and management information and reporting. The company primarily processes cardholder accounts for customers issuing Visa, MasterCard, and Diner's Club credit cards, along with corporate cards, private-label cards, and ATM cards.

Founded in 1887, Synovus has about 10,000 employees and 16,000 shareholders. It has a market capitalization of about $9 billion.

EARNINGS PER SHARE GROWTH ★ ★

Past 5 years: 109 percent (16 percent per year)
Past 10 years: 338 percent (16 percent per year)

STOCK GROWTH ★ ★ ★ ★

Past 10 years: 837 percent (25 percent per year)
Dollar growth: $10,000 over 10 years (including reinvested dividends) would have grown to about $110,000.
Average annual compounded rate of return (including reinvested dividends): 27 percent

CONSISTENCY   ★ ★ ★ ★

Increased earnings per share: 18 consecutive years

DIVIDEND   ★ ★ ★

Dividend yield: 1.7 percent
Increased dividend: 21 consecutive years
Past 5-year increase: 193 percent (24 percent per year)
Good dividend reinvestment and stock purchase plan; voluntary stock purchase plan allows contributions of $50 to $250,000 per year. The company also offers a direct purchase plan with a minimum initial investment of $250.

SYNOVUS FINANCIAL AT A GLANCE

Fiscal year ended: Dec. 31
Total assets and net income in $millions

	1995	1996	1997	1998	1999	2000	5-Year Growth Avg. Annual (%)	5-Year Growth Total (%)
Total assets ($)	7,928	8,612	9,260	10,498	12,547	14,908	13	88
Net income ($)	115	140	165	187	225	263	18	129
Earnings/share ($)	0.44	0.53	0.62	0.70	0.80	0.92	16	109
Dividends/share ($)	0.15	0.20	0.24	0.29	0.36	0.44	24	193
Dividend yield (%)	2.2	1.4	1.7	1.2	1.8	1.6		
PE range	10–19	14–28	20–35	24–36	21–31	15–29		

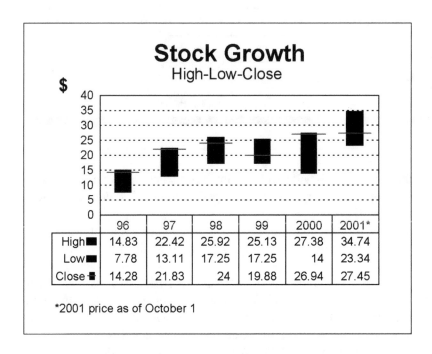

Stock Growth
High-Low-Close

	96	97	98	99	2000	2001*
High	14.83	22.42	25.92	25.13	27.38	34.74
Low	7.78	13.11	17.25	17.25	14	23.34
Close	14.28	21.83	24	19.88	26.94	27.45

*2001 price as of October 1

18

Omnicom Group, Inc.

Omnicom

437 Madison Avenue
New York, NY 10022
212-415-3600
NYSE: OMC
www.omnicomgroup.com

Chairman: Bruce Crawford
President and CEO: John D. Wren

Earnings Growth	★ ★ ★ ★
Stock Growth	★ ★ ★ ★
Consistency	★ ★ ★ ★
Dividend	★
Total	**13 Points**

Talk about your worldwide web. Omnicom, the global advertising conglomerate, operates more than 1,400 separate companies, with customers in more than 100 countries.

The Madison Avenue agency is responsible for some of America's leading ad campaigns, such as "Got Milk" and Budweiser's "Louie the Lizard."

The crown jewel of the Omnicom empire is BBDO Worldwide, which operates more than 300 offices in 76 countries. Its client list is teeming with household names—Pepsi, Visa, Wrigley, GE, Bayer, British Telecom, Fed Ex, Frito-Lay, Gillette, Pizza Hut, Campbell Soup, and Texaco.

Omnicom also operates DDB Worldwide, which has 200 offices in 99 countries, and TBWA Worldwide, which has 182 offices in 57 countries.

DDB handles the advertising for such corporate clients as ExxonMobil, Dell Computer, Volkswagen, Hasbro Toys, and Royal Philips Electronics. TBWA has run campaigns for Taco Bell, Kmart, Apple Computer, and Sony Playstation.

In all, Omnicom serves about 5,000 clients around the world. The company provides a wide range of services, including creation and production of advertising, marketing consultation, strategic media planning and buying, financial and business-to-business advertising, directory advertising, health care communications, managed care consulting, recruitment communications, branding consulting, digital communications, and contract publishing.

The company also offers direct database marketing, field marketing, integrated promotional marketing, public affairs, corporate and financial public relations, reputation management, sports and event marketing, telemarketing, and Internet and digital media development.

Omnicom generates about 50 percent of its revenue from its international operations.

The company was created in 1986 through the merger of three large marketing and corporate communications agencies, BBDO, Doyle Dane Bernbach (DDB), and Needham Harper. Omnicom has 56,000 employees and 4,200 shareholders. It has a market capitalization of $17 billion.

EARNINGS PER SHARE GROWTH ★ ★ ★ ★

Past 5 years: 153 percent (21 percent per year)
Past 10 years: 380 percent (17 percent per year)

STOCK GROWTH ★ ★ ★ ★

Past 10 years: 1,230 percent (29.5 percent per year)
Dollar growth: $10,000 over 10 years (including reinvested dividends) would have grown to about $170,000.
Average annual compounded rate of return (including reinvested dividends): 32 percent

CONSISTENCY ★ ★ ★ ★

Increased earnings per share: 15 consecutive years
Increased sales: 14 consecutive years

DIVIDEND   ★

Dividend yield: 1.0 percent
Increased dividend: 9 of the past 10 years
Past 5-year increase: 112 percent (16 percent per year)
The company does not offer a dividend reinvestment plan.

OMNICOM GROUP AT A GLANCE

Fiscal year ended: Dec. 31
Revenue and net income in $millions

	1995	1996	1997	1998	1999	2000	5-Year Growth Avg. Annual (%)	Total (%)
Revenue ($)	2,257	2,776	3,296	4,291	5,130	6,154	22	173
Net income ($)	140	162	217	279	363	435	25	211
Earnings/share ($)	0.95	1.15	1.28	1.57	2.01	2.40	21	153
Dividends/share ($)	0.33	0.37	0.45	0.53	0.63	0.70	16	112
Dividend yield (%)	2.2	1.6	1.3	1.1	0.7	0.8		
PE range	11–19	15–23	17–33	23–37	27–53	24–36		

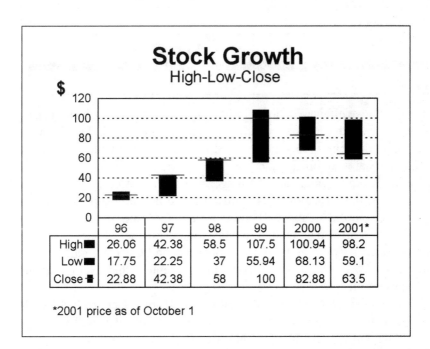

Stock Growth
High-Low-Close

	96	97	98	99	2000	2001*
High■	26.06	42.38	58.5	107.5	100.94	98.2
Low■	17.75	22.25	37	55.94	68.13	59.1
Close■	22.88	42.38	58	100	82.88	63.5

*2001 price as of October 1

19

Home Depot, Inc.

2455 Paces Ferry Road NW
Atlanta, GA 30339
770-433-8211
NYSE: HD
www.homedepot.com

Chairman: Bernard Marcus
President and CEO: Robert L. Nardelli

Earnings Growth	★ ★ ★ ★
Stock Growth	★ ★ ★ ★
Consistency	★ ★ ★ ★
Dividend	★
Total	**13 Points**

Americans' love affair with home improvement has helped turn Home Depot into one of the most successful retailers in the world. The Atlanta-based operation has about 1,150 stores, including 1,029 Home Depots in the United States, 67 in Canada, and 7 in South America. It also operates 30 EXPO Design Centers and 4 Villager's Hardware stores.

With its long aisles of tools, hardware, and building supplies, Home Depot stores average about 100,000 square feet and stock 40,000 to 50,000 different items, including nuts, bolts, brushes, boards, carpet, screens, saws, spades, power tools, appliances, and lawn and garden supplies. The newer stores also include garden centers that average about 25,000 square feet.

The company also offers installation services of select products, such as carpeting and kitchen cabinets. In select test markets, it also offers roofing, siding, and window installation services.

Home Depot has built its business by offering its vast selection of merchandise at low prices. The company avoids special sales but routinely offers wholesale-type prices on all of its merchandise. In addition to the aisles and aisles of hardware, most stores also feature a small stage and bleachers for how-to clinics.

One of the secrets to Home Depot's success is its well-trained salesforce. Store employees are cross-trained in all departments, and many have a background in the building industry. Customers with questions about home projects can usually learn all they need to know by talking with sales clerks. About 95 percent of the company's employees are full-time, and the company offers above-average salaries and benefits to keep its employees in the fold.

Home Depot's primary customers are do-it-yourself homeowners, although many are remodeling contractors and building maintenance professionals who buy supplies at Home Depot stores.

Of the company's $46 billion in annual revenue, 24 percent comes from building materials, lumber, and floor and wall coverings; 28 percent comes from plumbing, heating, lighting, and electrical supplies; 28 percent from hardware and seasonal products; and 20 percent from paint, flooring, and wall coverings.

The Home Depot was founded in 1978 by Bernard Marcus (who still serves as the company's chairman), Arthur Blank (former Home Depot president and CEO), and Kenneth G. Langone (a company board of directors member).

The company has about 227,000 employees and 61,000 shareholders. It has a market capitalization of about $110 billion.

EARNINGS PER SHARE GROWTH　　★ ★ ★ ★

Past 5 years: 223 percent (26 percent per year)
Past 10 years: 1,000 percent (27 percent per year)

STOCK GROWTH　　★ ★ ★ ★

Past 10 years: 1,536 percent (33 percent per year)
Dollar growth: $10,000 over 10 years (including reinvested dividends) would have grown to $164,000.
Average annual compounded rate of return (including reinvested dividends): 33 percent

CONSISTENCY　　★ ★ ★ ★

Increased earnings per share: 14 consecutive years
Increased sales: 20 consecutive years

DIVIDEND   ★

Dividend yield: 0.3 percent
Increased dividend: 13 consecutive years
Past 5-year increase: 300 percent (32 percent per year)
Home Depot offers a good direct stock purchase plan that requires a minimum $250 initial investment.

HOME DEPOT AT A GLANCE

Fiscal year ended: Jan. 31
Revenue and net income in $millions

	1996	1997	1998	1999	2000	2001	5-Year Growth Avg. Annual (%)	Total (%)
Revenue ($)	15,470	19,535	24,146	30,219	38,434	45,738	24	196
Net income ($)	732	938	1,160	1,614	2,320	2,581	29	252
Earnings/share ($)	0.34	0.43	0.55	0.71	1.00	1.10	26	223
Dividends/share ($)	0.04	0.05	0.06	0.08	0.11	0.16	32	300
Dividend yield (%)	0.4	0.4	0.3	0.3	0.2	0.3		
PE range	21–32	27–38	24–46	35–79	48–98	34–70		

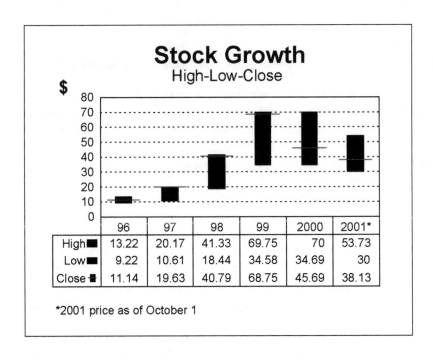

Stock Growth
High-Low-Close

	96	97	98	99	2000	2001*
High■	13.22	20.17	41.33	69.75	70	53.73
Low■	9.22	10.61	18.44	34.58	34.69	30
Close ■	11.14	19.63	40.79	68.75	45.69	38.13

*2001 price as of October 1

MBNA Corporation

1100 North King Street
c/o MBNA America Bank NA
Wilmington, DE 19884
800-362-6255
NYSE: KRB
www.MBNA.com

Chairman and CEO: Alfred Lerner

Earnings Growth	★ ★ ★ ★
Stock Growth	★ ★ ★ ★
Consistency	★ ★ ★ ★
Dividend	★
Total	**13 Points**

MBNA Corporation may be in the credit card business, but its real focus is on consumer marketing. The Wilmington, Delaware operation has become the world's leading independent credit card lender through an aggressive mass mailing campaign and a telemarketing department that encompasses 18 facilities in nine states staffed by 3,500 employees.

In other words, you may know MBNA as the guys who call you during dinner or pepper your mailbox with special offers for "low introductory rates."

But MBNA's marketing pitch has an appealing twist for many consumers. MBNA is the leading issuer of "affinity credit cards," which are specially designed cards endorsed by organizations, universities, associations, and other groups. In other words, it's not just any junk mail—it's junk mail from your alma mater, your club, your favorite sports team, or even your favorite charity or environmental group. Belong to the National Audubon Society? MBNA has a card for you. AAA member? There's a credit card waiting for you as well.

In all, MBNA has more than 50 million credit card customers and associations with about 5,000 organizations. It adds about 14 million new customers a year and about 500 new affinity groups, including such recent enrollees as United Tennis Association, the Atlanta Braves, the Fraternal Order of Police, Rotary International, and United Parcel Service.

Under the affinity group arrangement, MBNA gives the endorsing group a small percentage of the profits on all the transactions registered on the cards sold through that association—a fact that is built into the marketing campaign to encourage customers to sign up. The cards issued to affinity group members usually carry custom graphics and the name and logo of the endorsing organization.

MBNA has also enjoyed growing success marketing its cards over the Internet. Its Web site, MBNA.com, was launched in 2000 and generated more than 2 million new card customers in the first 18 months.

The company has about 23,000 employees and 2,800 shareholders. It has a market capitalization of about $8 billion.

EARNINGS PER SHARE GROWTH ★ ★ ★ ★

Past 5 years: 233 percent (27 percent per year)
Past 9 years: 665 percent (23 percent per year)

STOCK GROWTH ★ ★ ★ ★

Past 9 years: 1,339 percent (31 percent per year)
Dollar growth: $10,000 over 10 years (including reinvested dividends) would have grown to $175,000.
Average annual compounded rate of return (including reinvested dividends): 33 percent

CONSISTENCY ★ ★ ★ ★

Increased earnings per share: 9 consecutive years (since initial offering in 1991)
Increased sales: 9 consecutive years

DIVIDEND ★

Dividend yield: 1.1 percent
Increased dividend: 8 of the past 9 years
Past 5-year increase: 88 percent (13 percent per year)
MBNA does not offer a dividend reinvestment plan.

MBNA AT A GLANCE

Fiscal year ended: Dec. 31
Total assets and net income in $millions

	1995	1996	1997	1998	1999	2000	5-Year Growth Avg. Annual (%)	5-Year Growth Total (%)
Total assets ($)	31,805	45,530	59,523	71,980	85,451	107,514	27.5	238
Net income ($)	353	474	623	776	1,024	1,313	29	272
Earnings/share ($)	0.46	0.59	0.77	0.97	1.21	1.53	27	233
Dividends/share ($)	0.17	0.19	0.21	0.23	0.28	0.32	13	88
Dividend yield (%)	2.4	1.5	1.2	1.1	1.1	1.0		
PE range	11–16	11–21	15–26	13–26	17–27	12–26		

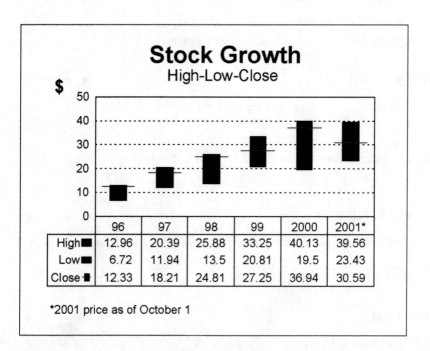

Stock Growth
High-Low-Close

$		96	97	98	99	2000	2001*
	High■	12.96	20.39	25.88	33.25	40.13	39.56
	Low■	6.72	11.94	13.5	20.81	19.5	23.43
	Close■	12.33	18.21	24.81	27.25	36.94	30.59

*2001 price as of October 1

Cintas Corporation

6800 Cintas Boulevard
P.O. Box 65737
Cincinnati, OH 45262
513-459-1200
Nasdaq: CTAS
www.cintas-corp.com

Chairman: Richard Farmer
President: Scott Farmer
CEO: Robert Kohlhepp

Earnings Growth	★ ★ ★ ★
Stock Growth	★ ★ ★ ★
Consistency	★ ★ ★ ★
Dividend	★
Total	**13 Points**

Four million Americans wear a Cintas uniform to work each day. The Cincinnati operation is the nation's largest provider of corporate uniforms, supplying the clothing for a wide range of businesses, from delivery services and airlines to service stations and retail chains.

Cintas has been one of the most consistent companies in America, with 32 consecutive years of record sales and earnings.

Cintas operates facilities in more than 200 cities throughout North America. It has about 140 processing plants, 6 distribution centers, about 15 manufacturing facilities, and 10 direct sales offices. The company's customer base extends from coast to coast and includes more than 400,000 corporate customers.

The company rents or sells the uniforms to customer companies and typically provides the laundry services as well. Cintas designs and manufactures most of the uniforms it supplies for customers.

Uniform rentals account for about 74 percent of the company's $2.2 billion in revenue. Other services combine for the other 26 percent.

Much of the company's growth has come through acquisitions. Since going public in 1983, Cintas has acquired about 100 smaller regional uniform companies. And with more than 700 mostly family-owned uniform rental companies still operating in the United States, Cintas plans to continue its aggressive acquisition policy.

Cintas launched a first aid and safety division in 1997, which provides first aid supplies for companies throughout the United States. It currently has more than 40 first aid supply operations in more than 30 major cities.

In addition to uniforms, the company also supplies rain gear, caps, gloves, long underwear, socks, and work shoes.

Cintas was founded in 1968 and went public with its initial stock offering in 1983. It has about 22,500 employees and 26,000 shareholders. The company has a market capitalization of about $8 billion.

EARNINGS PER SHARE GROWTH ★ ★ ★ ★

Past 5 years: 145 percent (20 percent per year)
Past 10 years: 432 percent (18 percent per year)

STOCK GROWTH ★ ★ ★ ★

Past 10 years: 810 percent (25 percent per year)
Dollar growth: $10,000 over 10 years (including reinvested dividends) would have grown to $95,000.
Average annual compounded rate of return (including reinvested dividends): 25.5 percent

CONSISTENCY ★ ★ ★ ★

Increased earnings per share: 32 consecutive years
Increased sales: 32 consecutive years

DIVIDEND ★

Dividend yield: 0.5 percent
Increased dividend: 17 consecutive years
Past 5-year increase: 175 percent (22 percent per year)
The company offers no dividend reinvestment plan.

CINTAS AT A GLANCE

Fiscal year ended: May 31
Revenue and net income in $millions

	1996	1997	1998	1999	2000	2001	5-Year Growth Avg. Annual (%)	Total (%)
Revenue ($)	730	840	1,198	1,751	1,902	2,160	24	195
Net income ($)	75	91	118	167	193	222	24	196
Earnings/share ($)	0.53	0.64	0.76	0.99	1.14	1.30	20	145
Dividends/share ($)	0.08	0.10	0.12	0.15	0.19	0.22	22	175
Dividend yield (%)	0.4	0.5	0.4	0.4	0.5	0.5		
PE range	23–36	22–38	31–58	31–63	20–47	20–42		

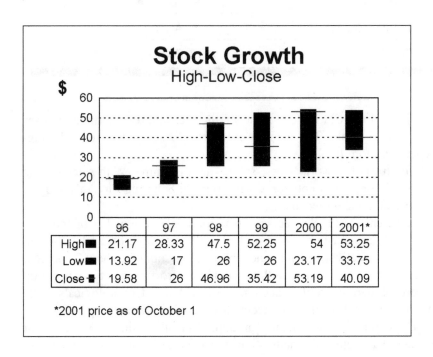

Stock Growth
High-Low-Close

	96	97	98	99	2000	2001*
High■	21.17	28.33	47.5	52.25	54	53.25
Low■	13.92	17	26	26	23.17	33.75
Close■	19.58	26	46.96	35.42	53.19	40.09

*2001 price as of October 1

22
Schering-Plough Corporation

2000 Galloping Hill Road
Kenilworth, NJ 07033
908-298-4000
NYSE: SGP
www.schering-plough.com

Chairman and CEO: Richard J. Kogan

Earnings Growth	★ ★ ★
Stock Growth	★ ★ ★
Consistency	★ ★ ★ ★
Dividend	★ ★ ★
Total	**13 Points**

In a single dose, Claritin can fight off allergies and relieve running noses for a full 24 hours. The wonder drug also does wonders for Schering-Plough's bottom line.

Claritin is the world's best-selling antihistamine. With sales of just over $3 billion, it accounts for nearly a third of Schering-Plough's $10 billion in total annual revenue.

The Kenilworth, New Jersey operation is also the maker of Intron A (Rebetron), an anti-infective drug that generates more than $1 billion in sales. Anti-infectives and anticancer products account for about 20 percent of Schering's total revenue. Allergy and respiratory medications make up 42 percent, cardiovasculars account for 8 percent, dermatologicals make up 7 percent, and other pharmaceuticals account for about 7 percent.

The company also operates an animal health business (8 percent of revenue) that focuses on medications for dogs, cats, cattle, and other farm animals.

Schering is the parent company of Dr. Scholl's foot care products, which markets a broad line of products for aching feet. In addition to its well-known shoe cushions, the company sells Cushlin Gel Corn Wraps, Bunion Guard, and Pedicure Essential foot grooming products. The company also makes Lotramin AF, which is the nation's leading athlete's foot medication, and ("fast-actin'") Tinactin antifungal medication.

Schering-Plough is also a world leader in sun care products. It is the maker of Coppertone, Solarcaine, and Tropical Blend lotions. Sun care products account for 2 percent of the company's revenue, while over-the-counter medications make up 2 percent and foot products account for about 4 percent.

Schering-Plough sells its products worldwide, generating 36 percent of its revenue in foreign markets. Europe is its leading overseas market, although the company also has substantial sales in Latin America, Canada, Asia, and Africa.

The company has about 28,000 employees and 49,000 shareholders. It has a market capitalization of about $56 billion.

EARNINGS PER SHARE GROWTH   ★ ★ ★

Past 5 years: 131 percent (18.5 percent per year)
Past 10 years: 429 percent (18 percent per year)

STOCK GROWTH   ★ ★ ★

Past 10 years: 582 percent (21 percent per year)
Dollar growth: $10,000 over 10 years (including reinvested dividends) would have grown to about $79,000.
Average annual compounded rate of return (including reinvested dividends): 23 percent

CONSISTENCY   ★ ★ ★ ★

Increased earnings per share: 19 consecutive years
Increased sales: 21 consecutive years

DIVIDEND   ★ ★ ★

Dividend yield: 1.7 percent
Increased dividend: 14 consecutive years
Past 5-year increase: 96 percent (14 percent per year)
Good dividend reinvestment and stock purchase plan; voluntary stock purchase plan allows contributions of $25 to $36,000 annually.

SCHERING-PLOUGH AT A GLANCE

Fiscal year ended: Dec. 31
Revenue and net income in $millions

	1995	1996	1997	1998	1999	2000	5-Year Growth Avg. Annual (%)	5-Year Growth Total (%)
Revenue ($)	5,076	5,627	6,745	8,027	9,116	9,815	14	93
Net income ($)	1,053	1,213	1,444	1,756	2,110	2,423	15	103
Earnings/share ($)	0.71	0.83	0.99	1.18	1.42	1.64	18.5	131
Dividends/share ($)	0.28	0.32	0.37	0.43	0.49	0.55	14	96
Dividend yield (%)	2.5	2.1	1.5	0.9	1.0	1.2		
PE range	11–19	15–22	16–32	25–48	28–42	18–36		

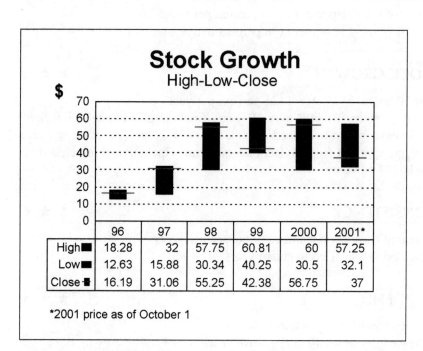

Stock Growth
High-Low-Close

$						
	96	97	98	99	2000	2001*
High	18.28	32	57.75	60.81	60	57.25
Low	12.63	15.88	30.34	40.25	30.5	32.1
Close	16.19	31.06	55.25	42.38	56.75	37

*2001 price as of October 1

Household International, Inc.

HOUSEHOLD

2700 Sanders Road
Prospect Heights, IL 60070
847-205-7490
NYSE: HI
www.household.com

Chairman and CEO: William F. Aldinger

Earnings Growth	★ ★ ★ ★
Stock Growth	★ ★ ★ ★
Consistency	★ ★ ★
Dividend	★ ★
Total	**13 Points**

Household International has become one of the nation's leading lenders by targeting the customers no one else wants. The company's prime target are consumers who have limited credit histories, modest incomes, high debt-to-income ratios, or previous credit problems.

Why court the problem borrowers? Because Household can charge a higher interest rate to those customers to compensate for the additional risk.

Household operates 1,400 branch offices in 46 states and claims about 3.5 million customers. The branches are operated under the company's subsidiaries, HFC and Beneficial Finance.

Household is the second largest consumer finance company in the United States and one of the nation's top independent providers of auto financing for customers who don't have access to traditional lending sources. Household extends its car loans through about 8,500 auto dealerships nationwide.

The Prospect Heights, Illinois operation is also the third largest credit insurance company in the United States, offering credit life, accident, disability, and health insurance.

Household is also one of the largest consumer finance companies in the United Kingdom. The company has about 180 branches throughout the UK. Canada is Household's other major market, with about 100 branch offices in ten provinces.

The company is also the second largest provider of third-party, private-label, or cobranded credit cards in the United States. Its merchant customers include such companies as Best Buy, GM, Mitsubishi, and Yamaha. The cobranded cards offer special benefits to cardholders. For instance, for the GM credit cards—issued through Household's alliance with General Motors—customers can earn discounts on the purchase or lease of a new GM vehicle. The company also offers cobranded cards for the AFL-CIO and its 67 affiliated national and international labor unions.

Household's managed receivables break down this way: credit cards, 34 percent; home equity and other secured loans, 48 percent; and unsecured loans, 18 percent.

Founded in 1878, Household has about 29,000 employees and a market capitalization of about $32 billion.

EARNINGS PER SHARE GROWTH   ★ ★ ★ ★

Past 5 years: 146 percent (20 percent per year)
Past 10 years: 251 percent (13 percent per year)

STOCK GROWTH   ★ ★ ★ ★

Past 10 years: 810 percent (25 percent per year)
Dollar growth: $10,000 over 10 years (including reinvested dividends) would have grown to $109,000.
Average annual compounded rate of return (including reinvested dividends): 27 percent

CONSISTENCY   ★ ★ ★

Increased earnings per share: 9 of the past 10 years
Increased sales: 7 of the past 10 years

DIVIDEND ★ ★

Dividend yield: 1.5 percent

Increased dividend: 10 consecutive years

Past 5-year increase: 68 percent (11 percent per year)

Good dividend reinvestment and stock purchase plan; the plan allows participating shareholder to purchase shares at a 2.5 percent discount from the market price and allows purchase of fractional shares. Investors may purchase up to $5,000 per quarter.

HOUSEHOLD INTERNATIONAL AT A GLANCE

Fiscal year ended: Dec. 31
Revenue and net income in $millions

	1995	1996	1997	1998	1999	2000	5-Year Growth Avg. Annual (%)	Total (%)
Revenue ($)	5,144	5,059	5,503	8,708	9,500	11,961	18	133
Net income ($)	453	820	940	1,157	1,486	1,701	31	275
Earnings/share ($)	1.44	1.77	2.17	2.32	3.07	3.55	20	146
Dividends/share ($)	0.44	0.49	0.55	0.60	0.68	0.74	11	68
Dividend yield (%)	2.6	1.6	1.3	1.5	1.8	1.4		
PE range	10–14	10–18	13–22	22–52	11–17	8–16		

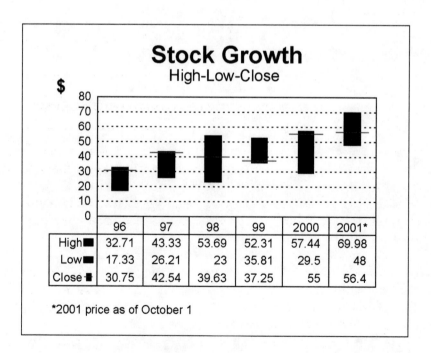

Stock Growth
High-Low-Close

	96	97	98	99	2000	2001*
High■	32.71	43.33	53.69	52.31	57.44	69.98
Low■	17.33	26.21	23	35.81	29.5	48
Close■	30.75	42.54	39.63	37.25	55	56.4

*2001 price as of October 1

M&T Bank Corporation

M&T Bank Corporation

One M&T Plaza
Buffalo, NY 14203
716-842-5445
NYSE: MTB
www.mandtbank.com

Chairman, President, and CEO: Robert G. Willmers

Earnings Growth	★ ★
Stock Growth	★ ★ ★ ★
Consistency	★ ★ ★ ★
Dividend	★ ★ ★
Total	**13 Points**

Founded more than 140 years ago, the M&T Bank Corp. (formerly known as First Empire State Corp.) has been growing rapidly recently through a series of acquisitions. The company does most of its business through two wholly owned banking subsidiaries, Manufacturers and Traders Trust Company and the M&T Bank. M&T is the nation's 30th largest banking organization.

The company has about 500 branch offices throughout New York, Pennsylvania, Maryland, and West Virginia. Recent acquisitions include Premier National Bancorp, a New York state bank with 34 branches, and Keystone Financial, a Pennsylvania-based bank with branch offices in its home state as well as Maryland and West Virginia.

M&T offers the standard banking services, such as savings, checking, and loan services for consumers, businesses, and other clients.

M&T also conducts business through a number of subsidiaries, including M&T Capital Corp., which provides equity capital and long-term credit to small businesses; M&T Credit Corp., which offers credit services for consumers; M&T Mortgage, which has offices in several states and specializes in residential home mortgage loans and mortgage services; M&T Financial, which specializes in capital equipment leasing; M&T Real Estate, which specializes in commercial real estate lending and servicing; and M&T Securities, which provides securities brokerage and advisory services for bank customers.

The company has established a solid presence in New York City, particularly in the area of multiple-unit housing financing.

M&T breaks its operations into several key divisions, including commercial banking, auditing, credit, facilities management, finance, retail banking, and trust and investment services.

The company's loan portfolio breaks down this way: commercial loans, 22 percent; commercial real estate, 38 percent; consumer real estate, 21 percent; and other consumer loans, 19 percent.

M&T has about 9,000 employees and 5,000 shareholders. It has a market capitalization of about $7 billion.

EARNINGS PER SHARE GROWTH

Past 5 years: 94 percent (14 percent per year)
Past 10 years: 361 percent (16.5 percent per year)

STOCK GROWTH ★ ★ ★ ★

Past 10 years: 1,078 percent (28 percent per year)
Dollar growth: $10,000 over 10 years (including reinvested dividends) would have grown to $128,000.
Average annual compounded rate of return (including reinvested dividends): 29 percent

CONSISTENCY ★ ★ ★ ★

Increased earnings per share: 13 consecutive years
Increased sales: 10 consecutive years

DIVIDEND

Dividend yield: 1.4 percent
Increased dividend: More than 20 consecutive years
Past 5-year increase: 152 percent (20 percent per year)
Good dividend reinvestment and stock purchase plan; voluntary stock purchase plan allows contributions of $10 to $1,000 per quarter.

M&T BANK AT A GLANCE

Fiscal year ended: Dec. 31
Total assets and net income in $millions

	1995	1996	1997	1998	1999	2000	5-Year Growth Avg. Annual (%)	Total (%)
Total assets ($)	11,956	12,944	14,003	20,584	22,409	28,949	19	142
Net income ($)	131	151	176	222	266	303	18	131
Earnings/share ($)	1.88	2.13	2.53	2.79	3.28	3.64	14	94
Dividends/share ($)	0.25	0.28	0.32	0.38	0.45	0.63	20	152
Dividend yield (%)	1.4	1.1	0.8	0.7	1.1	1.1		
PE range	7–11	9–13	11–18	15–22	12–17	10–19		

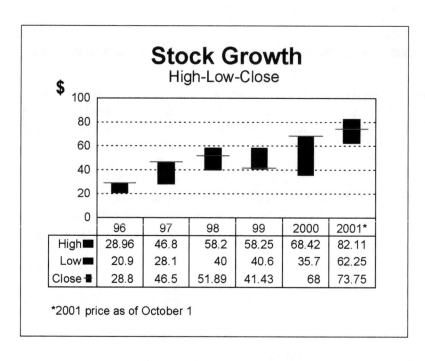

Stock Growth
High-Low-Close

	96	97	98	99	2000	2001*
High■	28.96	46.8	58.2	58.25	68.42	82.11
Low■	20.9	28.1	40	40.6	35.7	62.25
Close■	28.8	46.5	51.89	41.43	68	73.75

*2001 price as of October 1

25
BB&T Corporation

200 West Second Street
Winston-Salem, NC 27101
336-733-2000
NYSE: BBT
www.bbandt.com

Chairman and CEO: John A. Allison
President: Kelly S. King

Earnings Growth	★ ★
Stock Growth	★ ★ ★
Consistency	★ ★ ★ ★
Dividend	★ ★ ★ ★
Total	**13 Points**

BB&T (formerly Branch Banking and Trust) has used a corporate buying binge the past ten years to transform itself from a small regional bank to one of the larger financial services companies in the southeastern United States. The Winston-Salem, North Carolina institution has acquired more than 50 banks and thrifts, 47 insurance agencies, and 14 financial services providers over the past decade.

BB&T has about 930 branch offices in North and South Carolina, Virginia, Maryland, Georgia, Tennessee, West Virginia, Alabama, Kentucky, and Washington, D.C. The largest concentration of branches is in its home state of North Carolina, with about 335 offices.

The company offers a wide range of services, including small business lending, commercial middle market lending, retail lending, home equity and mortgage lending, sales finance, leasing, asset management, and trust services.

It also offers agency insurance, treasury services, investment and mutual fund sales, capital markets, factoring, asset-based lending, international banking services, cash management, electronic payment services, and credit and debit card services.

BB&T also operates two subsidiaries: Scott & Stringfellow, a broker-dealer in Richmond, Virginia, and Regional Acceptance Corporation, a consumer finance company specializing in indirect used-auto lending.

The company's loan portfolio breaks down this way: commercial, 53 percent; consumer, 24 percent; mortgages, 21 percent; and other, 2 percent.

BB&T is the largest originator of residential mortgage loans in the Carolinas, with about $5 billion a year in new loans.

The company's commercial lending program is targeted to small and midsize companies with sales of $200 million or less. It also offers a number of construction loans for new homes and commercial buildings, including industrial facilities, apartments, shopping centers, office buildings, hotels, and warehouses.

Founded in 1872, BB&T is the oldest bank headquartered in North Carolina. The company has about 17,500 employees and a market capitalization of about $15 billion.

EARNINGS PER SHARE GROWTH ★ ★

Past 5 years: 85 percent (13 percent per year)
Past 9 years: 219 percent (13.5 percent per year)

STOCK GROWTH ★ ★ ★

Past 10 years: 546 percent (21 percent per year)
Dollar growth: $10,000 over 10 years (including reinvested dividends) would have grown to $86,000.
Average annual compounded rate of return (including reinvested dividends): 24 percent

CONSISTENCY ★ ★ ★ ★

Increased earnings per share: 10 consecutive years
Increased sales: 10 consecutive years

DIVIDEND ★ ★ ★ ★

Dividend yield: 2.8 percent
Increased dividend: 10 consecutive years
Past 5-year increase: 95 percent (14 percent per year)
Good dividend reinvestment and stock purchase plan; voluntary stock purchase plan allows contributions of at least $25 to $10,000 per month.

BB&T AT A GLANCE

Fiscal year ended: Dec. 31
Total assets and net income in $millions

	1995	1996	1997	1998	1999	2000	5-Year Growth Avg. Annual (%)	Total (%)
Total assets ($)	20,493	21,247	29,178	34,427	43,481	59,340	24	190
Net income ($)	355	467	502	652	706	626	12	76
Earnings/share ($)	1.17	1.27	1.30	1.75	1.83	2.17	13	85
Dividends/share ($)	0.43	0.50	0.58	0.66	0.75	0.86	14	95
Dividend yield (%)	3.7	3.3	2.5	2.0	2.1	3.1		
PE range	8–12	11–15	14–26	16–24	15–23	13–24		

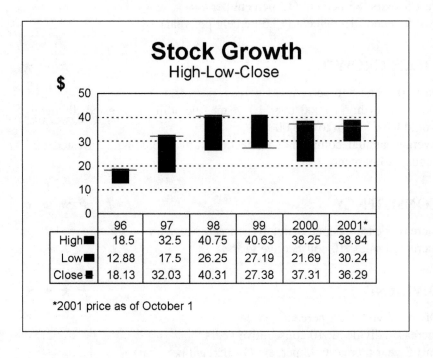

Stock Growth
High-Low-Close

	96	97	98	99	2000	2001*
High■	18.5	32.5	40.75	40.63	38.25	38.84
Low■	12.88	17.5	26.25	27.19	21.69	30.24
Close ■	18.13	32.03	40.31	27.38	37.31	36.29

*2001 price as of October 1

Kohl's Corporation

KOHL'S

N56 W17000 Ridgewood Drive
Menomonee Falls, WI 53051
262-703-7000
NYSE: KSS
www.kohls.com

Chairman: William S. Kellogg
CEO: Lawrence Montgomery

Earnings Growth	★ ★ ★ ★
Stock Growth	★ ★ ★ ★
Consistency	★ ★ ★ ★
Dividend	
Total	**12 Points**

Name-brand merchandise at modest prices has helped Kohl's become one of the nation's fastest growing retailers.

The Menomonee Falls, Wisconsin department store chain has grown from 40 stores in 1986 to more than 350 stores today. Its stores are located in 28 states throughout the United States, although about half are located in the Midwest. Kohl's plans to open about 70 new stores each year. The company jumped feetfirst into the New York area in 2000, opening 35 new stores in New York, New Jersey, and Connecticut.

Kohl's sells moderately priced apparel; shoes; accessories; soft home products such as towels, sheets, and pillows; housewares; and a variety of other goods. It gears its merchandise to middle-income customers shopping for their families. Women's apparel accounts for about 30 percent of the company's $6 billion in annual revenue. Other departments include men's products, 21 percent of revenue; shoes, 9 percent; children's goods, 13 percent; home products, 19 percent; and accessories, 8 percent.

Kohl's stores have fewer departments than traditional department stores, but they offer customers a broad assortment of merchandise displayed in complete selections of styles, colors, and sizes.

The company focuses strongly on cost controls, with lean staffing levels, sophisticated management information systems, and operating efficiencies resulting from centralized buying, advertising, and distribution. The strategy has worked extremely well for Kohl's, which has posted record earnings and revenue all ten years since it began reporting its financial results. The company went public with its initial stock offering in 1992.

Most of Kohl's stores are located in shopping centers. The company supplies its stores through its four distribution centers in Wisconsin, Virginia, Missouri, and Ohio.

Kohl's has about 17,000 full-time and 27,000 part-time employees and 6,000 shareholders. The company has a market capitalization of about $19 billion.

EARNINGS PER SHARE GROWTH   ★ ★ ★ ★

Past 5 years: 293 percent (32 percent per year)
Past 10 years: 5,400 percent (49 percent per year)

STOCK GROWTH   ★ ★ ★ ★

Past 10 years: 1,593 percent (32 percent per year)
Dollar growth: $10,000 over 10 years (including reinvested dividends) would have grown to $170,000.
Average annual compounded rate of return (including reinvested dividends): 32 percent

CONSISTENCY   ★ ★ ★ ★

Increased earnings per share: 10 consecutive years
Increased sales: 10 consecutive years

DIVIDEND

Kohl's pays no dividend.

KOHL'S AT A GLANCE

Fiscal year ended: Dec. 31
Revenue and net income in $millions

	1995	1996	1997	1998	1999	2000	5-Year Growth Avg. Annual (%)	5-Year Growth Total (%)
Revenue ($)	1,926	2,388	3,060	3,682	4,557	6,152	26	219
Net income ($)	81	103	141	192	258	372	36	359
Earnings/share ($)	0.28	0.35	0.46	0.59	0.77	1.10	32	293
Dividends/share ($)	—	—	—	—	—	—		
Dividend yield (%)	—	—	—	—	—	—		
PE range	19–28	25–42	26–55	35–67	48–68	43–86		

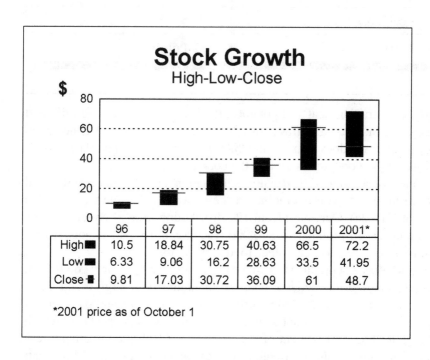

Stock Growth
High-Low-Close

$

	96	97	98	99	2000	2001*
High	10.5	18.84	30.75	40.63	66.5	72.2
Low	6.33	9.06	16.2	28.63	33.5	41.95
Close	9.81	17.03	30.72	36.09	61	48.7

*2001 price as of October 1

27

Sysco Corporation

1390 Enclave Parkway
Houston, TX 77077
281-584-1390
NYSE: SYY
www.sysco.com

Chairman and CEO: Charles H. Cotros
President: Richard Schnieders

Earnings Growth	★ ★
Stock Growth	★ ★ ★
Consistency	★ ★ ★ ★
Dividend	★ ★ ★
Total	**12 Points**

Sysco delivers the meat and potatoes, the bread and butter, the milk and honey, the biscuits and gravy, the green eggs and ham—OK, no green eggs—but Sysco does ship about 275,000 food products and related goods to food service operations around the country.

The Houston-based distributor is the nation's largest marketer of food service products, with operations in the nation's 150 largest cities (plus parts of Canada). Operating from 124 distribution centers, Sysco delivers food and related products to 370,000 restaurants, hotels, schools, hospitals, retirement homes, and other food service operations.

Sysco does not produce its own products but rather procures goods from several thousand independent sources, including both large brand-name food producers and independent private-label processors and packers.

Sysco's leading product segment is canned and dry products, which account for about 21 percent of the company's $19 billion in annual revenue. Other significant contributors are fresh and frozen meats, 14 percent; frozen fruits, vegetables, and bakery goods, 14 percent; dairy products, 9 percent; paper and disposables, 8 percent; and poultry, 10 percent. The company also handles beverages, fresh produce, janitorial products, seafood, and medical supplies.

Restaurant sales account for 65 percent of Sysco's annual revenue, while hospitals and nursing homes account for 10 percent; schools and colleges make up 6 percent; hotels and motels generate 5 percent; and other sources such as retail groceries account for 14 percent.

The company's 10,000 sales and service representatives also help food service clients with menu planning and inventory control, as well as contract services for installing kitchen equipment and beverage dispensers.

Founded in 1969 through the merger of nine small food distributors, Sysco has grown rapidly through a series of acquisitions. In all, the company has acquired more than 50 other food-related business.

The company has 40,000 employees and 15,000 shareholders. Sysco has a market capitalization of $19 billion.

EARNINGS PER SHARE GROWTH   ★ ★

Past 5 years: 94 percent (14 percent per year)
Past 10 years: 277 percent (14 percent per year)

STOCK GROWTH   ★ ★ ★

Past 10 years: 460 percent (19 percent per year)
Dollar growth: $10,000 over 10 years (including reinvested dividends) would have grown to about $62,000.
Average annual compounded rate of return (including reinvested dividends): 20 percent

CONSISTENCY   ★ ★ ★ ★

Increased earnings per share: 24 consecutive years
Increased sales: 24 consecutive years

DIVIDEND   ★ ★ ★

Dividend yield: 1.1 percent
Increased dividend: 30 consecutive years
Past 5-year increase: 130 percent (18 percent per year)
Good dividend reinvestment and stock purchase plan; voluntary stock purchase plan allows contributions of $100 to $10,000 per month.

SYSCO AT A GLANCE

Fiscal year ended: Dec. 31
Revenue and net income in $millions

	1995	1996	1997	1998	1999	2000	5-Year Growth Avg. Annual (%)	Total (%)
Revenue ($)	12,118	13,395	14,455	15,328	17,423	19,003	9	57
Net income ($)	252	277	302	325	362	454	12.5	80
Earnings/share ($)	0.35	0.38	0.43	0.48	0.54	0.68	14	94
Dividends/share ($)	0.10	0.13	0.15	0.17	0.19	0.23	18	130
Dividend yield (%)	1.5	1.6	1.6	1.5	1.4	1.3		
PE range	16–22	18–23	17–27	21–30	23–38	14–34		

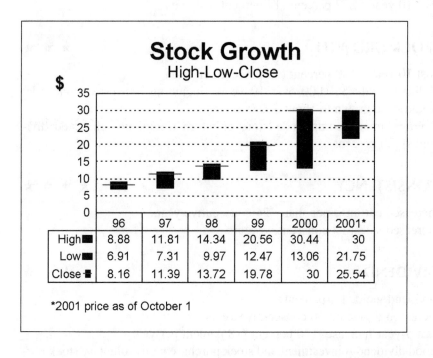

Stock Growth
High-Low-Close

$	96	97	98	99	2000	2001*
High■	8.88	11.81	14.34	20.56	30.44	30
Low■	6.91	7.31	9.97	12.47	13.06	21.75
Close■	8.16	11.39	13.72	19.78	30	25.54

*2001 price as of October 1

28
Wal-Mart Stores, Inc.

WAL★MART®

702 Southwest 8th Street
Bentonville, AR 72716
501-273-4000
NYSE: WMT
www.walmartstores.com

Chairman: S. Robinson Walton
President and CEO: H. Lee Scott, Jr.

Earnings Growth	★ ★ ★
Stock Growth	★ ★ ★
Consistency	★ ★ ★ ★
Dividend	★ ★
Total	**12 Points**

First America, then the world. Wal-Mart has taken its low prices to markets the world over. In recent years, the company has opened more than 1,000 stores in Europe, Asia, and Latin America.

Wal-Mart is the world's largest retail chain, with more than 4,000 stores in all. In addition to its 1,100 foreign Wal-Mart stores, the company operates about 1,750 discount stores in the United States, plus 900 Supercenters, 500 Sam's Clubs, and 19 Neighborhood Markets.

Wal-Mart's Supercenter stores are its fastest-growing segment. First introduced in 1989, the stores range in size from 170,000 to 200,000 square feet and offer a wide selection of groceries, general merchandise, and customer services, including pharmacy, dry cleaning, portrait studios, photo finishing, hair salons, and optical shops.

Wal-Mart's product sales break down this way: hard goods (hardware, housewares, auto supplies, and small appliances), 21 percent; soft goods (apparel, towels, sheets, etc.), 19 percent; grocery, candy, and tobacco, 19 percent; pharmaceuticals, 10 percent; sporting goods and toys, 7 percent; health and beauty aids, 7 percent; records and electronics, 8 percent; stationery, 3 percent; shoes, 2 percent; and jewelry, 2 percent.

The company has posted consistent earnings and revenue growth for many years, including 31 consecutive years of record sales and earnings dating back to 1969, the year the company went public.

Wal-Mart was founded in 1962 by Sam Walton, who ultimately became a legend of American business and the nation's richest man before his death in 1992. Walton entered the retailing business in 1945 when he opened a Ben Franklin variety store franchise in Newport, Arkansas. His first Wal-Mart store (called Wal-Mart Discount City) was opened in Rogers, Arkansas, in 1962.

Walton achieved his early success largely by locating stores in rural locations like Rogers where there was no competition from other discounters. The retailer's everyday low prices attracted throngs of shoppers wherever the new stores appeared. The company has been able to keep its prices low by buying its merchandise in large volume and turning it over quickly, incurring a minimum of overhead in the process.

Wal-Mart stores have since invaded urban areas en masse, where they compete toe-to-toe with Target, Kmart, and other discounters. Even though the competition is stiffer, the urban-based Wal-Marts have still proven very profitable.

Wal-Mart has 1,250,000 employees and 300,000 shareholders. The company has a market capitalization of $230 billion.

EARNINGS PER SHARE GROWTH ★ ★ ★

Past 5 years: 133 percent (18 percent per year)
Past 10 years: 382 percent (17 percent per year)

STOCK GROWTH ★ ★ ★

Past 10 years: 372 percent (17 percent per year)
Dollar growth: $10,000 over 10 years (including reinvested dividends) would have grown to about $50,000.
Average annual compounded rate of return (including reinvested dividends): 17.5 percent

CONSISTENCY

Increased earnings per share: 31 consecutive years (every year since going public in 1969)
Increased sales: 31 consecutive years

DIVIDEND

Dividend yield: 0.5 percent
Increased dividend: 23 consecutive years
Past 5-year increase: 140 percent (19 percent per year)
Excellent dividend reinvestment and stock purchase program; voluntary stock purchase plan allows contributions of $50 to $150,000 per year. Investors may also elect to have $25 a month (or more) automatically deducted from their checking account and invested in Wal-Mart stock. Persons who are not shareholders may also enroll in the program either by investing as little as $250 or by authorizing automatic monthly withdrawals of at least $25.

WAL-MART STORES AT A GLANCE

Fiscal year ended: Jan. 31
Revenue and net income in $millions

	1996	1997	1998	1999	2000	2001	5-Year Growth Avg. Annual (%)	Total (%)
Revenue ($)	93,627	104,859	117,958	137,634	165,013	191,329	15	104
Net income ($)	2,740	3,056	3,526	4,430	5,377	6,295	17	130
Earnings/share ($)	0.60	0.67	0.78	0.99	1.28	1.40	18	133
Dividends/share ($)	0.10	0.11	0.14	0.16	0.20	0.24	19	140
Dividend yield (%)	0.8	0.9	0.8	0.5	0.4	0.4		
PE range	16–23	16–31	24–53	39–71	33–55	—		

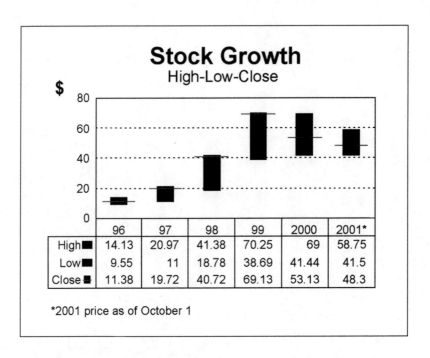

Stock Growth
High-Low-Close

	96	97	98	99	2000	2001*
High	14.13	20.97	41.38	70.25	69	58.75
Low	9.55	11	18.78	38.69	41.44	41.5
Close	11.38	19.72	40.72	69.13	53.13	48.3

*2001 price as of October 1

Fiserv, Inc.

255 Fiserv Drive
Brookfield, WI 53054
262-879-5000
Nasdaq: FISV
www.fiserv.com

Chairman: Donald F. Dillon
President and CEO: Leslie Muma

Earnings Growth	★ ★ ★ ★
Stock Growth	★ ★ ★ ★
Consistency	★ ★ ★ ★
Dividend	
Total	**12 Points**

Fiserv helps bankers keep track of their money. The Milwaukee-area operation is the nation's largest data processing provider for banks and savings institutions.

The company provides a wide range of data processing services for nearly 8,000 financial clients, including banks, brokerage companies, credit unions, financial planners and investment advisors, insurance companies, leasing companies, mortgage banks, and savings institutions.

Fiserv has customers in more than 85 countries, although its U.S. operations still generate the vast majority of its $1.65 billion in annual revenue.

The company provides a wide range of data processing services, including software systems for account, item, and financial transaction processing and recordkeeping, regulatory reporting, electronic funds transfer, and related database management. The company offers services in four general categories, including:

- **Financial institution solutions.** The company provides account and transaction processing services, lending systems, auto leasing systems, revolving credit services, plastic card services, and a variety of related services for more than 7,500 financial institutions. It processes more than 4 billion checks annually.

- **Insurance solutions.** Fiserv offers systems and software for life, health, and property and casualty insurance, and workers' compensation, as well as claims management services for about 3,000 insurance companies.
- **Securities solutions.** The firm provides clearing, execution, and facilitation of investment transactions for more than 400 Internet and traditional brokerage companies.
- **Trust services solutions.** The company offers retirement plan administrative services, mutual fund custody, and financial marketing services for financial planners and investment advisors.

Fiserv was formed in 1984 by George Dalton and Leslie Muma (who continues to serve as president and CEO) through the merger of two regional data processing firms. Since then, the Milwaukee-area operation has made more than 100 acquisitions.

Fiserv has about 14,000 employees and 20,000 shareholders. The company has a market capitalization of about $7 billion.

EARNINGS PER SHARE GROWTH ★ ★ ★ ★

Past 5 years: 172 percent (22 percent per year)
Past 10 years: 548 percent (21 percent per year)

STOCK GROWTH ★ ★ ★ ★

Past 10 years: 931 percent (26 percent per year)
Dollar growth: $10,000 over 10 years would have grown to $100,000.
Average annual compounded rate of return: 26 percent

CONSISTENCY ★ ★ ★ ★

Increased earnings per share: 15 consecutive years
Increased sales: 15 consecutive years

DIVIDEND

Fiserv pays no dividend, nor does it offer a stock purchase plan.

FISERV AT A GLANCE

Fiscal year ended: Dec. 31
Revenue and net income in $millions

	1995	1996	1997	1998	1999	2000	5-Year Growth Avg. Annual (%)	Total (%)
Revenue ($)	703	798	974	1,234	1,408	1,654	19	135
Net income ($)	50	62	91	114	138	172	28	244
Earnings/share ($)	0.50	0.60	0.76	0.90	1.09	1.36	22	172
Dividends/share ($)	—	—	—	—	—	—		
Dividend yield (%)	—	—	—	—	—	—		
PE range	17–28	16–26	19–30	22–39	22–37	17–45		

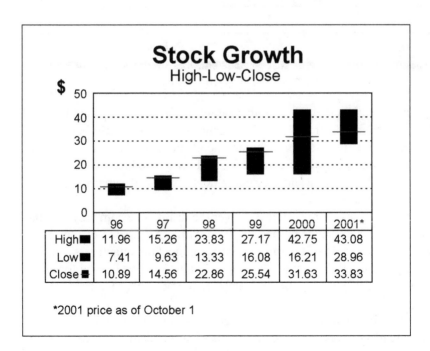

Stock Growth
High-Low-Close

	96	97	98	99	2000	2001*
High■	11.96	15.26	23.83	27.17	42.75	43.08
Low■	7.41	9.63	13.33	16.08	16.21	28.96
Close■	10.89	14.56	22.86	25.54	31.63	33.83

*2001 price as of October 1

30
Cardinal Health

7000 Cardinal Place
Dublin, OH 43017
614-757-5000
NYSE: CAH
www.cardinal.com

Chairman and CEO: Robert D. Walter
President: John Kane

Earnings Growth	★ ★ ★ ★
Stock Growth	★ ★ ★ ★
Consistency	★ ★ ★ ★
Dividend	
Total	**12 Points**

Cardinal Health serves as a lifeline between medical manufacturers and the health care industry. The Dublin, Ohio operation has used an aggressive series of acquisitions to become one of the nation's leading distributors of pharmaceuticals and related health care products to drugstores, hospitals, care centers, and pharmacy departments of supermarkets and mass merchandisers.

Cardinal does more than just deliver the drugs. The company also has about 1,600 pharmacists on hand to help with other phases of the operation. For instance, 15 of the top 20 pharmaceutical manufacturers use Cardinal subsidiary, R. P. Scherer, to help them develop new dosage forms for their drugs. Cardinal also offers contract manufacturing services for pharmaceutical companies.

Pharmaceutical distribution services account for about 75 percent of the company's operating revenue; its medical-surgical products and services segment for about 19 percent; pharmaceutical technologies and services, 4 percent; and automation and information services, 2 percent.

Its leading divisions include:

- **Cardinal Distribution and National Specialty Services,** which serves as a pharmaceutical distributor to retailers and health care facilities
- **Pyxis Corp.,** which is the nation's largest manufacturer of point-of-use systems that automate the distribution, management, and control of medications and supplies in hospitals and alternate care facilities
- **Allegiance Corp.,** which is a leading manufacturer and supplier of health care products and a provider of cost management services for hospitals, laboratories, and other health care facilities
- **PCI Services,** which provides integrated packaging services to pharmaceutical manufacturers

Cardinal's full-service national coverage, its integrated inventory management and marketing systems, coupled with guaranteed next-day delivery, have helped strengthen its relationships with customers. Cardinal's innovations have also caught the attention of drug manufacturers who increasingly prefer to work with technologically sophisticated distributors that can take larger, more diversified product lines to market.

Founded originally as a food wholesaler in 1971, Cardinal abandoned the food business long ago to focus solely on the health care business. The firm has acquired about 20 other companies since 1995.

Cardinal has about 42,000 employees and a market capitalization of about $32 billion.

EARNINGS PER SHARE GROWTH ★ ★ ★ ★

Past 5 years: 157 percent (21 percent per year)
Past 10 years: 683 percent (23 percent per year)

STOCK GROWTH ★ ★ ★ ★

Past 10 years: 1,625 percent (33 percent per year)
Dollar growth: $10,000 over 10 years (including reinvested dividends) would have grown to $180,000.
Average annual compounded rate of return (including reinvested dividends): 33 percent

CONSISTENCY ★ ★ ★ ★

Increased earnings per share: 12 consecutive years
Increased sales: 10 consecutive years

DIVIDEND

Dividend yield: 0.2 percent
Increased dividend: 5 of the past 10 years
Past 5-year increase: 60 percent (10 percent per year)
Cardinal does not offer a dividend reinvestment and stock purchase plan.

CARDINAL HEALTH AT A GLANCE

Fiscal year ended: June 30
Revenue and net income in $millions

	1996	1997	1998	1999	2000	2001	5-Year Growth Avg. Annual (%)	Total (%)
Revenue ($)	8,862	18,394	21,076	32,733	38,350	47,948	23.5	188
Net income ($)	160	334	448	499	718	857	40	435
Earnings/share ($)	0.73	0.82	1.05	1.12	1.60	1.88	21	157
Dividends/share ($)	0.04	0.04	0.05	0.06	0.07	0.08	10	60
Dividend yield (%)	0.2	0.2	0.2	0.1	0.2	0.2		
PE range	29–48	27–42	29–48	21–49	15–43			

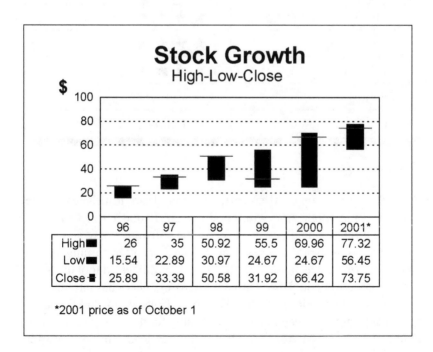

Stock Growth
High-Low-Close

	96	97	98	99	2000	2001*
High	26	35	50.92	55.5	69.96	77.32
Low	15.54	22.89	30.97	24.67	24.67	56.45
Close	25.89	33.39	50.58	31.92	66.42	73.75

*2001 price as of October 1

Microsoft Corporation

Microsoft ®

One Microsoft Way
Redmond, WA 98052
425-882-8080
Nasdaq: MSFT
www.microsoft.com

Chairman: William H. Gates
CEO: Steven A. Balmer
President: Richard Belluzzo

Earnings Growth	★ ★ ★ ★
Stock Growth	★ ★ ★ ★
Consistency	★ ★ ★ ★
Dividend	
Total	**12 Points**

There will be no breakup of Microsoft, which no doubt instills fear in the hearts of its competitors. And with good reason. Founder Bill Gates has proven to be a ruthless and powerful foe in the software wars.

Gates, who is the world's richest man, built Microsoft by turning a complex and powerful new technology into a useful, multifaceted tool that consumers the world over could use. Through Microsoft, Gates has introduced a long line of software products, such as Windows, DOS, Word, and Explorer, that have made computer technology user-friendly for the average consumer.

Founded in 1975, Microsoft is the worldwide leader in software for personal computers. The Redmond, Washington manufacturer helps maintain its edge in the market by spending generously on product development. It spends about $3 billion a year on research and development.

Microsoft has subsidiaries in about 60 countries around the world. Foreign sales have been growing quickly and currently account for about 54 percent of the company's total revenue.

Microsoft offers products in several key categories, including:

- **Platforms** (computer operating systems), including Windows 2000, Windows 2000 Professional, Windows 98, Windows NT Workstation, and Windows NT Server
- **Desktop applications,** including Microsoft Office (a software package that includes a wide range of business-related applications), Word (word processing), Excel (spreadsheet), PowerPoint (presentations), Access (database management), and Outlook (Internet e-mail)
- **Server applications,** including Windows NT Server for office networks, Microsoft Exchange Server, and SQL Server
- **Developer tools,** used by software developers to create new applications
- **Interactive media products,** including interactive entertainment and information products such as Microsoft Encarta encyclopedia, Microsoft Bookshelf, and other Internet and CD-ROM products

The company has also developed software for mobile devices, networks, and Web sites. Microsoft has about 39,000 employees and a market capitalization of about $300 billion.

EARNINGS PER SHARE GROWTH ★ ★ ★ ★

Past 5 years: 323 percent (33 percent per year)
Past 10 years: 1,720 percent (33 percent per year)

STOCK GROWTH ★ ★ ★ ★

Past 10 years: 3,282 percent (49 percent per year)
Dollar growth: $10,000 over 10 years would have grown to $550,000.
Average annual compounded rate of return: 49 percent

CONSISTENCY ★ ★ ★ ★

Increased earnings per share: 19 consecutive years
Increased sales: 19 consecutive years

DIVIDEND

Microsoft pays no dividend.

MICROSOFT AT A GLANCE

Fiscal year ended: June 30
Revenue and net income in $millions

	1996	1997	1998	1999	2000	2001	5-Year Growth Avg. Annual (%)	5-Year Growth Total (%)
Revenue ($)	9,050	11,936	15,262	19,747	22,956	25,296	23	179
Net income ($)	2,195	3,454	4,490	7,785	9,421	10,300	36	369
Earnings/share ($)	0.43	0.66	0.84	1.40	1.70	1.82	33	323
Dividends/share ($)	—	—	—	—	—	—		
Dividend yield (%)	—	—	—	—	—	—		
PE range	23–50	30–57	37–86	48–84	23–69			

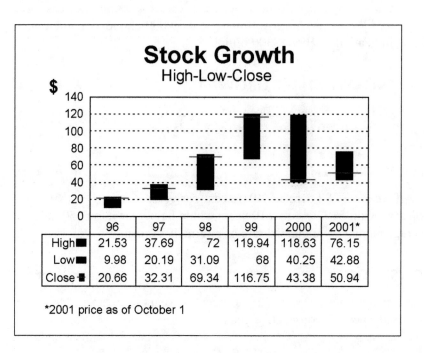

Stock Growth
High-Low-Close

	96	97	98	99	2000	2001*
High■	21.53	37.69	72	119.94	118.63	76.15
Low■	9.98	20.19	31.09	68	40.25	42.88
Close■	20.66	32.31	69.34	116.75	43.38	50.94

*2001 price as of October 1

32

Concord EFS, Inc.

2525 Horizon Lake Drive, Suite 120
Memphis, TN 38133
901-371-8000
Nasdaq: CEFT
www.concordefs.com

Chairman and CEO: Dan M. Palmer
President: Edward A. Labry III

Earnings Growth	★ ★ ★ ★
Stock Growth	★ ★ ★ ★
Consistency	★ ★ ★ ★
Dividend	
Total	**12 Points**

Concord EFS helps retailers take your money. The Memphis-based operation is the leading player in the merchant card electronic transaction processing business. Through all of its divisions, Concord is involved in 50 percent of all ATM debit transactions and 60 percent of all point-of-sale debit transactions in the United States.

Concord provides electronic transaction processing, authorization, data capture, settlement, and funds transfer services to restaurants, financial institutions, supermarkets, service stations, convenience stores, and other independent retailers.

The company also provides ATM processing, debit card processing, and debit network access for financial institutions.

Concord's payment service systems enable retailers to accept virtually any type of cashless payment, including credit and debit cards, electronic benefits transfer, fleet, prepaid, and automatic clearinghouse cards, as well as a variety of check-based options.

The company also provides special payment cards for truck drivers to purchase fuel and obtain cash advances at truck stops.

Payment services accounts for about 72 percent of the company's $1.2 billion in annual revenue. The other 28 percent comes from the company's network services division, which provides ATM processing, debit card processing, and debit network access for financial institutions.

Founded in 1970, the company has grown recently through several significant acquisitions. In 2000, it acquired National Payment Systems, a New York–based operation that provides card-based payment processing services to independent sales organizations, which in turn sell those services to retailers.

It also acquired Cash Station, a Midwest debit network based in Chicago; Star System, the nation's largest PIN-secured debit network; and Virtual Cyber Systems, a small Internet software development company.

The acquisitions have helped Concord build the nation's largest electronic funds transfer network, with about 180,000 ATMs, 720,000 point-of-sale merchants, and 6,500 associated financial institutions.

Concord has about 2,000 employees and a market capitalization of about $12 billion.

EARNINGS PER SHARE GROWTH ★ ★ ★ ★

Past 5 years: 500 percent (36 percent per year)
Past 10 years: 2,000 percent (35.5 percent per year)

STOCK GROWTH ★ ★ ★ ★

Past 10 years: 7,381 percent (53 percent per year)
Dollar growth: $10,000 over 10 years would have grown to $750,000.
Average annual compounded rate of return: 53 percent

CONSISTENCY ★ ★ ★ ★

Increased earnings per share: 10 consecutive years
Increased sales: 10 consecutive years

DIVIDEND

Concord pays no dividend.

CONCORD EFS AT A GLANCE

Fiscal year ended: Dec. 31
Revenue and net income in $millions

	1995	1996	1997	1998	1999	2000	5-Year Growth Avg. Annual (%)	5-Year Growth Total (%)
Revenue ($)	128	366	508	666	890	1,229	57	850
Net income ($)	18.3	38.9	60.1	91.1	138	196	60	971
Earnings/share ($)	0.14	0.21	0.30	0.44	0.51	0.84	36	500
Dividends/share ($)	—	—	—	—	—	—		
Dividend yield (%)	—	—	—	—	—	—		
PE range	27–38	26–66	23–47	20–66	33–65	18–57		

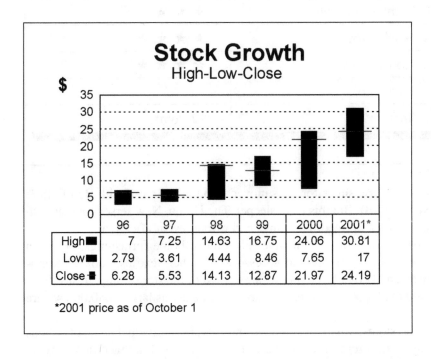

Stock Growth
High-Low-Close

	96	97	98	99	2000	2001*
High■	7	7.25	14.63	16.75	24.06	30.81
Low■	2.79	3.61	4.44	8.46	7.65	17
Close■	6.28	5.53	14.13	12.87	21.97	24.19

*2001 price as of October 1

33

Bed Bath & Beyond, Inc.

BED BATH & BEYOND®

650 Liberty Avenue
Union, NJ 07083
908-688-0888
Nasdaq: BBBY
www.bedbathandbeyond.com

Co-Chairman/Co-CEO: Warren Eisenberg
Co-Chairman/Co-CEO: Leonard Feinstein
President: Steven H. Temares

Earnings Growth	★ ★ ★ ★
Stock Growth	★ ★ ★ ★
Consistency	★ ★ ★ ★
Dividend	
Total	**12 Points**

The warehouse superstore has moved into the bedroom with Bed Bath & Beyond (BBB). But this is no sleeper. The Union, New Jersey retailer continues to rack up record earnings and revenue year after year.

BBB stores offer a massive selection of home furnishings, bedroom and bathroom furniture and accessories, kitchen textiles, cookware, dinnerware, and other basic housewares. Most of the stores range in size from 30,000 to 50,000 square feet, although some are as large as 80,000 square feet.

The stores, which are divided into several individual specialty shops featuring different product lines, are designed with a "racetrack" layout that leads shoppers from display to display. The aisles of merchandise, stacked from floor to ceiling throughout the store, feature warehouse prices, substantially below regular department store prices. And with more than 30,000 different items, the selection is far greater than that of department stores and other specialty retail stores. BBB's leading product line is bed linens, which accounts for about 20 percent of net sales.

The company operates about 316 stores in 43 states. Its leading concentration is in California (37 stores), followed by Texas (23), New York (16), and New Jersey (16).

The company opens about 70 new stores each year.

BBB was founded in 1971 when Leonard Feinstein and Warren Eisenberg opened two stores—one in New York, one in New Jersey—under the name Bed 'n Bath. Feinstein and Eisenberg continue to serve as co-CEOs of the company. Over the next 14 years, the pair opened additional stores in Connecticut and California. Then in 1985, they introduced a new superstore format and changed the name, two years later, to Bed Bath & Beyond.

BBB has about 12,000 employees and a market capitalization of about $7 billion.

EARNINGS PER SHARE GROWTH   ★ ★ ★ ★

Past 5 years: 321 percent (34 percent per year)
Past 8 years: 1,080 percent (35 percent per year)

STOCK GROWTH   ★ ★ ★ ★

Past 8 years: 1,628 percent (43 percent per year)
Dollar growth: $10,000 over 8 years would have grown to $170,000.
Average annual compounded rate of return: 43 percent

CONSISTENCY   ★ ★ ★ ★

Increased earnings per share: 10 consecutive years
Increased sales: 10 consecutive years

DIVIDEND

Bed Bath & Beyond does not pay a dividend.

BED BATH & BEYOND AT A GLANCE

Fiscal year ended: Feb. 28
Revenue and net income in $millions

	1996	1997	1998	1999	2000	2001	5-Year Growth Avg. Annual (%)	Total (%)
Revenue ($)	597.3	816.9	1,057	1,382	1,857	2,397	32	301
Net income ($)	.039	.055	.073	.097	131.2	171.9	35	341
Earnings/share ($)	0.14	0.20	0.26	0.34	0.46	0.59	34	321
Dividends/share ($)	—	—	—	—	—	—		
Dividend yield (%)	—	—	—	—	—	—		
PE range	28–55	29–50	33–68	37–57	23–58			

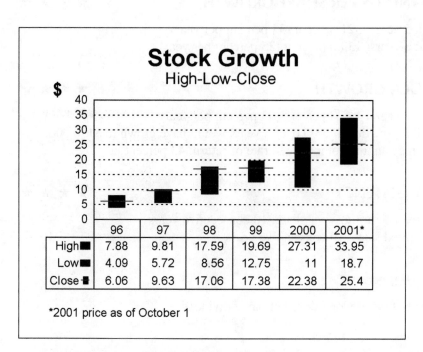

Stock Growth
High-Low-Close

$						
	96	97	98	99	2000	2001*
High■	7.88	9.81	17.59	19.69	27.31	33.95
Low■	4.09	5.72	8.56	12.75	11	18.7
Close■	6.06	9.63	17.06	17.38	22.38	25.4

*2001 price as of October 1

FASTENAL COMPANY

2001 Theurer Boulevard
Winona, MN 55987
507-454-5374
Nasdaq: FAST
www.fastenal.com

Chairman, President, and CEO: Robert A. Kierlin

Earnings Growth	★ ★ ★ ★
Stock Growth	★ ★ ★ ★
Consistency	★ ★ ★ ★
Dividend	
Total	**12 Points**

Need nuts, bolts, screws, or other fasteners? Fastenal can hook you up. The company operates about 900 stores throughout North America that offer 68,000 different types of threaded fasteners and related supplies. Fastenal also sells a variety of other tools, maintenance supplies, and electrical products. In all, the company sells about 200,000 different types of industrial and construction supplies.

In addition to its stores, the Winona, Minnesota operation makes a significant share of its sales through direct calls on customers by store personnel. Most of its customers are in the construction or manufacturing business, including plumbers, electricians, sheet metal contractors, and road construction companies.

Fastenal divides its offerings into nine product categories, including:

- Threaded fasteners and supplies
- 51,000 types of tools

- 24,000 types of metal cutting tool blades
- 23,000 types of fluid transfer components and accessories for hydraulic and pneumatic power
- 8,000 types of material handling and storage products
- 4,000 types of janitorial and paper products
- 7,000 types of electrical supplies
- 7,000 types of welding supplies
- 3,000 types of safety supplies

Threaded fasteners account for about 55 percent of Fastenal's total revenue. In addition to its product offerings, the company also operates a special manufacturing division that can, as the company puts it, "produce anything that can be cut, machined, or formed from metal bars." It can also modify standard fasteners to meet customer specifications. Aside from its custom-made products, however, all of the products the company sells are manufactured by other companies.

Fastenal was founded in 1967 by company president Bob Kierlin, whose original concept was to make a vending machine that would dispense nuts and washers to customers. Fastenal, which went public with its initial stock offering in 1987, has posted record sales and earnings per share every year since then.

The company has about 7,000 employees and 2,200 shareholders, and a market capitalization of about $2.5 billion.

EARNINGS PER SHARE GROWTH ★ ★ ★ ★

Past 5 years: 196 percent (24 percent per year)
Past 10 years: 1,153 percent (29 percent per year)

STOCK GROWTH ★ ★ ★ ★

Past 10 years: 1,269 percent (30 percent per year)
Dollar growth: $10,000 over 10 years (including reinvested dividends) would have grown to $138,000.
Average annual compounded rate of return (including reinvested dividends): 30 percent

CONSISTENCY ★ ★ ★ ★

Increased earnings per share: 13 consecutive years
Increased sales: 13 consecutive years

DIVIDEND

Dividend yield: 0.1 percent
Increased dividend: 3 of the past 10 years
Past 5-year increase: 300 percent (32 percent per year)
The company offers no dividend reinvestment and stock purchase plan.

FASTENAL AT A GLANCE

Fiscal year ended: Dec. 31
Revenue and net income in $millions

	1995	1996	1997	1998	1999	2000	5-Year Growth Avg. Annual (%)	Total (%)
Revenue ($)	223	288	398	503	609	746	27	234
Net income ($)	27	32	41	53	65	81	25	200
Earnings/share ($)	0.72	0.86	1.08	1.40	1.73	2.13	24	196
Dividends/share ($)	0.02	0.02	0.02	0.02	0.04	0.08	32	300
Dividend yield (%)	0.1	0.04	0.05	005	0.1	0.15		
PE range	27–59	34–58	28–56	14–40	19–35	16–34		

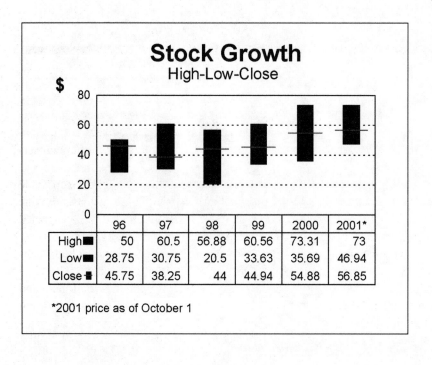

Stock Growth
High-Low-Close

$	96	97	98	99	2000	2001*
High■	50	60.5	56.88	60.56	73.31	73
Low■	28.75	30.75	20.5	33.63	35.69	46.94
Close✚	45.75	38.25	44	44.94	54.88	56.85

*2001 price as of October 1

35

Legg Mason, Inc.

100 Light Street
Baltimore, MD 21202
877-534-4627
NYSE: LM
www.leggmason.com

Chairman, President, and CEO: Raymond A. Mason

Earnings Growth	★ ★ ★ ★
Stock Growth	★ ★ ★ ★
Consistency	★ ★ ★
Dividend	★
Total	**12 Points**

Legg Mason is a financial services conglomerate that stretches like an octopus through much of the investment market. The Baltimore operation has a network of subsidiaries—some formed from within, others acquired—that cover the gamut of both the institutional and individual financial services market.

Known most of all for its family of mutual funds, Legg Mason made one of its most significant acquisitions in 1998 when it bought Brandywine Asset Management. Brandywine operated a small family of well-respected mutual funds and a well-rated institutional investment service.

Other key divisions include Western Asset Management, which manages fixed-income and currency assets for institutional clients; Batterymarch Financial Management, which manages U.S., international, and emerging markets portfolios for institutional clients; and Legg Mason Capital Management, which manages stock portfolios primarily for institutional accounts. Three other subsidiaries manage portfolios for wealthy individuals, endowments, and foundations: Barrett Associates, Berkshire Asset Management, and Gray, Seifert & Co.

The company also operates Perigee Investment Counsel, a Canadian institutional firm, and LeggMason Investors Holdings PLC, which manages stock mutual funds in the United Kingdom.

Legg Mason also acquired Private Capital Management, a leading high-net-worth money manager, and Royce & Associates, which operates a well-rated family of small-cap and microcap mutual funds, in 2001.

Legg Mason divides its operations into three main segments:

- **Asset management.** The company manages an extensive family of mutual funds totaling about $27 billion in assets. It also offers institutional investment management services through its various subsidiaries, with total assets under management of about $135 billion.
- **Private clients.** Legg Mason offers brokerage services, insurance, and financial planning for individual investors. The company has about 144 offices in the United States.
- **Capital markets.** The company offers a variety of services for the investment market, including stock and bond institutional sales and trading, and corporate and public finance services.

Legg Mason has about 5,400 employees and 2,300 shareholders. It has a market capitalization of about $3 billion.

EARNINGS PER SHARE GROWTH ★ ★ ★ ★

Past 5 years: 184 percent (23 percent per year)
Past 10 years: 400 percent (17.5 percent per year)

STOCK GROWTH ★ ★ ★ ★

Past 10 years: 922 percent (26 percent per year)
Dollar growth: $10,000 over 10 years (including reinvested dividends) would have grown to $110,000.
Average annual compounded rate of return (including reinvested dividends): 27 percent

CONSISTENCY ★ ★ ★

Increased earnings per share: 9 of the past 10 years
Increased sales: 9 of the past 10 years

DIVIDEND ★

Dividend yield: 0.9 percent
Increased dividend: 9 of the past 10 years
Past 5-year increase: 94 percent (14 percent per year)
Legg Mason does not offer a dividend reinvestment plan.

LEGG MASON AT A GLANCE

Fiscal year ended: March 31
Revenue and net income in $millions

	1996	1997	1998	1999	2000	2001	5-Year Growth Avg. Annual (%)	Total (%)
Revenue ($)	516	640	869	1,046	1,399	1,536	24.5	197
Net income ($)	38	57	76	93	150	156	33	310
Earnings/share ($)	0.81	1.11	1.32	1.55	2.33	2.30	23	184
Dividends/share ($)	0.18	0.19	0.21	0.25	0.31	0.35	14	94
Dividend yield (%)	0.9	1.2	0.8	0.7	0.7	0.6		
PE range	11–16	13–20	13–27	13–24	17–28	13–26		

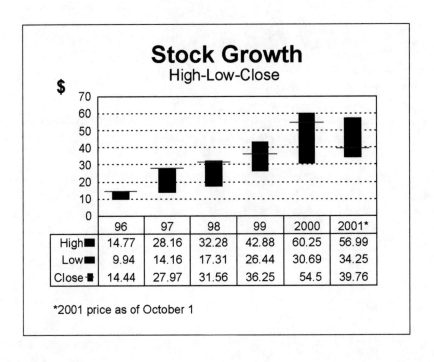

Stock Growth
High-Low-Close

	96	97	98	99	2000	2001*
High	14.77	28.16	32.28	42.88	60.25	56.99
Low	9.94	14.16	17.31	26.44	30.69	34.25
Close	14.44	27.97	31.56	36.25	54.5	39.76

*2001 price as of October 1

Stryker Corporation

stryker

P.O. Box 4085
Kalamazoo, MI 49003
616-385-2600
NYSE: SYK
www.strykercorp.com

Chairman, President, and CEO:
John W. Brown

Earnings Growth	★ ★ ★ ★
Stock Growth	★ ★ ★ ★
Consistency	★ ★ ★ ★
Dividend	
Total	**12 Points**

Known for its surgical instruments and orthopedic implants, Stryker is becoming increasingly diversified in its medical offerings. With 23 consecutive years of increased earnings and revenue, the Kalamazoo, Michigan operation continues to keep its customers at the leading edge of medical technology.

Artificial limbs and related orthopedic products account for about 57 percent of Stryker's $2.2 billion in annual revenue. The company is a leading maker of hip, knee, and shoulder implants.

In addition to its orthopedic products, Stryker breaks its offerings into several key groups, including:

- **Trauma systems.** Products include nailing, plating, and external fixation systems, instruments, and related products used for craniomaxillofacial surgery, and specialized video systems for image-guided surgery.

- **Surgical instruments and equipment.** Stryker makes powered surgical instruments, such as cement injection systems. It also makes video-imaging equipment and instruments for arthroscopy and general surgery.
- **Medical equipment.** Stryker makes a line of specialty stretchers and beds and other patient-handling equipment. Its critical care beds enable physicians to weigh patients, take X rays, and perform other functions without removing the patient from the bed.
- **Rehabilitative medical services.** The company offers physical, occupational, and speech therapy services to patients recovering from orthopedic or neurological illness and injury through a network of more than 250 outpatient physical therapy centers throughout the United States.

Medical surgical equipment makes up 36 percent of total revenues, and other medical products account for the remaining 7 percent.

Stryker markets its products in more than 100 countries. Foreign operations make up 39 percent of total revenue.

Stryker was founded in 1941 by Dr. Homer H. Stryker, a prominent orthopedic surgeon and the inventor of several leading orthopedic products. The company has about 12,000 employees and 3,000 stockholders. It has a market capitalization of $11 billion.

EARNINGS PER SHARE GROWTH   ★ ★ ★ ★

Past 5 years: 144 percent (19.5 percent per year)
Past 10 years: 746 percent (24 percent per year)

STOCK GROWTH   ★ ★ ★ ★

Past 10 years: 1,464 percent (32 percent per year)
Dollar growth: $10,000 over 10 years (including reinvested dividends) would have grown to about $170,000.
Average annual compounded rate of return (including reinvested dividends): 32 percent

CONSISTENCY

Increased earnings per share: 23 consecutive years
Increased sales: 23 consecutive years

DIVIDEND

Dividend yield: 0.1 percent
Increased dividend: 8 consecutive years
Past 5-year increase: 300 percent (33 percent per year)
Stryker does not offer a dividend reinvestment plan.

STRYKER AT A GLANCE

Fiscal year ended: Dec. 31
Revenue and net income in $millions

	1995	1996	1997	1998	1999	2000	5-Year Growth Avg. Annual (%)	5-Year Growth Total (%)
Revenue ($)	872	910	980	1,103	2,104	2,289	21	162
Net income ($)	87	101	125	150	160	221	20	154
Earnings/share ($)	0.45	0.52	0.64	0.77	0.81	1.10	19.5	144
Dividends/share ($)	0.02	0.05	0.06	0.06	0.07	0.08	33	300
Dividend yield (%)	0.2	0.4	0.3	0.3	0.2	0.2		
PE range	19–27	18–30	18–35	50–91	226–373	22–52		

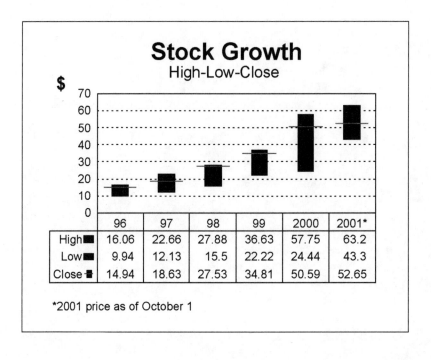

Stock Growth
High-Low-Close

	96	97	98	99	2000	2001*
High	16.06	22.66	27.88	36.63	57.75	63.2
Low	9.94	12.13	15.5	22.22	24.44	43.3
Close	14.94	18.63	27.53	34.81	50.59	52.65

*2001 price as of October 1

Oracle Corporation

ORACLE ®

500 Oracle Parkway
Redwood Shores, CA 94065
650-506-7000
Nasdaq: ORCL
www.oracle.com

Chairman and CEO: Lawrence Ellison

Earnings Growth	★ ★ ★ ★
Stock Growth	★ ★ ★ ★
Consistency	★ ★ ★ ★
Dividend	
Total	**12 Points**

Oracle is the world's second largest software maker behind Microsoft. The Redwood Shores, California operation specializes in database and development software, business applications for sales and service, manufacturing and supply chain applications, and finance and human resources software.

With Oracle software, computer users can tap into computer resources anywhere, anytime. Its Oracle relational database management systems enable users to define, retrieve, manipulate, and control data stored on multiple computers, and to manage video, audio, text, messaging, and spatial data.

The company's e-business software suite is designed to put a company's entire business on the Internet, including marketing, sales, service, procurement, supply chain, manufacturing, accounting, and human resources. "All the applications in our suite are designed and engineered to work together," says Oracle founder and CEO Larry Ellison, "so customers buying the entire suite don't need to do any systems integration."

Oracle makes software products that fit into three different categories: server technologies, application development and business intelligence tools, and business applications.

The company's server technology products include database servers, connectivity products, and gateways. Its application development tools consist of a set of software products used to build database applications for both client server and Web environments. Oracle's business application products consist of more than 45 integrated software modules for financial management, supply chain management, manufacturing, project systems, human resources, and front office applications.

The company's principal products run on a broad range of computers, including mainframes, minicomputers, workstations, personal computers, and laptops. Oracle software can function on 85 different operating systems, including UNIX, Windows, and Windows NT.

Oracle markets its products in 145 countries around the world. International sales account for about half of its total revenue.

Founded in 1977, Oracle has about 41,000 employees and a market capitalization of $100 billion.

EARNINGS PER SHARE GROWTH ★ ★ ★ ★

Past 5 years: 300 percent (32 percent per year)
Past 10 years: 4,300 percent

STOCK GROWTH ★ ★ ★ ★

Past 10 years: 2,762 percent (40 percent per year)
Dollar growth: $10,000 over 10 years would have grown to $287,000.
Average annual compounded rate of return: 40 percent

CONSISTENCY ★ ★ ★ ★

Increased earnings per share: 10 consecutive years
Increased sales: 15 consecutive years

DIVIDEND

Oracle pays no dividend.

ORACLE AT A GLANCE

Fiscal year ended: May 31
Revenue and net income in $millions

	1996	1997	1998	1999	2000	2001	5-Year Growth Avg. Annual (%)	5-Year Growth Total (%)
Revenue ($)	4,223	5,684	7,144	8,827	10,130	10,860	21	157
Net income ($)	603	821	814	1,290	2,055	2,561	34	324
Earnings/share ($)	0.11	0.14	0.16	0.22	0.35	0.44	32	300
Dividends/share ($)	—	—	—	—	—	—		
Dividend yield (%)	—	—	—	—	—	—		
PE range	29–56	25–51	21–54	24–130	20–44	10–41		

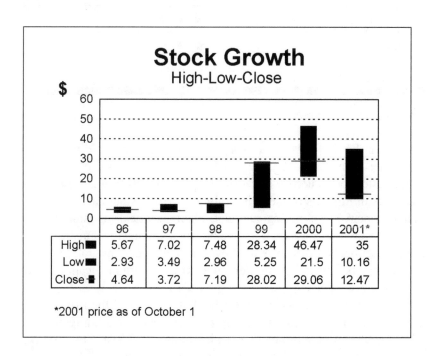

Stock Growth
High-Low-Close

	96	97	98	99	2000	2001*
High■	5.67	7.02	7.48	28.34	46.47	35
Low■	2.93	3.49	2.96	5.25	21.5	10.16
Close-■	4.64	3.72	7.19	28.02	29.06	12.47

*2001 price as of October 1

38

Bristol-Myers Squibb Company

345 Park Avenue
New York, NY 10154
212-546-4000
NYSE: BMY
www.bms.com

Chairman: Charles A. Heimbold, Jr.
President and CEO: Peter Dolan

Earnings Growth	★ ★ ★ ★
Stock Growth	★ ★
Consistency	★ ★ ★
Dividend	★ ★ ★
Total	**12 Points**

Bristol-Myers Squibb puts out a long list of products designed to combat cancer, squelch headaches, and heal heart conditions. Its line of over-the-counter medications, such as Excedrin, Nuprin, and Bufferin, are permanent fixtures in millions of medicine cabinets across America.

The company's leading segment is its pharmaceuticals division, which accounts for about 80 percent of its $18 billion in annual revenue. Its leading pharmaceuticals segment is cardiovascular medications, followed by anticancer agents, anti-infectives, central nervous system medications, and analgesics.

Nutritional supplements make up about 10 percent of the firm's total revenue. The company produces Enfamil, Prosobee, Nutramigen, and Lactofree infant formula products; Isocal, Nutrament, Boost, Choco Milk, and Sustagen nutritional supplements; and Pusssz, Poly-Vi-Sol, and Natalins vitamins.

Medical devices account for about 10 percent of sales, including knee and hip replacement systems, ostomy care products, and wound care products. The company recently announced plans to sell its Clairol division (hair care products) to Procter & Gamble.

Bristol-Myers has several medications that generate in excess of $1 billion in sales, including:

- **Pravachol** ($1.8 billion in annual revenue). Used to treat high cholesterol, Pravachol's patent in the United States expires in October 2005 and in international markets from 2001 through 2010.
- **Glucophage** ($1.7 billion). An oral antidiabetes agent for type 2 non-insulin-dependent diabetes, its patent expired in September 2000, but it has not been affected by generic competition.
- **Taxol** ($1.6 billion). The drug is used in the treatment of refractory ovarian cancer and certain AIDS-related conditions, as well as in the treatment of metastatic breast cancer.

Bristol-Myers does a strong international business, with sales in more than 100 countries. Foreign sales account for about 32 percent of the company's total revenue.

Founded in 1887, Bristol-Myers merged with Squibb in 1989. The company has about 55,000 employees and 135,000 shareholders. It has a market capitalization of about $110 billion.

EARNINGS PER SHARE GROWTH ★ ★ ★ ★

Past 5 years: 173 percent (22 percent per year)
Past 10 years: 184 percent (23 percent per year)

STOCK GROWTH ★ ★

Past 10 years: 282 percent (14.5 percent per year)
Dollar growth: $10,000 over 10 years (including reinvested dividends) would have grown to $48,000.
Average annual compounded rate of return (including reinvested dividends): 17 percent

CONSISTENCY ★ ★ ★

Increased earnings per share: 9 of the past 10 years
Increased sales: 7 of the past 10 years

DIVIDEND   ★ ★ ★

Dividend yield: 2 percent
Increased dividend: 28 consecutive years
Past 5-year increase: 32 percent (6 percent per year)
Good dividend reinvestment and stock purchase plan; voluntary stock purchase plan allows contributions of $105 to $10,025 per month for those holding 50 shares or more.

BRISTOL-MYERS SQUIBB AT A GLANCE

Fiscal year ended: Dec. 31
Revenue and net income in $millions

	1995	1996	1997	1998	1999	2000	5-Year Growth Avg. Annual (%)	Total (%)
Revenue ($)	11,320	12,268	13,698	15,061	16,878	18,216	10	61
Net income ($)	1,934	3,423	3,738	3,638	5,158	5,478	23	183
Earnings/share ($)	0.75	1.22	1.34	1.36	1.87	2.05	22	173
Dividends/share ($)	0.74	0.75	0.76	0.78	0.86	0.98	6	32
Dividend yield (%)	4.3	2.8	1.6	1.2	1.3	1.3		
PE range	16–24	13–20	16–31	32–49	30–42	20–36		

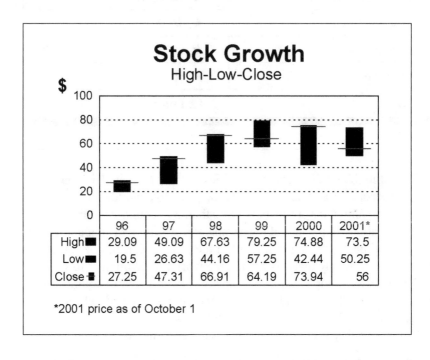

Stock Growth
High-Low-Close

	96	97	98	99	2000	2001*
High	29.09	49.09	67.63	79.25	74.88	73.5
Low	19.5	26.63	44.16	57.25	42.44	50.25
Close	27.25	47.31	66.91	64.19	73.94	56

*2001 price as of October 1

39

Colgate-Palmolive Company

 **COLGATE-PALMOLIVE** COMPANY

300 Park Avenue
New York, NY 10022
212-310-2000
NYSE: CL
www.colgatepalmolive.com

Chairman and CEO: Reuben Mark
President: William Shanahan

Earnings Growth	★ ★ ★ ★
Stock Growth	★ ★ ★
Consistency	★ ★ ★
Dividend	★ ★
Total	**12 Points**

Colgate-Palmolive helps fend off cavities the world over. The New York operation accounts for about half of all toothpaste sold worldwide. It markets its toothpaste and other products in more than 200 countries. Foreign sales account for about 70 percent of the company's $9 billion in annual revenue.

But toothpaste is just a small part of the grocery cart full of household products the company markets around the world. In addition to its Colgate and Ultra Brite toothpastes, the company makes a line of toothbrushes, dental floss, mouthwash, and professional dental products. Oral care products account for about 34 percent of total sales.

Colgate's other four major product segments include:

- **Personal care products** (24 percent of revenue). The company makes a variety of soaps and related products, such as Irish Spring and Palmolive bar soap, Softsoap liquid soap, Wash 'n Dri disposable towel-ettes, Speedstick and Irish Spring deodorants, Baby Magic baby care products, and Colgate and Palmolive shave cream, Skin Bracer, and Afta Aftershave.

- **Household surface care** (16 percent). Its leading brands include Ajax cleaners, Palmolive cleaners and detergents, and Murphy Oil Soap cleaner.
- **Fabric care** (14 percent). The company makes Fab and Dynamo, Ajax Ultra, and Fresh Start laundry detergents.
- **Pet nutrition** (12 percent). Its Science Diet line of pet foods is one of the fastest-growing brands in the business.

Colgate has long been one of the leading global marketers. It has been generating more than half its sales in foreign markets since 1960, and has been selling toothpaste in Latin America since 1925.

The company's new product development process begins by analyzing consumer insights from targeted countries to create universal products. To improve the odds of success, potential new products are test-marketed in lead countries that represent both developing and mature economies. New products introduced in the past five years account for nearly 40 percent of the company's total revenue.

Colgate has about 38,000 employees and 45,000 shareholders. It has a market capitalization of about $34 billion.

EARNINGS PER SHARE GROWTH   ★ ★ ★ ★

Past 5 years: 554 percent (46 percent per year)
Past 10 years: 198 percent (11 percent per year)

STOCK GROWTH   ★ ★ ★

Past 10 years: 585 percent (21 percent per year)
Dollar growth: $10,000 over 10 years (including reinvested dividends) would have grown to $75,000.
Average annual compounded rate of return (including reinvested dividends): 22 percent

CONSISTENCY   ★ ★ ★

Increased earnings per share: 9 of the past 10 years
Increased sales: 9 of the past 10 years

DIVIDEND   ★ ★

Dividend yield: 1.3 percent
Increased dividend: 23 consecutive years
Past 5-year increase: 43 percent (7 percent per year)
Good dividend reinvestment and stock purchase plan; voluntary stock purchase plan allows contributions of $20 per month up to $60,000 per year.

COLGATE-PALMOLIVE AT A GLANCE

Fiscal year ended: Dec. 31
Revenue and net income in $millions

	1995	1996	1997	1998	1999	2000	5-Year Growth Avg. Annual (%)	Total (%)
Revenue ($)	8,358	8,749	9,057	8,972	9,118	9,358	2	12
Net income ($)	172	635	740	849	937	1,064	44	519
Earnings/share ($)	0.26	0.98	1.13	1.30	1.47	1.70	46	554
Dividends/share ($)	0.44	0.47	0.53	0.55	0.59	0.63	7	43
Dividend yield (%)	2.6	2.0	1.4	1.2	0.9	1.0		
PE range	56–75	17–24	19–34	24–37	24–44	23–39		

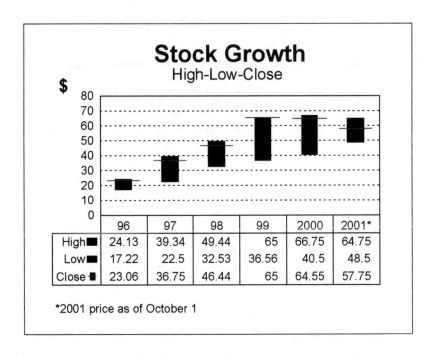

Stock Growth
High-Low-Close

$	96	97	98	99	2000	2001*
High■	24.13	39.34	49.44	65	66.75	64.75
Low■	17.22	22.5	32.53	36.56	40.5	48.5
Close ■	23.06	36.75	46.44	65	64.55	57.75

*2001 price as of October 1

AFLAC, Inc.

1932 Wynnton Road
Columbus, GA 31999
706-323-3431
NYSE: AFL
www.aflac.com

Chairman and CEO: Daniel Amos
President: Kriss Cloninger III

Earnings Growth	★ ★
Stock Growth	★ ★ ★ ★
Consistency	★ ★ ★ ★
Dividend	★ ★
Total	**12 Points**

AFLAC sells a line of supplemental insurance that is big in the United States and huge in Japan. In fact, one out of every five Japanese workers is insured by AFLAC, and its policies are offered to employees of 96 percent of the companies listed on the Tokyo Stock Exchange.

AFLAC specializes in supplemental cancer coverage that helps fill the gaps in its customers' primary policies. It is the leading writer of cancer expense insurance worldwide. The company also sells life, accident, Medicare supplement, and long-term convalescent care policies.

About 80 percent of AFLAC's revenue comes from its Japanese operations—most of it from supplemental cancer insurance policies. Japanese are attracted to AFLAC policies because of the company's solid financial standing. By contrast, many of its Japanese competitors are strapped with large holdings of low-priced stocks and bad loans.

Japan is also a prime target for AFLAC's supplemental coverage, because most Japanese are covered by the national health insurance system, which is not particularly comprehensive. The AFLAC policies cover medical and nonmedical costs that are not reimbursed under the national system.

AFLAC's cancer life insurance, which is the main product offered by the company, provides a fixed daily indemnity benefit for hospitalization and outpatient services related to cancer, and a lump-sum benefit upon initial diagnosis of internal cancer. The policies also provide a death benefit and cash surrender values.

In the United States, AFLAC is the leading provider of supplemental insurance at work sites. Its policies are offered to more than 170,000 payroll groups.

In all, AFLAC insures more than 40 million people worldwide, the vast majority of whom hold supplemental insurance policies. About 45,000 agents sell AFLAC polices in Japan, while about 40,000 agents sell for AFLAC in the U.S. market.

The Columbus, Georgia operation was incorporated in 1973. AFLAC has about 4,000 employees and 89,000 shareholders. The company has a market capitalization of about $15 billion.

EARNINGS PER SHARE GROWTH ★ ★

Past 5 years: 113 percent (16 percent per year)
Past 10 years: 531 percent (20 percent per year)

STOCK GROWTH ★ ★ ★ ★

Past 10 years: 761 percent (24 percent per year)
Dollar growth: $10,000 over 10 years (including reinvested dividends) would have grown to $93,000.
Average annual compounded rate of return (including reinvested dividends): 25 percent

CONSISTENCY ★ ★ ★ ★

Increased earnings per share: 11 consecutive years
Increased sales: 2 consecutive years

DIVIDEND ★ ★

Dividend yield: 0.7 percent
Increased dividend: Every year since 1992
Past 5-year increase: 89 percent (14 percent per year)
Good dividend reinvestment and stock purchase plan; voluntary stock purchase plan allows contributions of $50 to $120,000 per year.

AFLAC AT A GLANCE

Fiscal year ended: Dec. 31
Premium income and net income in $millions

	1995	1996	1997	1998	1999	2000	5-Year Growth Avg. Annual (%)	Total (%)
Premium income ($)	7.19	7.1	7.25	7.1	8.64	9.72	6	35
Net income ($)	0.349	0.394	0.585	0.487	0.571	0.687	14	97
Earnings/share ($)	0.59	0.68	1.04	0.88	1.04	1.26	16	113
Dividends/share ($)	0.09	0.10	0.11	0.12	0.15	0.17	14	89
Dividend yield (%)	1.1	0.91	0.88	0.58	0.61	0.46		
PE range	9–12	10–16	9–13	12–25	18–27	13–29		

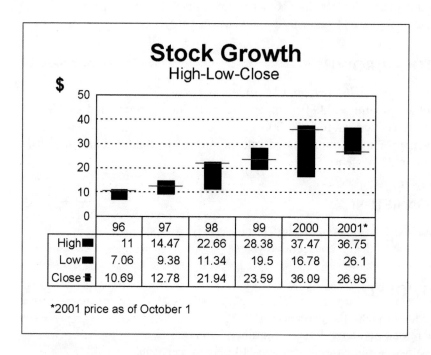

Stock Growth
High-Low-Close

$	96	97	98	99	2000	2001*
High	11	14.47	22.66	28.38	37.47	36.75
Low	7.06	9.38	11.34	19.5	16.78	26.1
Close	10.69	12.78	21.94	23.59	36.09	26.95

*2001 price as of October 1

Intel Corporation

2200 Mission College Boulevard
Santa Clara, CA 95052
408-765-8080
Nasdaq: INTC
www.intel.com

Chairman: Andrew S. Grove
President and CEO: Craig R. Barrett

Earnings Growth	★ ★ ★ ★
Stock Growth	★ ★ ★ ★
Consistency	★ ★ ★
Dividend	★
Total	**12 Points**

The semiconductor market has had its ups and downs over the years, but there's no question that microchips are here to stay. They're in our cars, our phones, our TVs, and many of our home appliances. In fact, microchips serve as the brains of a whole new realm of technology. Intel is the world's leading manufacturer of microchips. Its line of Pentium chips has been installed in millions of computers, serving as the control center of the personal computer by processing system data and controlling other devices in the system.

The more advanced the microprocessing chips, the faster and more powerful the computer. Intel's ability to develop ever-faster chips has kept it at the forefront of the computer revolution. With its Pentium 4 chips, Intel continues to be the dominant player in the worldwide microprocessor market.

Intel's computer microchips process system data and control input, output, and peripheral and memory devices in the PC. They are also used to control the operation of communications systems, automobile control applications, robotics, electronic instrumentation, keyboards, home video machines, and a wide range of other electronics products.

Microprocessor sales account for more than 80 percent of Intel's total revenue. Intel's computing enhancement group, including chipsets, embedded processors, microcontrollers, flash memory, and graphics products, accounts for about 15 percent of total revenue. Its network communications group, which makes network and Internet connectivity products, accounts for less than 5 percent of revenue.

Founded in 1968, the Santa Clara, California company has been the world leader in the microchip market since the mid-1980s, after designing the original microprocessor for the IBM PC. It has maintained its lead by first turning out its popular 286 chip, followed by the 386, then the 486, and finally the Pentium generation of chips. Worldwide, well over 100 million PCs are based on Intel architecture. Intel's primary customers are computer manufacturers who incorporate the chips into their computers.

Intel has about 70,000 employees and a market capitalization of $200 billion.

EARNINGS PER SHARE GROWTH ★ ★ ★ ★

Past 5 years: 202 percent (25 percent per year)
Past 10 years: 1,410 percent (14 percent per year)

STOCK GROWTH ★ ★ ★ ★

Past 10 years: 1,942 percent (35 percent per year)
Dollar growth: $10,000 over 10 years (including reinvested dividends) would have grown to $205,000.
Average annual compounded rate of return (including reinvested dividends): 35 percent

CONSISTENCY ★ ★ ★

Increased earnings per share: 9 of the past 10 years
Increased sales: 14 consecutive years

DIVIDEND ★

Dividend yield: 0.3 percent
Increased dividend: 5 of the past 8 years
Past 5-year increase: 250 percent (28.5 percent per year)
Good dividend reinvestment and stock purchase plan; voluntary stock purchase plan allows contributions of $25 to $15,000 per month.

INTEL AT A GLANCE

Fiscal year ended: Dec. 31
Revenue and net income in $millions

	1995	1996	1997	1998	1999	2000	5-Year Growth Avg. Annual (%)	Total (%)
Revenue ($)	16,202	20,847	25,070	26,273	29,389	33,726	16	108
Net income ($)	3,566	5,157	6,945	6,068	7,314	10,535	24	195
Earnings/share ($)	0.50	0.73	0.97	0.86	1.05	1.51	25	202
Dividends/share ($)	0.02	0.02	0.03	0.03	0.05	0.07	28.5	250
Dividend yield (%)	0.3	0.2	0.2	0.1	0.1	0.2		
PE range	7–18	8–24	16–26	19–36	23–42	19–50		

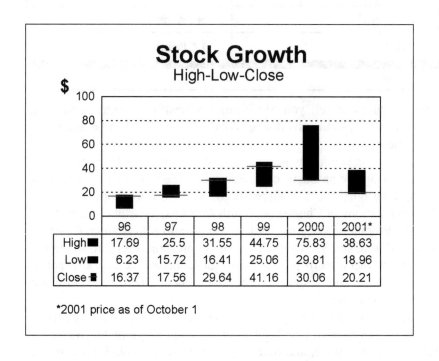

Stock Growth
High-Low-Close

	96	97	98	99	2000	2001*
High■	17.69	25.5	31.55	44.75	75.83	38.63
Low■	6.23	15.72	16.41	25.06	29.81	18.96
Close■	16.37	17.56	29.64	41.16	30.06	20.21

*2001 price as of October 1

Jefferson-Pilot
Corporation

100 North Greene Street
Greensboro, NC 27401
336-691-3000
NYSE: JP
www.jpfinancial.com

Chairman, President, and CEO: D. Stonecipher

Earnings Growth	★ ★
Stock Growth	★ ★ ★
Consistency	★ ★ ★ ★
Dividend	★ ★ ★
Total	**12 Points**

Jefferson-Pilot can sell you life insurance, health insurance, and annuities—as well as some advertising spots on its group of radio and television stations.

Although the company generates most of its revenue from its growing group of insurance products, it has also established a small presence in the broadcasting business. The Greensboro, North Carolina operation owns television stations in Charleston, South Carolina, Charlotte, North Carolina, and Richmond, Virginia, and 17 radio stations in Atlanta, Charlotte, Denver, Miami, and San Diego. The communications division, which also produces television sports programs covering college basketball and football and professional motor sports, accounts for about 7 percent of Jefferson-Pilot's total revenue.

The rest of the company's revenue comes from its insurance groups. Founded in 1890, Jefferson-Pilot offers a broad range of life insurance, group health insurance, and other types of insurance policies and investment products. The company has posted 13 consecutive years of record sales and revenue.

Through its Jefferson-Pilot and Alexander Hamilton life insurance companies, the company offers continuous and limited-pay life and endowment policies, universal life policies, retirement income plans, and level and decreasing term insurance. Life insurance products account for about 54 percent of Jefferson-Pilot's operating income.

Jefferson-Pilot also offers a range of investment products and services, including several types of annuities and mutual funds. Annuities and investment products generate about 20 percent of operating income. Other operations, such as benefit partners and corporate services and investments, make up the other 19 percent.

The company's life insurance and investment products are marketed by a staff of more than 400 full-time agents and thousands of independent agents. They are also sold by about 60 financial institutions and 36 brokerage companies.

Jefferson-Pilot has about 3,800 employees and 10,000 shareholders. The company has a market capitalization of about $7 billion.

EARNINGS PER SHARE GROWTH   ★ ★

Past 5 years: 108 percent (16 percent per year)
Past 10 years: 260 percent (14 percent per year)

STOCK GROWTH   ★ ★ ★

Past 10 years: 474 percent (19 percent per year)
Dollar growth: $10,000 over 10 years (including reinvested dividends) would have grown to $73,000.
Average annual compounded rate of return (including reinvested dividends): 22 percent

CONSISTENCY   ★ ★ ★ ★

Increased earnings per share: 13 consecutive years
Increased sales: 13 consecutive years

DIVIDEND   ★ ★ ★

Dividend yield: 2.4 percent
Increased dividend: 19 consecutive years
Past 5-year increase: 71 percent (11 percent per year)
Good dividend reinvestment and stock purchase plan; voluntary stock purchase plan allows contributions of $20 to $2,000 per month.

JEFFERSON-PILOT AT A GLANCE

Fiscal year ended: Dec. 31
Revenue and net income in $millions

	1995	1996	1997	1998	1999	2000	5-Year Growth Avg. Annual (%)	5-Year Growth Total (%)
Revenue ($)	1,521	2,125	2,578	2,610	2,561	3,238	16	113
Net income ($)	255	294	396	444	495	537	16	111
Earnings/share ($)	1.58	1.82	2.32	2.61	2.95	3.29	16	108
Dividends/share ($)	0.56	0.62	0.69	0.77	0.86	0.96	11	71
Dividend yield (%)	3.1	2.5	2.1	1.6	1.9	1.9		
PE range	9–13	11–14	9–16	12–20	13–17	10–15		

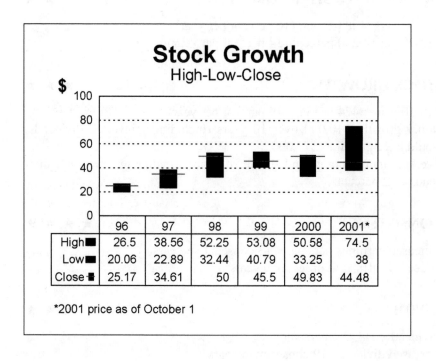

Stock Growth
High-Low-Close

$						
	96	97	98	99	2000	2001*
High■	26.5	38.56	52.25	53.08	50.58	74.5
Low■	20.06	22.89	32.44	40.79	33.25	38
Close-■	25.17	34.61	50	45.5	49.83	44.48

*2001 price as of October 1

370 N. Wabasha Street
St. Paul, MN 55102
651-293-2233
NYSE: ECL
www.ecolab.com

Chairman, President, and CEO: Allan Schuman

Earnings Growth	★ ★
Stock Growth	★ ★ ★ ★
Consistency	★ ★ ★
Dividend	★ ★ ★
Total	**12 Points**

Ecolab may not scrub behind your ears, but the company offers a broad range of cleaning and sanitizing products that helps keep the world cleaner, fresher, and more sanitary. Ecolab is one of the world's leading manufacturers of maintenance products and services for the hospitality, institutional, and industrial markets.

The St. Paul operation sells its products to hotels, restaurants, food service operations, laundries, dairy plants and farms, light industry, and health care and educational facilities. Ecolab has operations in 40 countries and sales in more than 150 countries. International sales account for about 21 percent of total revenue.

Ecolab divides its operations into seven key segments, including:

- **Institutional.** The company sells specialized cleaners and sanitizers for washing dishes, laundry, and general housekeeping. The division also provides pool and spa treatment programs for commercial and hospitality customers and products and services for the vehicle wash industry.

- **Kay.** The Kay line of products includes chemical cleaning and sanitizing products primarily for the fast-food industry, including fast-food restaurants and other places that prepare and serve fast food, such as convenience stores, airports, stadiums, discount stores, and grocery store delis.
- **Textile care.** Provides chemical laundry products and proprietary dispensing systems and related services to institutional and commercial laundries.
- **Food and beverage.** Ecolab sells detergents, cleaners, sanitizers, lubricants, animal health, and water treatment products to dairy plants, livestock farms, breweries, soft-drink bottling plants, pharmaceutical and cosmetic plants, and meat, poultry, and other food processors.
- **Professional products.** The company produces a line of infection prevention and janitorial products for the medical and janitorial markets. Products include detergents, general purpose cleaners, carpet care, furniture polishes, disinfectants, floor care products, hand soaps, deodorizers, infection control, and gym floor products.
- **Vehicle care.** Provides soaps, polishes, wheel and tire treatments, and air fresheners for vehicle rental, fleet, and consumer car wash and detail operations.
- **Water care services.** Ecolab provides water and wastewater treatment products as well as services and systems for commercial and institutional customers.

Founded in 1923, Ecolab has about 13,000 employees and 6,000 shareholders. The company has a market capitalization of about $5 billion.

EARNINGS PER SHARE GROWTH ★ ★

Past 5 years: 99 percent (15 percent per year)
Past 10 years: 204 percent (12 percent per year)

STOCK GROWTH ★ ★ ★ ★

Past 10 years: 565 percent (21 percent per year)
Dollar growth: $10,000 over 10 years (including reinvested dividends) would have grown to $75,000.
Average annual compounded rate of return (including reinvested dividends): 22 percent

CONSISTENCY ★ ★ ★

Increased earnings per share: 9 consecutive years
Increased sales: 9 consecutive years

DIVIDEND ★ ★ ★

Dividend yield: 1.1 percent
Increased dividend: 16 consecutive years
Past 5-year increase: 85 percent (13 percent per year)
Good dividend reinvestment and stock purchase plan; voluntary stock purchase plan allows contributions of $10 to $60,000 per year.

ECOLAB AT A GLANCE

Fiscal year ended: Dec. 31
Revenue and net income in $millions

	1995	1996	1997	1998	1999	2000	5-Year Growth Avg. Annual (%)	Total (%)
Revenue ($)	1,341	1,490	1,640	1,888	2,080	2,264	11	69
Net income ($)	99.2	113	134	154	176	198	15	100
Earnings/share ($)	0.75	0.88	1.00	1.15	1.30	1.49	15	99
Dividends/share ($)	0.26	0.29	0.34	0.38	0.42	0.48	13	85
Dividend yield (%)	2.0	1.5	1.2	1.1	1.1	1.1	—	–45
PE range	13–21	17–23	18–27	22–32	24–33	17–28		

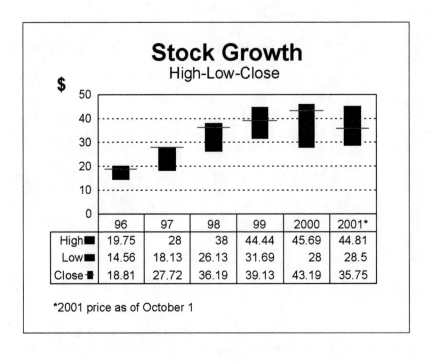

Stock Growth
High-Low-Close

$	96	97	98	99	2000	2001*
High■	19.75	28	38	44.44	45.69	44.81
Low■	14.56	18.13	26.13	31.69	28	28.5
Close■	18.81	27.72	36.19	39.13	43.19	35.75

*2001 price as of October 1

Donaldson Company, Inc.

1400 West 94th Street
Minneapolis, MN 55431
952-887-3131
NYSE: DCI
www.donaldson.com

Chairman, President, and CEO: William G. Van Dyke

Earnings Growth	★ ★
Stock Growth	★ ★ ★
Consistency	★ ★ ★ ★
Dividend	★ ★ ★
Total	**12 Points**

Donaldson has declared war on dust, grime, and flying particles. The Minneapolis-based operation manufactures filters and purifiers for trucks, turbines, and a broad range of industrial and agricultural equipment.

The company's biggest market is engine products, which account for about 61 percent of its total revenue. Donaldson makes liquid filters, air cleaners and accessories, mufflers, and other exhaust products for the construction, industrial, mining, and agricultural markets, as well as for medium and heavy-duty trucks and automobiles. It also sells filters to military contractors for land-based military equipment such as tanks. Nearly half of the company's engine products sales are through the aftermarket as replacement parts.

Industrial products account for the other 39 percent of Donaldson's sales. Leading industrial products divisions include:

- **Dust collection.** The company's Torit, DCE, and Aercology divisions make dust, fume, and mist collectors for manufacturing and assembly plants. The company also offers replacement filter cartridges, bags, and spare parts.

- **Gas turbine systems.** Donaldson manufactures static and pulse-clean air filter systems, exhaust silencers, chiller coils, and anti-icing systems for turbine engines for use in the electric power generation and oil and gas industries.
- **Special applications.** The firm makes specialized air filtration systems for computer disk drives, aircraft and automotive cabins, industrial and hospital clean rooms, business machines, room air cleaners, personal respirators, and air emission control.

Donaldson sells its products worldwide, with 11 foreign manufacturing plants and joint ventures and subsidiaries throughout Europe and Asia, as well as in Mexico, South Africa, and Australia. Foreign sales account for about 37 percent of total revenue.

Donaldson was founded in 1915 by Frank Donaldson, whose first filter was a tin can and Spanish moss air filter he made for a farmer's tractor. By the late 1920s, Donaldson had developed a spark-arresting muffler designed to cut the incidence of crop fires from engine sparks.

The company has about 8,500 employees and a market capitalization of about $1.5 billion.

EARNINGS PER SHARE GROWTH   ★ ★

Past 5 years: 97 percent (15 percent per year)
Past 10 years: 295 percent (15 percent per year)

STOCK GROWTH   ★ ★ ★

Past 10 years: 540 percent (20 percent per year)
Dollar growth: $10,000 over 10 years (including reinvested dividends) would have grown to $67,000.
Average annual compounded rate of return (including reinvested dividends): 21 percent

CONSISTENCY   ★ ★ ★ ★

Increased earnings per share: 13 consecutive years
Increased sales: 16 consecutive years

DIVIDEND ★ ★ ★

Dividend yield: 1.0 percent
Increased dividend: 14 consecutive years
Past 5-year increase: 100 percent (15 percent per year)
Good dividend reinvestment and stock purchase plan; voluntary stock purchase plan allows contributions of $10 to $1,000 per month.

DONALDSON AT A GLANCE

Fiscal year ended: July 31
Revenue and net income in $millions

	1996	1997	1998	1999	2000	2001	Avg. Annual (%)	Total (%)
							5-Year Growth	
Revenue ($)	759	833	940	944	1,092	1,137	8	49
Net income ($)	43	51	57	62	70	76	12	76
Earnings/share ($)	0.84	0.99	1.14	1.31	1.51	1.66	15	97
Dividends/share ($)	0.15	0.17	0.19	0.23	0.27	0.30	15	100
Dividend yield (%)	2.0	2.2	1.7	1.1	0.6	1.0		
PE range	16–21	110–141	18–29	22–35	36–80	10–25		

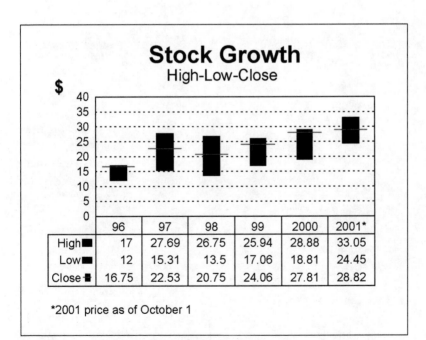

Stock Growth
High-Low-Close

$	96	97	98	99	2000	2001*
High■	17	27.69	26.75	25.94	28.88	33.05
Low■	12	15.31	13.5	17.06	18.81	24.45
Close■	16.75	22.53	20.75	24.06	27.81	28.82

*2001 price as of October 1

Franklin Resources, Inc.

777 Mariners Island Boulevard
San Mateo, CA 94404
650-312-2000
NYSE: BEN
www.franklintempleton.com

Chairman and CEO: Charles B. Johnson

Earnings Growth	★ ★
Stock Growth	★ ★ ★ ★
Consistency	★ ★ ★ ★
Dividend	★ ★
Total	**12 Points**

Franklin Resources rode the crest of the 1990s bull market to become one of the leading investment companies in the world. The 54-year-old operation used aggressive marketing and strategic acquisitions to establish a global presence for its growing universe of investment products.

The firm manages more than $200 billion in mutual funds and other investments for individuals, institutions, and corporate pension plans. It has offices in 29 countries and clients in more than 130 countries. In all, Franklin offers about 240 mutual funds.

The San Mateo, California operation has long been known for its line of Franklin municipal bond funds, which offer tax-exempt interest income. In recent years, Franklin has bolstered its offerings with other types of funds through some key acquisitions, including the Templeton Funds in 1992 and the Mutual Series family of funds in 1996.

The company offers more than 30 types of state municipal bond funds. Other leading fund categories include global stock funds (8), growth funds (8), sector funds (8), and growth and income funds (7).

In terms of assets under management, equity funds lead the list, accounting for about 66 percent of assets, followed by fixed-income funds

(28 percent), hybrid funds such as asset allocation and balanced funds (4 percent), and money market funds (2 percent).

In addition to its investment management operations, the company owns the Franklin Bank (formerly the Pacific Union Bank & Trust Company), which has about $120 million in assets. It also operates real estate and insurance divisions and a capital corporation that specializes in auto loans. However, those services account for less than 1 percent of the company's $2.3 billion in annual revenue.

Founded in New York City in 1947, Franklin has about 4,000 shareholders and 6,300 employees. It has a market capitalization of about $12 billion.

EARNINGS PER SHARE GROWTH

Past 5 years: 111 percent (16 percent per year)
Past 10 years: 500 percent (20 percent per year)

STOCK GROWTH ★ ★ ★ ★

Past 10 years: 727 percent (24 percent per year)
Dollar growth: $10,000 over 10 years (including reinvested dividends) would have grown to about $93,000.
Average annual compounded rate of return (including reinvested dividends): 25 percent

CONSISTENCY ★ ★ ★ ★

Increased earnings per share: 17 consecutive years
Increased sales: 9 of the past 10 years

DIVIDEND

Dividend yield: 0.6 percent
Increased dividend: 9 of the past 10 years
Past 5-year increase: 85 percent (13 percent per year)
Good dividend reinvestment and stock purchase plan; voluntary stock purchase plan allows contributions of $10 to $5,000 per quarter.

FRANKLIN RESOURCES AT A GLANCE

Fiscal year ended: Sept. 30
Revenue and net income in $millions

	1995	1996	1997	1998	1999	2000	5-Year Growth Avg. Annual (%)	Total (%)
Revenue ($)	876	1,520	2,163	2,577	2,263	2,340	22	167
Net income ($)	269	315	434	500	427	562	16	109
Earnings/share ($)	1.08	1.26	1.72	1.98	1.85	2.28	16	111
Dividends/share ($)	0.13	0.15	0.17	0.20	0.22	0.24	13	85
Dividend yield (%)	1.0	0.6	0.4	0.6	0.7	0.6		
PE range	10–18	12–19	12–30	13–29	16–26	10–20		

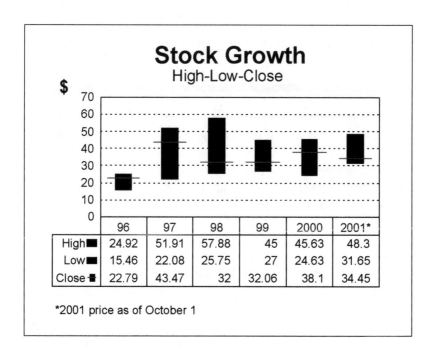

Stock Growth
High-Low-Close

$	96	97	98	99	2000	2001*
High■	24.92	51.91	57.88	45	45.63	48.3
Low■	15.46	22.08	25.75	27	24.63	31.65
Close-■	22.79	43.47	32	32.06	38.1	34.45

*2001 price as of October 1

Automatic Data Processing, Inc.

One ADP Boulevard
Roseland, NJ 07068
973-974-5000
NYSE: ADP
www.adp.com

Chairman and CEO: Arthur F. Weinbach
President: Gary C. Butler

Earnings Growth	★ ★
Stock Growth	★ ★ ★ ★
Consistency	★ ★ ★ ★
Dividend	★
Total	**11 Points**

Automatic Data Processing (ADP) cuts the checks for more than 29 million workers a week. The company is the leading provider of payroll and tax filing processing, offering transaction processing, data communications, and information services for about 500,000 corporate clients.

In terms of earnings growth, ADP has been the most consistent company in America. Since it was opened in 1949, the Roseland, New Jersey operation has posted record sales and earnings for 51 consecutive years.

ADP is considered a pioneer in the outsourcing business, in which companies farm out tasks that don't directly relate to their core competencies.

ADP's oldest business is Employer Services, which generates 58 percent of the company's $9.3 billion in annual revenue. The division provides a comprehensive range of payroll, tax deposit and reporting, benefits outsourcing, 401(k) recordkeeping, and unemployment compensation management services.

Its employer services are also offered throughout Europe, where the company has more than 20,000 corporate clients.

ADP also operates in three other key segments:

- **Brokerage services** (23 percent of revenue). ADP provides data services, recordkeeping, order entry, proxy processing, and other services for the financial services industry. ADP is the leading provider of third-party processing and retail equity information in North America. It processes more than 25 percent of all online trades in the United States and Canada, handling more than 1.2 million trades per day.
- **Dealer services** (12 percent). The company provides some computing, data, and professional services to more than 18,000 automobile, truck, and farm equipment dealers and 30 manufacturers in 13 countries. Auto dealers use ADP's on-site systems to manage their accounting, factory communications, inventory, sales, and service activities. To help auto dealers eliminate paperwork, ADP systems can digitize and store records that can be retrieved from workstations for viewing, faxing, or printing.
- **Claims services and other income** (7 percent). The company provides auto collision estimates and parts availability services to insurance companies, claims adjusters, repair shops, and salvage yards.

ADP has 40,000 employees and about 25,000 shareholders. The company has a market capitalization of about $35 billion.

EARNINGS PER SHARE GROWTH

Past 5 years: 82 percent (13 percent per year)
Past 10 years: 251 percent (13 percent per year)

STOCK GROWTH

Past 10 years: 703 percent (23 percent per year)
Dollar growth: $10,000 over 10 years (including reinvested dividends) would have grown to $86,000.
Average annual compounded rate of return (including reinvested dividends): 24 percent

CONSISTENCY ★ ★ ★ ★

Increased earnings per share: 51 consecutive years
Increased sales: 51 consecutive years

DIVIDEND   ★

Dividend yield: 0.7 percent
Increased dividend: 26 consecutive years
Past 5-year increase: 105 percent (15 percent per year)
The company offers no dividend reinvestment and stock purchase plan.

AUTOMATIC DATA PROCESSING AT A GLANCE

Fiscal year ended: June 30
Revenue and net income in $millions

	1996	1997	1998	1999	2000	2001	5-Year Growth Avg. Annual (%)	Total (%)
Revenue ($)	3,567	4,112	4,798	5,540	6,287	7,018	14	96
Net income ($)	455	524	605	697	841	925	15	103
Earnings/share ($)	0.79	0.90	0.99	1.10	1.31	1.44	13	82
Dividends/share ($)	0.20	0.22	0.26	0.30	0.34	0.41	15	105
Dividend yield (%)	1.1	1.1	1.0	0.9	0.7	0.8		
PE range	23–30	23–36	29–42	32–49	30–53	31–52		

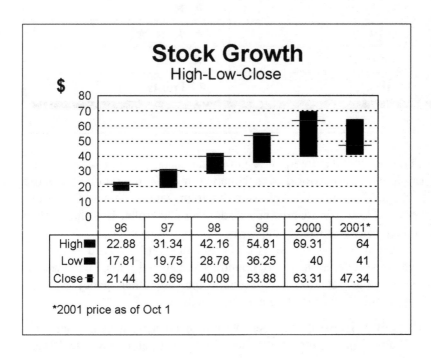

Stock Growth
High-Low-Close

	96	97	98	99	2000	2001*
High	22.88	31.34	42.16	54.81	69.31	64
Low	17.81	19.75	28.78	36.25	40	41
Close	21.44	30.69	40.09	53.88	63.31	47.34

*2001 price as of Oct 1

Interpublic Group of Companies

1271 Avenue of the Americas
New York, NY 10020
212-399-8000
NYSE: IPG
www.interpublic.com

Chairman, President, and CEO: John J. Dooner, Jr.

Earnings Growth	★ ★
Stock Growth	★ ★
Consistency	★ ★ ★ ★
Dividend	★ ★ ★
Total	**11 Points**

For the past century, Interpublic Group has been pushing products and polishing images the world over. Founded in 1902, Interpublic has more than 40 agencies and related divisions and represents such world-class operations as Coca-Cola, Unilever, Nestlé, and Chevrolet. It is the world's second largest advertising group.

Interpublic's crown jewel is McCann-Erickson Worldwide Advertising, which has operations in 110 countries and agencies in 67 countries. It handles more global advertising accounts than any other agency.

Interpublic's other leading agencies include:

- **The Lowe Group,** the number four global advertising agency network, including Lowe Lintas & Partners Advertising and Lowe Healthcare Group

48

Linear Technology Corporation

1630 McCarthy Boulevard
Milpitas, CA 95035
408-432-1900
Nasdaq: LLTC
www.linear-tech.com

Chairman and CEO: Robert Swanson
President: Clive Davies

nings Growth	★ ★ ★ ★
ck Growth	★ ★ ★ ★
sistency	★ ★ ★
idend	
l	**11 Points**

hnology makes microchips that are used in a wide range of ap-
including wireless communications, notebook and handheld
computer peripherals, medical systems, factory automation,
oducts, satellites, military and space systems, and automotive

the volatile swings in microchip demand that have sent most
acturers through a series of ups and downs, Linear Technology
ed to rack up impressive growth of revenue and earnings for

lpitas, California operation makes a broad line of high-perfor-
-integrated circuits (in which a number of transistors and other
combined to form more complicated electronic circuits).

- **Draft Worldwide,** the largest domestic company specializing in brand-building direct and promotional marketing
- **Octagon,** a global sports marketing agency
- **Initiative Media Worldwide,** the world's largest independent media management company
- **Weber Shandwick Worldwide,** the world's largest public relations company

Other agencies within Interpublic include Golin/Harris International, Jack Morton Worldwide, NFO WorldGroup, Campbell-Ewald, Campbell Mithun, Carmichael Lynch, Daily & Associates, Deutsch, Gotham, Hill Holliday, the Martin Agency, Mullen, and Suissa Miller.

In all, Interpublic Group has more than 4,000 advertising clients in 110 countries. About half of Interpublic's income comes from foreign operations.

Interpublic has handled advertising campaigns for Levi-Strauss, Nestlé, GMAC, Camel cigarettes, L'Oreal, Gillette, Mennen, Black & Decker, Delta faucets, Johnson & Johnson, Maybelline, Goodyear, Exxon, Casio, Microsoft, and Del Monte fruits. Interpublic gave Chevrolet the "heartbeat of America," deemed Coke "the real thing," and made UPS the "tightest ship in the shipping business."

In addition to advertising creations, Interpublic agencies plan campaigns and place advertising on TV and radio and in magazines, newspapers, and direct response mailers. They also offer related services, such as corporate identity promotions, graphic design, management consulting, marketing research, sales promotion, interactive services, sales meetings and events, and brand equity promotion.

Interpublic was founded in 1902 by A.W. Erickson (and in 1911 by Harrison K. McCann). The agency has been pitching General Motors cars since 1916. It was first incorporated in 1930 as McCann-Erickson and has been operating under the name Interpublic Group since 1961.

The New York–based agency has about 48,000 employees and 3,500 shareholders. It has a market capitalization of about $12 billion.

EARNINGS PER SHARE GROWTH   ★ ★

Past 5 years: 110 percent (16 percent per year)
Past 10 years: 277 percent (14 percent per year)

STOCK GROWTH ★ ★

Past 10 years: 388 percent (17 percent per year)
Dollar growth: $10,000 over 10 years (including reinvested dividends) would have grown to $54,000.
Average annual compounded rate of return (including reinvested dividends): 18.5 percent

CONSISTENCY ★ ★ ★ ★

Increased earnings per share: 19 consecutive years
Increased sales: 9 of the past 10 years

DIVIDEND ★ ★ ★

Dividend yield: 1.5 percent
Increased dividend: 17 consecutive years
Past 5-year increase: 85 percent (13 percent per year)
Good dividend reinvestment and stock purchase plan; voluntary stock purchase plan allows contributions of $10 to $3,000 per quarter.

INTERPUBLIC GROUP AT A GLANCE

Fiscal year ended: Dec. 31
Revenue and net income in $millions

	1995	1996	1997	1998	1999
Revenue ($)	2,180	3,053	3,611	4,218	4,978
Net income ($)	168	229	224	340	331
Earnings/share ($)	0.72	0.85	0.95	1.11	1.29
Dividends/share ($)	0.20	0.22	0.25	0.29	0.33
Dividend yield (%)	1.6	1.5	1.2	1.0	0.8
PE range	19–25	16–20	20–34	43–77	35–

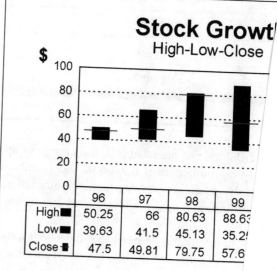

Stock Growth
High-Low-Close

$	96	97	98	99
High	50.25	66	80.63	88.63
Low	39.63	41.5	45.13	35.2
Close	47.5	49.81	79.75	57.6

*2001 price as of October 1

Linear Te
plications,
computers
network p
electronics

Despit
chip manuf
has continu
many years
The Mi
mance linea
elements ar

Semiconductor components are the electronic building blocks used in electronic systems and equipment. Linear circuits, which are a form of semiconductor, are used primarily to monitor, condition, amplify, and transform continuous analog signals associated with physical properties, such as temperature, pressure, weight, light, sound, or speed.

In all, the company sells about 5,600 products, including:

- **Amplifiers,** which amplify the voltage or output current of a device
- **High-speed amplifiers,** which are used to amplify signals above 5MHz for applications such as video, fast data acquisition, and data communication
- **Voltage regulators,** which control the voltage of a device or circuit at a specified level
- **Voltage reference circuits,** which serve as electronic benchmarks providing a constant voltage for system usage
- **Data converters,** which change linear (analog) signals into digital signals, or vice versa

The company's other linear circuits include buffers, battery monitors, motor controllers, hot swap circuits, comparators, sample-and-hold devices, and filters.

Linear markets its products worldwide to about 15,000 original manufacturers.

Founded in 1981, the company has about 2,800 employees and a market capitalization of about $14 billion.

EARNINGS PER SHARE GROWTH ★ ★ ★ ★

Past 5 years: 200 percent (25 percent per year)
Past 10 years: 1,512 percent (31 percent per year)

STOCK GROWTH ★ ★ ★ ★

Past 10 years: 5,589 percent (49 percent per year)
Dollar growth: $10,000 over 10 years (including reinvested dividends) would have grown to $570,000.
Average annual compounded rate of return (including reinvested dividends): 49 percent

CONSISTENCY   ★ ★ ★

Increased earnings per share: 9 of the past 10 years
Increased sales: 11 consecutive years

DIVIDEND

Dividend yield: 0.4 percent
Increased dividend: 9 consecutive years
Past 5-year increase: 250 percent (28 percent per year)
Linear Technology does not offer a dividend reinvestment and stock purchase plan.

LINEAR TECHNOLOGY AT A GLANCE

Fiscal year ended: June 30
Revenue and net income in $millions

	1996	1997	1998	1999	2000	2001	5-Year Growth Avg. Annual (%)	5-Year Growth Total (%)
Revenue ($)	378	379	485	507	706	973	21	157
Net income ($)	134	134	181	194	288	427	26	218
Earnings/share ($)	0.43	0.43	0.57	0.61	0.88	1.29	25	200
Dividends/share ($)	0.04	0.05	0.06	0.07	0.08	0.14	28	250
Dividend yield (%)	0.4	0.4	0.3	0.3	0.2	0.4		
PE range	12–29	23–43	17–39	34–68	39–85	32–55		

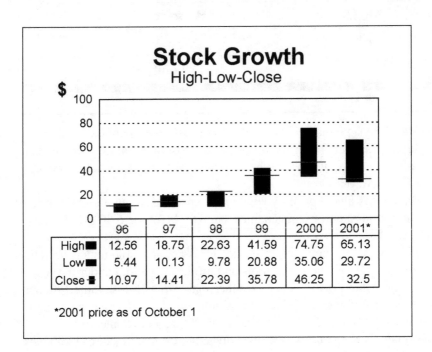

Stock Growth
High-Low-Close

$	96	97	98	99	2000	2001*
High	12.56	18.75	22.63	41.59	74.75	65.13
Low	5.44	10.13	9.78	20.88	35.06	29.72
Close	10.97	14.41	22.39	35.78	46.25	32.5

*2001 price as of October 1

49

Danaher Corporation

2099 Pennsylvania Avenue
12th Floor
Washington, DC 20006
202-828-0850
NYSE: DHR
www.danaher.com

Chairman: Steven M. Rales
President and CEO: H. Lawrence Culp, Jr.

Earnings Growth	★ ★ ★ ★
Stock Growth	★ ★ ★ ★
Consistency	★ ★ ★
Dividend	
Total	**11 Points**

The Danaher name may not be familiar to you, but if you know hand tools, you know Danaher. The Washington, D.C.–based operation is the maker of Craftsman tools, which have been a staple of Sears, Roebuck and Company for many years.

Danaher is also a primary supplier of specialized automotive service tools and general purpose mechanics' hand tools for the 6,500 NAPA auto parts stores.

The company's automotive service tools are also sold under the K-D Tools brand, and its industrial tools and products are sold under the Armstrong and Allen brand names. Danaher makes the Holo-Krome fastener tools and manufactures tools under a number of other brand names, including Matco Tools, Jacobs Chuck, Iseli, Delta, and Hennessy.

Danaher's tools and components division also manufactures toolboxes and storage devices, diesel engine retarders, wheel service equipment, drill chucks, hardware, and components for the power generation and transmission industries. Tools and components account for about 45 percent of the company's $3.8 billion in annual sales.

The company's other product segment, process and environmental controls, accounts for the other 55 percent of revenue. Danaher makes a broad range of monitoring, sensing, controlling, measuring, counting, and electrical power quality products, systems, and components. It also makes electronic test tools, underground storage tank leak detection systems, and motion, position, speed, temperature, level, and position instruments and sensing devices.

The District of Columbia–based manufacturer has operations in about 30 countries. Foreign sales account for about 20 percent of total revenue.

Originally established as a Massachusetts real estate investment trust in 1969, Danaher has about 24,000 employees and 4,200 shareholders. The company has a market capitalization of about $8 billion.

EARNINGS PER SHARE GROWTH

Past 5 years: 150 percent (20 percent per year)
Past 10 years: 431 percent (18 percent per year)

STOCK GROWTH

Past 10 years: 1,104 percent (28 percent per year)
Dollar growth: $10,000 over 10 years (including reinvested dividends) would have grown to $120,000.
Average annual compounded rate of return (including reinvested dividends): 28 percent

CONSISTENCY

Increased earnings per share: 9 of the past 10 years
Increased sales: 10 consecutive years

DIVIDEND

Dividend yield: 0.1 percent
Increased dividend: 3 of the past 7 years
Past 5-year increase: 75 percent (12 percent per year)
Danaher does not offer a dividend reinvestment and stock purchase plan.

DANAHER AT A GLANCE

Fiscal year ended: Dec. 31
Revenue and net income in $millions

	1995	1996	1997	1998	1999	2000	5-Year Growth Avg. Annual (%)	Total (%)
Revenue ($)	1,487	2,352	2,619	3,047	3,197	3,778	21	154
Net income ($)	106	246	188	192	261	324	25	205
Earnings/share ($)	0.89	1.17	1.31	1.36	1.84	2.23	20	150
Dividends/share ($)	0.04	0.10	0.10	0.09	0.07	0.07	12	75
Dividend yield (%)	0.3	0.2	0.3	0.2	0.15	0.1		
PE range	13–19	12–20	14–24	20–41	23–38	16–31		

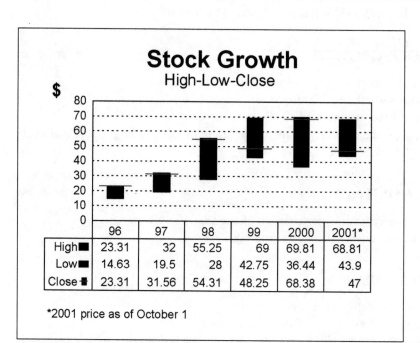

Stock Growth
High-Low-Close

	96	97	98	99	2000	2001*
High■	23.31	32	55.25	69	69.81	68.81
Low■	14.63	19.5	28	42.75	36.44	43.9
Close■	23.31	31.56	54.31	48.25	68.38	47

*2001 price as of October 1

AMGEN

One Amgen Center Drive
Thousand Oaks, CA 91320
805-447-1000
Nasdaq: AMGN
www.Amgen.com

Chairman, President, and CEO: Kevin W. Sharer

Earnings Growth	★ ★ ★
Stock Growth	★ ★ ★ ★
Consistency	★ ★ ★ ★
Dividend	
Total	**11 Points**

Long before stem cells and human cloning were part of the American vernacular, Amgen was quietly researching and developing the new frontiers of medical technology. Founded in 1980, Amgen is one of the true pioneers of the biotechnology revolution. The Silicon Valley operation is the world's largest independent biotechnology company.

Amgen has been a leader in discovering, developing, and manufacturing cost-effective human therapeutics that are based on advances in cellular and molecular biology.

Its profits are driven by three highly successful drugs:

- **Epogen.** This is the company's oldest and most profitable drug, with annual sales of about $2 billion, making it one of the top-selling pharmaceuticals in the world. First patented in 1987, Epogen stimulates and regulates the production of red blood cells.

- **Infergen.** The newest of Amgen's three main products, Infergen was approved by the FDA for the treatment of chronic hepatitis C viral (HCV) infection.
- **Neupogen.** With annual sales of about $1.2 billion, Neupogen is used for a variety of cancer-related applications. It helps reduce the incidence of infection associated with some forms of chemotherapy, and it is used to shorten the recovery time for some chemotherapy patients.

Amgen has a number of new products in the pipeline that focus on such areas as oncology, hephrology, and rheumatology. The company often develops new treatments in collaboration with other companies, including Praecis Pharmaceuticals, Regeneron, Yamanouchi Pharmaceutical, and the Massachusetts Institute of Technology. In 1997, Amgen formed a collaboration with Guilford Pharmaceuticals, which granted Amgen worldwide rights for Guilford's FKBP-neuroimmunophilin ligands, a class of small molecule neurotrophic agents that is being investigated for the treatment of neurodegenerative disorders.

The company is worldwide in scope, with offices throughout Europe, China, Australia, and North America. Amgen has about 7,300 employees and a market capitalization of about $67 billion.

EARNINGS PER SHARE GROWTH ★ ★ ★

Past 5 years: 119 percent (17 percent per year)
Past 10 years: 1,225 percent (29.5 percent per year)

STOCK GROWTH ★ ★ ★ ★

Past 10 years: 3,476 percent (43 percent per year)
Dollar growth: $10,000 over 10 years would have grown to $357,000.

CONSISTENCY ★ ★ ★ ★

Increased earnings per share: 11 consecutive years
Increased sales: 10 consecutive years

DIVIDEND

Amgen pays no dividend.

AMGEN AT A GLANCE

Fiscal year ended: Dec. 31
Revenue and net income in $millions

	1995	1996	1997	1998	1999	2000	5-Year Growth Avg. Annual (%)	Total (%)
Revenue ($)	1,940	2,225	2,381	2,718	3,340	3,629	13.5	87
Net income ($)	538	670	726	863	1,062	1,138	16	111
Earnings/share ($)	0.48	0.60	0.69	0.82	1.02	1.05	17	119
Dividends/share ($)	—	—	—	—	—	—		
Dividend yield (%)	—	—	—	—	—	—		
PE range	17–25	21–27	19–29	14–33	25–65	47–76		

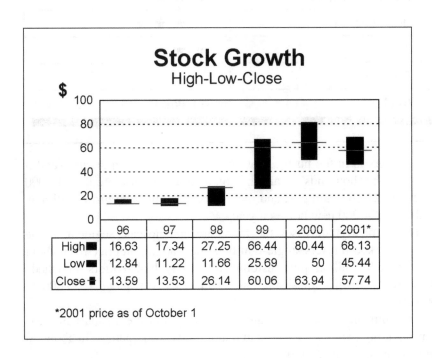

Stock Growth
High-Low-Close

	96	97	98	99	2000	2001*
High	16.63	17.34	27.25	66.44	80.44	68.13
Low	12.84	11.22	11.66	25.69	50	45.44
Close	13.59	13.53	26.14	60.06	63.94	57.74

*2001 price as of October 1

Toll Brothers

3103 Philmont Avenue
Huntingdon Valley, PA 19006
215-938-8000
NYSE: TOL
www.tollbrothers.com

Chairman and CEO: Robert I. Toll
President: Zvi Barzilay

Earnings Growth	★ ★ ★ ★
Stock Growth	★ ★ ★ ★
Consistency	★ ★ ★
Dividend	
Total	**11 Points**

Toll Brothers is in the business of building the American dream—and it does it by the thousands. In all, the company has built more than 15,000 homes in 321 communities, and the numbers continue to grow. Toll now builds about 4,000 new homes a year.

The company addresses the moderate and upscale segment of the housing market. It offers single-family homes ranging in price from about $185,000 to $1 million (plus customized options). It also offers "attached" homes (flats, town homes, and carriage homes) for about $150,000 to $600,000.

The company generally locates its houses in affluent suburban areas near major highways with access to major cities. Toll operates in about 20 states throughout the country.

Toll also develops entire planned communities that contain golf courses and other country club–type amenities. It currently has communities in

Michigan, Florida, North Carolina, and Virginia. The company expects to have ten communities up and running by the end of 2002.

Homebuyers in the planned communities are given a choice of at least four different floor plans, each with substantially different architectural styles. Buyers can also choose from a variety of additional options, such as additional rooms, finished lofts, and extra fireplaces.

Toll is able to offer its homes at competitive prices because of its efficiencies of scale. The company operates its own land development operation, as well as architectural, engineering, mortgage, title, security monitoring, landscape, cable TV, broadband Internet access, lumber distribution, house component assembly, and manufacturing operations.

Toll was founded in 1967 by Bob and Bruce Toll, whose father was also in the homebuilding business. The brothers still run the Huntingdon Valley, Pennsylvania business, Bob as chairman and CEO, and Bruce as vice chairman.

The company has about 2,500 employees and about 765 shareholders of record. Bob and Bruce Toll own about 34 percent of the stock. The company has a market capitalization of about $1.5 billion.

EARNINGS PER SHARE GROWTH   ★ ★ ★ ★

Past 5 years: 175 percent (22.5 percent per year)
Past 10 years: 1,193 percent (29 percent per year)

STOCK GROWTH   ★ ★ ★ ★

Past 10 years: 420 percent (20 percent per year)
Dollar growth: $10,000 over 10 years (including reinvested dividends) would have grown to about $75,000.
Average annual compounded rate of return (including reinvested dividends): 22 percent

CONSISTENCY   ★ ★ ★

Increased earnings per share: 9 consecutive years
Increased sales: 9 consecutive years

DIVIDEND

Toll Brothers does not pay a dividend.

TOLL BROTHERS AT A GLANCE

Fiscal year ended: Oct. 31
Revenue and net income in $millions

	1995	1996	1997	1998	1999	2000	5-Year Growth Avg. Annual (%)	5-Year Growth Total (%)
Revenue ($)	646	761	972	1,211	1,464	1,814	23	181
Net income ($)	50	54	65	85	101	146	24	192
Earnings/share ($)	1.41	1.50	1.86	2.25	2.75	3.88	22.5	175
Dividends/share ($)	—	—	—	—	—	—		
Dividend yield (%)	—	—	—	—	—	—		
PE range	7–12	9–15	9–14	7–14	5–8	4–10		

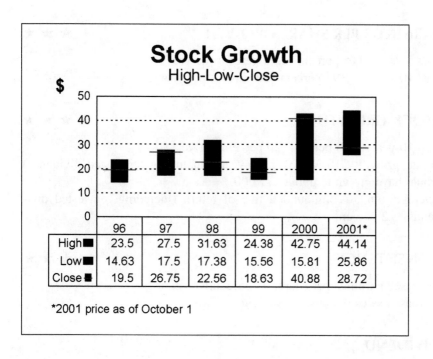

Stock Growth
High-Low-Close

$	96	97	98	99	2000	2001*
High■	23.5	27.5	31.63	24.38	42.75	44.14
Low■	14.63	17.5	17.38	15.56	15.81	25.86
Close■	19.5	26.75	22.56	18.63	40.88	28.72

*2001 price as of October 1

52

Anheuser-Busch Companies, Inc.

One Busch Place
St. Louis, MO 63118
314-577-2000
NYSE: BUD
www.anheuser-busch.com

President and Chairman: August A. Busch III

Earnings Growth	★ ★ ★ ★	
Stock Growth	★ ★	
Consistency	★ ★ ★	
Dividend	★ ★	
Total	**11 Points**	

The suds keep flowing and the profits keep growing for Anheuser-Busch, the world's leading brewery. Over the past quarter century, the St. Louis operation has more than doubled its share of the domestic beer market, from about 23 percent in the late 1970s to about 50 percent in 2001. Its two closest rivals combined (Miller and Coors) fall far short of Anheuser's market dominance. Miller commands about 22 percent of the domestic beer market, and Coors controls about 11 percent.

Anheuser-Busch is the world's largest brewer worldwide, accounting for about 10 percent of all beer sales. It sells about 121 million barrels a year out of 1.2 billion total barrels of beer sold worldwide. It boasts the top-selling regular beer (Budweiser) and the top-selling light beer (Bud Light). The company operates 14 breweries, including 12 in the United States and 2 overseas. It sells its products in more than 80 countries.

Beer sales account for about 95 percent of the St. Louis–based brewing company's $14.3 billion in annual revenue.

Among the company's other leading brands are Busch, Natural Light, O'Doul's (nonalcoholic), Elk Mountain Amber Ale, Red Wolf Lager, Hurricane Malt Liquor, Tequiza, King Cobra, ZiegenBock Amber, and Natural Pilsner. Its Michelob brand includes several varieties, including Michelob, Michelob Golden Draft, Light, Dry, Classic Dark, Malt, Amber Bock, Pale Ale, Honey Lager, Porter, and Hefe-Weizen.

Busch's brewing business is fully integrated. In addition to its breweries, it owns a beverage can manufacturer, a bottle making plant, a barley processing plant, a label printing operation, and a refrigerated railcar transportation subsidiary. It is the nation's second-largest manufacturer of aluminum beverage containers and the world's largest recycler of aluminum beverage cans.

The firm also owns and operates several theme parks, including two Busch Gardens parks (in Tampa, Florida, and Williamsburg, Virginia); Adventure Island in Tampa; Sesame Place in Pennsylvania; three Sea World parks; Discovery Cove in Orlando, Florida; and Water Country USA in Williamsburg. The company also operates the Baseball City Sports Complex near Orlando.

Anheuser-Busch traces its roots to a small St. Louis brewery started in 1852. After a few years of lackluster results, the original owner, George Schneider, sold out the struggling operation to an investment group headed by St. Louis soap tycoon Eberhard Anheuser. Anheuser ultimately turned the business over to his son-in-law, a portly, gregarious man by the name of Adolphus Busch.

Mr. Busch, who converted the small brewery into a national force, is generally recognized as the founder of Anheuser-Busch. Budweiser, which Mr. Busch helped develop in 1876, was one of the first beers to achieve widespread distribution. Michelob, the company's premium beer, was first brought to market in 1896. When Adolphus Busch died in 1913, his son August A. Busch assumed control of the business. The reins have since passed through two more generations of the Busch family. August A. Busch III, 63, now directs the company as its chairman of the board and president.

The company has about 24,000 employees and 60,000 shareholders. It has a market capitalization of about $36 billion.

EARNINGS PER SHARE GROWTH   ★ ★ ★ ★

Past 5 years: 172 percent (22 percent per year)
Past 10 years: 118 percent (8.5 percent per year)

STOCK GROWTH

Past 10 years: 347 percent (16 percent per year)
Dollar growth: $10,000 over 10 years (including reinvested dividends) would have grown to $52,000.
Average annual compounded rate of return (including reinvested dividends): 18 percent

CONSISTENCY

Increased earnings per share: 9 of the past 10 years
Increased sales: 9 of the past 10 years

DIVIDEND

Dividend yield: 1.6 percent
Increased dividend: 28 consecutive years
Past 5-year increase: 50 percent (8.5 percent per year)
Good dividend reinvestment and stock purchase plan; voluntary stock purchase plan allows contributions of $25 to $5,000 per month.

ANHEUSER-BUSCH AT A GLANCE

Fiscal year ended: Dec. 31
Revenue and net income in $millions

	1995	1996	1997	1998	1999	2000	5-Year Growth Avg. Annual (%)	5-Year Growth Total (%)
Revenue ($)	12,004	12,621	12,832	13,208	13,723	14,297	3	19
Net income ($)	642.3	1,190	1,170	1,233	1,402	1,552	19	142
Earnings/share ($)	0.62	1.17	1.17	1.27	1.47	1.69	22	172
Dividends/share ($)	0.42	0.46	0.50	0.54	0.58	0.63	8.5	50
Dividend yield (%)	2.8	2.3	2.27	1.65	1.64	1.38		
PE range	15–20	14–19	16–20	16–26	21–28	16–29		

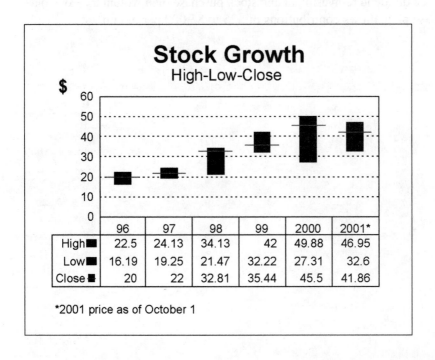

Stock Growth
High-Low-Close

$	96	97	98	99	2000	2001*
High	22.5	24.13	34.13	42	49.88	46.95
Low	16.19	19.25	21.47	32.22	27.31	32.6
Close	20	22	32.81	35.44	45.5	41.86

*2001 price as of October 1

53

Starbucks Corporation

2401 Utah Avenue South
P.O. Box 34067
Seattle, WA 98134
206-318-1575
Nasdaq: SBUX
www.starbucks.com

Chairman: Howard Schultz
President and CEO: Orin C. Smith

Earnings Growth	★ ★ ★ ★
Stock Growth	★ ★ ★ ★
Consistency	★ ★ ★
Dividend	
Total	**11 Points**

Starbucks has turned the coffeehouse experience into a $2 billion operation. Coffee drinkers can now get their morning caffeine buzz at more than 4,500 Starbucks restaurants across America and around the world.

Although the restaurants vary in size and design, a running theme of Starbucks is their laid-back atmosphere, where customers can kick back, read a book, chat with friends, or just silently sip their morning brew.

The restaurants serve a wide selection of regular and decaffeinated coffees, including a "coffee of the day," as well as a broad selection of Italian espressos, cold blended beverages, teas, and roasted whole bean coffees. Starbucks stores also offer pastries and other foods, sodas, and juices. And for the do-it-yourselfer, Starbucks sells coffee grinders, coffeemakers, espresso machines, coffee filters, tumblers, and mugs.

About 8 percent of the company's revenue comes from its whole bean coffees; 73 percent from its other coffees, teas, and other specialized beverages; 14 percent from food items; and 5 percent from coffeemaking equipment and accessories.

The company has stores in about 35 states and 17 foreign countries. The restaurants are typically located in high-traffic, high-visibility areas, such as downtown and suburban retail centers, office buildings, super-market foyers, and university campuses.

Starbucks opens 400 to 500 new restaurants a year. Most of its restaurants are company-owned, although some stores—particularly outside the United States—are owned by independent concessionaires who operate them under special licensing arrangements.

In addition to its retail sales, Starbucks sells coffee wholesale to office coffee distributors and institutional food service companies. The company also has a joint venture with Pepsi-Cola to develop bottled coffee drinks and with Breyer's to develop coffee ice creams.

Founded in 1971, Starbucks has about 47,000 employees and 9,000 shareholders. It has a market capitalization of about $7 billion.

EARNINGS PER SHARE GROWTH ★ ★ ★ ★

Past 5 years: 300 percent (32 percent per year)
Past 8 years: 1,700 percent (33 percent per year)

STOCK GROWTH ★ ★ ★ ★

Past 8 years: 789 percent (24 percent per year)
Dollar growth: $10,000 over 10 years would have grown to about $86,000.
Average annual compounded rate of return: 24 percent

CONSISTENCY ★ ★ ★

Increased earnings per share: 8 consecutive years (since its IPO in 1992)
Increased sales: 9 consecutive years

DIVIDEND

Starbucks pays no dividend.

STARBUCKS AT A GLANCE

Fiscal year ended: Dec. 31
Revenue and net income in $millions

	1995	1996	1997	1998	1999	2000	5-Year Growth Avg. Annual (%)	Total (%)
Revenue ($)	465	697	967	1,309	1,680	2,169	36	366
Net income ($)	26	36	57	81	102	137	39	427
Earnings/share ($)	0.09	0.12	0.18	0.22	0.27	0.36	32	300
Dividends/share ($)	—	—	—	—	—	—		
Dividend yield (%)	—	—	—	—	—	—		
PE range	35–50	28–78	42–73	38–80	36–75	47–103		

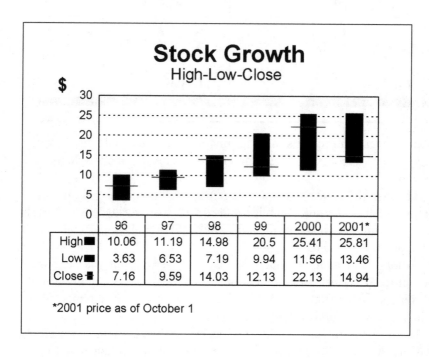

Stock Growth
High-Low-Close

	96	97	98	99	2000	2001*
High	10.06	11.19	14.98	20.5	25.41	25.81
Low	3.63	6.53	7.19	9.94	11.56	13.46
Close	7.16	9.59	14.03	12.13	22.13	14.94

*2001 price as of October 1

Maxim Integrated Products

120 San Gabriel Drive
Sunnyvale, CA 94086
408-737-7600
Nasdaq: MXIM
www.maxim-ic.com

Chairman, President, and CEO: John Gifford

Earnings Growth	★ ★ ★
Stock Growth	★ ★ ★ ★
Consistency	★ ★ ★ ★
Dividend	
Total	**11 Points**

Maxim Integrated Products makes semiconductors used in a wide variety of applications, from cell phones and test instruments to bar-code readers and cable TV.

The company specializes in integrated circuits that use digital technology to detect, measure, amplify, and convert real-world measures, such as temperature, pressure, speed, and sound, into digital signals that can be stored and processed on a computer.

Among its leading products are data converters, interface circuits, microprocessor supervisors, operational amplifiers, power supplies, multiplexers, switches, battery chargers, battery management circuits, fiber-optic transceivers, and voltage references.

In all, the Sunnyvale, California operation markets more than 2,000 products. Many of its products are used on microprocessor-based electronics equipment, such as personal computers and peripherals, test equipment, handheld devices, wireless phones and pagers, and video displays.

The company produces products for four key industries:

- **Communications.** It makes products for broadband networks, cable systems, central office switches, direct broadcast TV, fiber optics, pagers, cellular phones, satellite communications, and video communications.
- **Industrial control industry.** Its products are used to control temperature, velocity, flow, pressure, and position.
- **Instrumentation.** Maxim circuits are used for automatic test equipment, analyzers, data recorders, and instruments used to measure electricity, light, pressure, sound, speed, and temperature.
- **Data processing.** The firm's circuits are used for handheld computers, bar-code readers, disk drives, mainframes, minicomputers, personal computers, printers, point-of-sale terminals, tape drives, servers, and workstations.

The company also produces products for military, video, and medical equipment applications.

Maxim markets its products worldwide. International sales account for about 57 percent of its annual revenue.

The company spends more than $140 million a year on research and development and introduces about 250 products per year.

Founded in 1983, Maxim has about 4,200 employees and 1,000 shareholders. It has a market capitalization of about $15 billion.

EARNINGS PER SHARE GROWTH   ★ ★ ★

Past 5 years: 129 percent (18 percent per year)
Past 10 years: 1,920 percent (35 percent per year)

STOCK GROWTH   ★ ★ ★ ★

Past 10 years: 6,506 percent (53 percent per year)
Dollar growth: $10,000 over 10 years would have grown to $650,000.
Average annual compounded rate of return: 53 percent

CONSISTENCY   ★ ★ ★ ★

Increased earnings per share: 13 consecutive years
Increased sales: 13 consecutive years

DIVIDEND

Maxim does not pay a dividend.

MAXIM INTEGRATED PRODUCTS AT A GLANCE

Fiscal year ended: June 30
Revenue and net income in $millions

	1996	1997	1998	1999	2000	2001	5-Year Growth Avg. Annual (%)	Total (%)
Revenue ($)	422	434	560	607	865	1,577	27	237
Net income ($)	123	137	178	196	281	335	22	172
Earnings/share ($)	0.44	0.47	0.59	0.65	0.88	1.01	18	129
Dividends/share ($)	—	—	—	—	—	—		
Dividend yield (%)	—	—	—	—	—	—		
PE range	11–27	22–40	18–38	30–74	47–102	35–75		

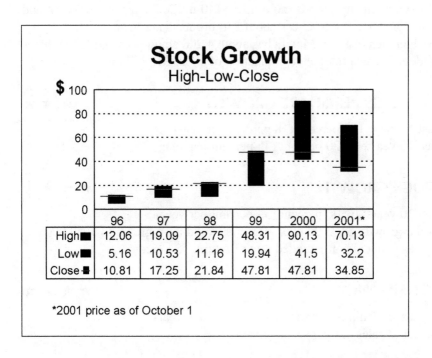

Stock Growth
High-Low-Close

	96	97	98	99	2000	2001*
High■	12.06	19.09	22.75	48.31	90.13	70.13
Low■	5.16	10.53	11.16	19.94	41.5	32.2
Close■	10.81	17.25	21.84	47.81	47.81	34.85

*2001 price as of October 1

55
Universal Health Services, Inc.

Universal Corporate Center
367 South Gulph Road
King of Prussia, PA 19406
610-768-3300
NYSE: UHS
www.uhsinc.com

Chairman, President, and CEO: Alan Miller

Earnings Growth	★ ★ ★ ★
Stock Growth	★ ★ ★ ★
Consistency	★ ★ ★
Dividend	
Total	**11 Points**

Care of the sick and injured is a growth industry in the United States, where the population is expanding and aging. Universal Health Services has been capitalizing on that trend by putting together a national chain of hospitals, behavioral health centers, ambulatory surgery centers, and radiation oncology centers.

The Pennsylvania-based operation has grown quickly through an aggressive series of acquisitions. It is the nation's third largest investor-owned hospital chain, with a total of about 100 facilities that includes more than 60 hospitals.

The company's strategy is to acquire or build health care facilities in rapidly growing markets. It is also responding to changes in the health care industry by focusing more on outpatient services now that a growing number of procedures are performed on an outpatient basis.

The company's hospitals offer a variety of services, including general surgery, internal medicine, obstetrics, emergency room care, radiology, oncology, diagnostic care, coronary care, pediatric services, and behavioral health services.

For its hospitals and other facilities, Universal provides capital resources and a variety of management services, including central purchasing, information services, finance and control systems, facilities planning, physician recruitment services, administrative personnel management, marketing, and public relations.

Including all of its facilities, the company reports a total of about 1 million patient days per year in acute care facilities, and 608,000 days in its behavioral health centers. Patient revenue breaks down this way: Medicare, 32 percent; Medicaid, 11.5 percent; HMOs and other managed care providers, 34.5 percent; and other sources, 22 percent.

The company has facilities in about 22 states (mostly in the Midwest and South), Puerto Rico, and France. Universal was founded in 1978 by Alan Miller, who still serves as president, CEO, and chairman.

The company has about 26,000 employees and a market capitalization of about $2.5 billion.

EARNINGS PER SHARE GROWTH ★ ★ ★ ★

Past 5 years: 151 percent (20 percent per year)
Past 10 years: 652 percent (22 percent per year)

STOCK GROWTH ★ ★ ★ ★

Past 10 years: 1,001 percent (27 percent per year)
Dollar growth: $10,000 over 10 years (including reinvested dividends) would have grown to $110,000.
Average annual compounded rate of return (including reinvested dividends): 27 percent

CONSISTENCY ★ ★ ★

Increased earnings per share: 9 of the past 10 years
Increased sales: 10 consecutive years

DIVIDEND

Universal Health Services pays no dividend.

UNIVERSAL HEALTH SERVICES AT A GLANCE

Fiscal year ended: Dec. 31
Revenue and net income in $millions

	1995	1996	1997	1998	1999	2000	5-Year Growth Avg. Annual (%)	5-Year Growth Total (%)
Revenue ($)	931	1,190	1,443	1,874	2,042	2,242	19	141
Net income ($)	35	51	67	80	79	94	22	168
Earnings/share ($)	1.26	1.64	2.03	2.45	2.48	3.16	20	151
Dividends/share ($)	—	—	—	—	—	—		
Dividend yield (%)	—	—	—	—	—	—		
PE range	8–16	13–19	14–25	16–25	9–23	12–37		

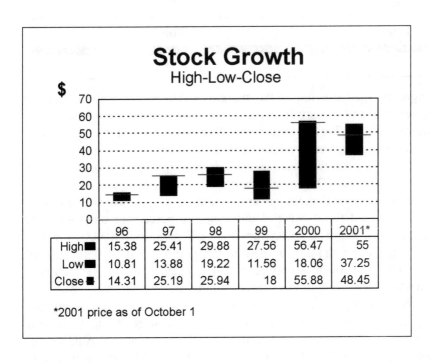

Stock Growth
High-Low-Close

	96	97	98	99	2000	2001*
High■	15.38	25.41	29.88	27.56	56.47	55
Low■	10.81	13.88	19.22	11.56	18.06	37.25
Close■	14.31	25.19	25.94	18	55.88	48.45

*2001 price as of October 1

Safeway, Inc.

5918 Stoneridge Mall Road
Pleasanton, CA 94588
925-467-3000
NYSE: SWY
www.safeway.com

Chairman, President, and CEO: Steven A. Burd

Earnings Growth	★ ★ ★ ★
Stock Growth	★ ★ ★ ★
Consistency	★ ★ ★
Dividend	
Total	**11 Points**

The grocery business runs on thin margins and keen competition. Safeway has managed to keep profits growing by expanding its store base and its offerings. With 1,700 stores in about 20 states and 4 Canadian provinces, Safeway is one of North America's biggest grocery store chains.

The newer Safeway stores are fairly large supermarkets of about 55,000 square feet. They carry a wide selection of both food and general merchandise. More than 90 percent of Safeway stores have specialty bakeries, delis, and floral centers, and about 70 percent of its stores have pharmacies. Most of its older stores range in size from 30,000 to 50,000 square feet, although many of its stores range in size from 5,000 to 29,000 square feet. The smaller stores are usually located in smaller communities or in areas with space limitations or community restrictions.

The company has also become more self-sufficient than most grocers. It operates 41 manufacturing and processing facilities, including 10 milk plants, 8 bread plants, 6 ice cream plants, 3 cheese and meat packaging plants, 4 soft drink bottling plants, 5 fruit and vegetable processing plants, 1 pet food plant, and 4 other food processing facilities.

Most of Safeway's 1,700 stores are located in the western United States and the western provinces of Canada. It also has stores in Alaska, Hawaii, Illinois, Pennsylvania, Maryland, and Virginia.

In addition to its namesake Safeway stores, the company also operates a number of other chains, including Pan 'n Save Foods, Vons, Pavilions, Dominick's, Carrs, and Tom Thumb.

Founded in 1925, Safeway was acquired by the investment firm of Kolberg Kravis Roberts and Company (KKR) in 1986 in a leveraged buy-out of its stock. In 1990, KKR brought the company public again with an initial stock offering. But after three years of disappointing financial results, the old management was swept out of power, and a new management team was hired to revive the company and bolster its sagging returns. To say the least, the operation was an unmitigated success.

From 1992 to 1998, earnings grew from $0.21 a share to $1.59—a 657 percent increase—and the stock price climbed from a low of $2.40 (split-adjusted) to $61—a 2,400 percent gain. In real-dollar terms, a $10,000 investment in the stock at its 1992 low would have grown to about $250,000 by the close of 1998.

Safeway has about 190,000 employees and a market capitalization of about $28 billion.

EARNINGS PER SHARE GROWTH　　　★ ★ ★ ★

Past 5 years: 213 percent (25.5 percent per year)
Past 10 years: 914 percent (26 percent per year)

STOCK GROWTH　　　★ ★ ★ ★

Past 10 years: 1,166 percent (27 percent per year)
Dollar growth: $10,000 over 10 years would have grown to about $109,000.
Average annual compounded rate of return: 27 percent

CONSISTENCY　　　★ ★ ★

Increased earnings per share: 9 of the past 10 years
Increased sales: 10 consecutive years

DIVIDEND

Safeway pays no dividend.

SAFEWAY AT A GLANCE

Fiscal year ended: Dec. 31
Revenue and net income in $millions

	1995	1996	1997	1998	1999	2000	5-Year Growth Avg. Annual (%)	Total (%)
Revenue ($)	16,398	17,269	22,484	24,484	28,860	31,977	14	95
Net income ($)	326	461	622	807	971	1,092	27	235
Earnings/share ($)	0.68	0.97	1.25	1.59	1.68	2.13	25.5	213
Dividends/share ($)	—	—	—	—	—	—		
Dividend yield (%)	—	—	—	—	—	—		
PE range	10–17	11–23	16–24	24–49	18–39	16–33		

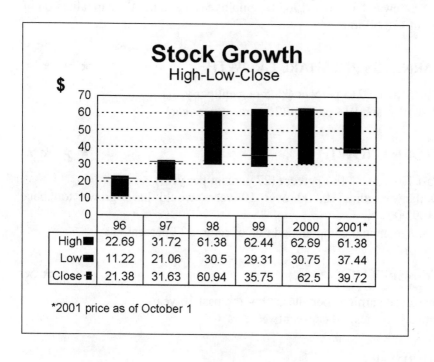

Stock Growth
High-Low-Close

	96	97	98	99	2000	2001*
High	22.69	31.72	61.38	62.44	62.69	61.38
Low	11.22	21.06	30.5	29.31	30.75	37.44
Close	21.38	31.63	60.94	35.75	62.5	39.72

*2001 price as of October 1

Dell Computer Corporation

One Dell Way
Round Rock, TX 78682
512-338-4400
Nasdaq: DELL
www.dell.com

Chairman and CEO: Michael Dell
Co-President: Kevin Rollins
Co-President: James Vanderslice

Earnings Growth	★ ★ ★ ★
Stock Growth	★ ★ ★ ★
Consistency	★ ★ ★
Dividend	
Total	**11 Points**

Dell has made its mark in the computer industry by going directly to the consumer. In fact, it has become the world's largest direct seller of computer systems. The Round Rock, Texas operation offers a wide range of desktop and notebook computers, workstations, and network server and storage products, and an extended selection of peripheral hardware and computing software.

Dell Computer founder Michael Dell built his business on the direct marketing approach, which cuts costs by eliminating the markups that would otherwise go to the wholesale and retail dealers. It also avoids the higher inventory costs associated with traditional distribution channels and reduces the high risk of product obsolescence in the rapidly changing computer market. The direct sales strategy also gives the company a better opportunity to maintain, monitor, and update its customer database.

Dell offers two lines of desktop computers, the OptiPlex line for corporate and institutional customers using a network, and the Dimension line for small businesses, workgroups, and individuals.

The company also offers a number of specialized services, including custom hardware and software integration, leasing and asset management, and network installation and support. Dell offers next-business-day delivery and extended training and support programs for many of its software offerings.

In addition to its own products, Dell also sells printers, scanners, digital cameras, monitors, and related products from other manufacturers.

Dell's customers range from large corporations, government agencies, and medical and educational institutions to small businesses and individuals. The company markets its products to the business sector through sales teams and to consumers through direct marketing advertising and the Internet.

The company sells its products worldwide. Sales outside of North America account for about 30 percent of total revenue.

Dell has manufacturing facilities in Texas, Tennessee, Brazil, Ireland, Malaysia, and China.

Founded in 1984, Dell has about 40,000 employees and a market capitalization of about $55 billion.

EARNINGS PER SHARE GROWTH ★ ★ ★ ★

Past 5 years: 925 percent (59 percent per year)
Past 10 years: 4,000 percent (45 percent per year)

STOCK GROWTH ★ ★ ★ ★

Past 10 years: 22,290 percent (71 percent per year)
Dollar growth: $10,000 over 10 years would have grown to $225,000.
Average annual compounded rate of return: 71 percent

CONSISTENCY ★ ★ ★

Increased earnings per share: 9 of the past 10 years
Increased sales: 10 consecutive years

DIVIDEND

Dell pays no dividend.

DELL COMPUTER AT A GLANCE

Fiscal year ended: Jan. 31
Revenue and net income in $millions

	1996	1997	1998	1999	2000	2001	5-Year Growth Avg. Annual (%)	Total (%)
Revenue ($)	5,296	7,759	12,327	18,243	25,265	31,888	43	502
Net income ($)	272	518	944	1,460	1,666	2,236	53	722
Earnings/share ($)	0.08	0.17	0.32	0.53	0.61	0.82	59	925
Dividends/share ($)	—	—	—	—	—	—		
Dividend yield (%)	—	—	—	—	—	—		
PE range	8–49	18–76	31–118	59–104	26–97	16–39		

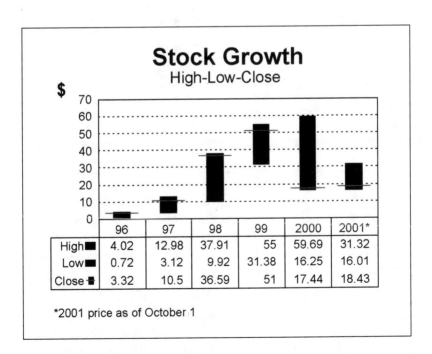

Stock Growth
High-Low-Close

	96	97	98	99	2000	2001*
High	4.02	12.98	37.91	55	59.69	31.32
Low	0.72	3.12	9.92	31.38	16.25	16.01
Close	3.32	10.5	36.59	51	17.44	18.43

*2001 price as of October 1

58

UnitedHealth Group, Inc.

UnitedHealth Group

UnitedHealth Group Center
9900 Bren Road East
Minnetonka, MN 55343
612-936-1300
NYSE:UNH
www.unitedhealthgroup.com

Chairman and CEO: William W. McGuire, M.D.
President: Stephen J. Hemsley

Earnings Growth	★ ★ ★ ★
Stock Growth	★ ★ ★ ★
Consistency	★ ★ ★
Dividend	
Total	**11 Points**

UnitedHealth Group is one of the nation's leading health maintenance organizations, with 35 million customers throughout the United States.

Founded in 1974, the company has grown rapidly by aggressively acquiring smaller HMOs. The firm operates through five divisions, including:

- **UnitedHealthcare** (68 percent of revenue). The company's largest division, UnitedHealthcare, serves about 7.5 million customers as part of health plans offered by employers and other groups of less than 5,000 individuals. It also provides services for about 400,000 Medicare customers and 549,000 Medicaid customers. UnitedHealthcare uses a network of about 350,000 physicians and 3,500 hospitals.

- **Ovations** (16 percent). Ovations is an HMO geared to individuals over 50. The company has a marketing arrangement with AARP that has helped recruit many of the 3.5 million customers who use Ovations' Medicare Supplement and Hospital Indemnity insurance.
- **Uniprise** (10 percent). Uniprise sets up customized health care services used by employees of its corporate customers. In all, Uniprise has about 260 corporate clients—including about one-fourth of all Fortune 500 companies—representing about 8 million individuals in all.
- **Ingenix** (2 percent). The company provides data and software products and services for the health care industry.
- **Specialized care** (4 percent). UnitedHealth offers some additional niche services, such as behavioral health and employee counseling programs, chronic care, dental services, and vision care. It has about 19 million behavioral health customers, 2.4 million dental customers, and 1.2 million vision customers.

UnitedHealth has managed to stay profitable and increase its earnings in recent years by focusing on cost control. The company has spent more than $400 million over the past two years to update its computer infrastructure to streamline core processes, such as claims, billing, and receiving.

The Minneapolis operation has about 30,000 employees and 4,600 shareholders. UnitedHealth has a market capitalization of about $17 billion.

EARNINGS PER SHARE GROWTH ★ ★ ★ ★

Past 5 years: 98 percent (15 percent per year)
Past 10 years: 1,300 percent (30 percent per year)

STOCK GROWTH ★ ★ ★ ★

Past 10 years: 800 percent (24.5 percent per year)
Dollar growth: $10,000 over 10 years (including reinvested dividends) would have grown to about $90,000.
Average annual compounded rate of return (including reinvested dividends): 24.6 percent

CONSISTENCY ★ ★ ★

Increased earnings per share: 9 of the past 10 years
Increased sales: 11 consecutive years

DIVIDEND

Dividend yield: 0.2 percent
Increased dividend: None
Past 5-year increase: None
UnitedHealth does not offer a dividend reinvestment plan.

UNITEDHEALTH GROUP AT A GLANCE

Fiscal year ended: Dec. 31
Revenue and net income in $millions

	1995	1996	1997	1998	1999	2000	5-Year Growth Avg. Annual (%)	Total (%)
Revenue ($)	5,671	10,074	11,794	17,355	19,562	21,122	30	272
Net income ($)	383	356	460	509	563	736	14	92
Earnings/share ($)	1.06	0.88	1.13	1.31	1.59	2.10	15	98
Dividends/share ($)	0.02	0.02	0.02	0.02	0.02	0.02	—	—
Dividend yield (%)	0.1	0.1	0.1	0.1	0.1	0.05		
PE range	17–24	17–39	18–26	—	12–21	10–29		

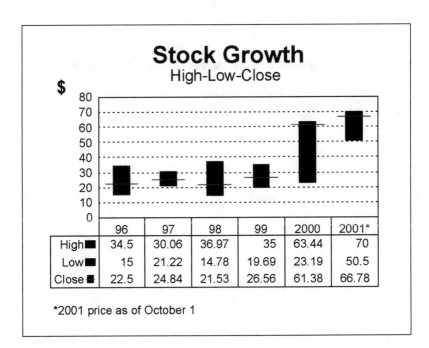

Stock Growth
High-Low-Close

	96	97	98	99	2000	2001*
High■	34.5	30.06	36.97	35	63.44	70
Low■	15	21.22	14.78	19.69	23.19	50.5
Close■	22.5	24.84	21.53	26.56	61.38	66.78

*2001 price as of October 1

59
EMC Corporation

EMC²
where information lives

35 Parkwood Drive
Hopkinton, MA 01748
508-435-1000
NYSE: EMC
www.emc.com

Chairman: Michael C. Reuttgers
President and CEO: Joseph M. Tucci

Earnings Growth	★ ★ ★ ★
Stock Growth	★ ★ ★ ★
Consistency	★ ★ ★
Dividend	
Total	**11 Points**

As corporations and institutions expand their computer networks, adding e-mail, e-commerce, voice, video, and graphics applications, they soon find themselves running short of digital storage space. EMC helps solve that storage shortage by offering a line of high-capacity digital storage systems.

The Massachusetts operation is the market leader in the enterprise data storage market, with more than a 50 percent share of the mainframe storage market.

EMC focuses on the growing trend toward networked information storage. Networked information storage involves connecting storage systems to servers via a networked environment instead of direct connections. The objective is to provide unlimited access to information, regardless of its location.

Founded in 1979, EMC originally focused on selling add-on memory for the minicomputer market. But as corporate computer networks grew larger and more sophisticated, EMC shifted its focus to address the voracious data storage appetites of the large corporate networks.

The company introduced its Symmetrix 4200 storage system in 1990 and has been upgrading and expanding the Symmetrix systems ever since. In 1994, the firm added to its product mix by introducing a mirroring software for business continuity and disaster recovery called the Symmetrix Remote Data Facility. Since then, the company has introduced more than a dozen software products, including EMC ControlCenter, EMCE Time-Finder, EMCData Manager, and EMC PowerPath, that enable customers to manage, protect, and share information across the computer enterprise.

EMC's customers include 95 of the Fortune 100, all of the world's top telecommunications companies, all of the 25 largest banks in the United States, 9 of the top 10 Internet service providers, and about 90 percent of the world's major reservation systems.

EMC has about 24,000 employees and a market capitalization of about $35 million.

EARNINGS PER SHARE GROWTH   ★ ★ ★ ★

Past 5 years: 316 percent (34 percent per year)
Past 10 years: 7,800 percent (55 percent per year)

STOCK GROWTH   ★ ★ ★ ★

Past 10 years: 9,767 percent (58 percent per year)
Dollar growth: $10,000 over 10 years would have grown to $980,000.
Average annual compounded rate of return: 58 percent

CONSISTENCY   ★ ★ ★

Increased earnings per share: 9 of the past 10 years
Increased sales: 10 consecutive years

DIVIDEND

EMC does not pay a dividend.

EMC AT A GLANCE

Fiscal year ended: Dec. 31
Revenue and net income in $millions

	1995	1996	1997	1998	1999	2000	5-Year Growth Avg. Annual (%)	Total (%)
Revenue ($)	1,921	2,274	2,938	3,974	6,716	8,873	36	362
Net income ($)	365	420	587	654	1,010	1,782	37	388
Earnings/share ($)	0.19	0.21	0.28	0.30	0.46	0.79	34	316
Dividends/share ($)	—	—	—	—	—	—		
Dividend yield (%)	—	—	—	—	—	—		
PE range	13–21	9–23	14–29	19–71	45–120	59–132		

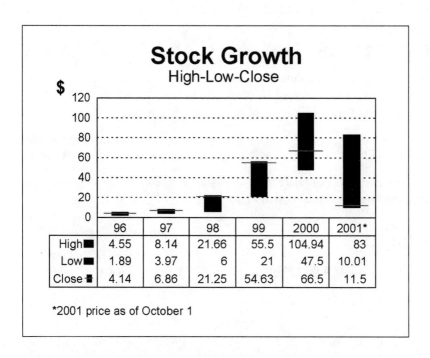

Stock Growth
High-Low-Close

	96	97	98	99	2000	2001*
High■	4.55	8.14	21.66	55.5	104.94	83
Low■	1.89	3.97	6	21	47.5	10.01
Close■	4.14	6.86	21.25	54.63	66.5	11.5

*2001 price as of October 1

Southwest Airlines Company

P.O. Box 36611
Dallas, TX 75235
214-792-4000
NYSE: LUV
www.southwest.com

Chairman: Herbert D. Kelleher
CEO: James F. Parker
President: C. C. Barrett

Earnings Growth	★ ★ ★ ★
Stock Growth	★ ★ ★ ★
Consistency	★ ★ ★
Dividend	
Total	**11 Points**

It has been choppy flying for most commercial airline operations the past few decades. They've had to contend with wide fluctuations in fuel prices, occasional economic slowdowns, and heightening competition.

But through it all, Southwest Airlines just keeps climbing. The Dallas-based carrier has been the most consistent company in the airline industry for many years by taking a totally different approach than the rest of the competition. Southwest is known for offering everyday low fares—with no frills—and frequent flights between its key destinations.

Rather than use a hub-and-spoke system for its flights—similar to the other major carriers—Southwest schedules shorter flights that travel point to point. The average flight distance for Southwest is about 500 miles. The point-to-point approach provides short-haul customers with more nonstop flights, while minimizing connections, delays, and total trip time.

Southwest also flies into smaller airports that are less congested and closer to the downtowns, such as Chicago Midway, Dallas Love Field, Houston Hobby, Oakland, Fort Lauderdale/Hollywood, and Long Island airports.

Southwest does not have working relationships with commuter feeder lines, nor does it schedule connecting flights with other carriers.

The company uses only one type of airplane (Boeing 737), which means maintenance crews and pilots need only learn to fly one type of plane.

Southwest was the first airline to offer ticketless travel in 1995, long before e-tickets became popular with other carriers.

The company has been growing at a steady, deliberate pace, adding new destinations that fit well into its national scheme. In all, only 57 cities in 29 states have Southwest Airlines service. But in the cities it serves, the service is extraordinary. Not only are fares cheaper, but also flights are more plentiful. For instance, Southwest has 180 flights a day departing from Phoenix, 166 from Las Vegas, 151 from Houston, and 139 from Dallas. In all, Southwest boasts 2,600 flights a day and 57 million passengers per year. It is the nation's fifth-largest carrier.

Founded in 1971, the company has about 30,000 employees and a market capitalization of about $14 billion.

EARNINGS PER SHARE GROWTH ★ ★ ★ ★

Past 5 years: 229 percent (27 percent per year)
Past 10 years: 1,028 percent (27 percent per year)

STOCK GROWTH ★ ★ ★ ★

Past 10 years: 1,530 percent (31 percent per year)
Dollar growth: $10,000 over 10 years (including reinvested dividends) would have grown to about $140,000.
Average annual compounded rate of return (including reinvested dividends): 31 percent

CONSISTENCY ★ ★ ★

Increased earnings per share: 9 of the past 10 years
Increased sales: 10 consecutive years

DIVIDEND

Dividend yield: 0.1 percent
Increased dividend: 12 consecutive years
Past 5-year increase: 100 percent (20 percent per year)
Southwest Airlines does not offer a dividend reinvestment and stock purchase plan.

SOUTHWEST AIRLINES AT A GLANCE

Fiscal year ended: Dec. 31
Revenue and net income in $millions

	1995	1996	1997	1998	1999	2000	5-Year Growth Avg. Annual (%)	Total (%)
Revenue ($)	2,873	3,406	3,817	4,164	4,736	5,650	14.5	97
Net income ($)	183	207	318	433	474	625	28	241
Earnings/share ($)	0.24	0.27	0.41	0.55	0.59	0.79	27	229
Dividends/share ($)	0.01	0.01	0.01	0.01	0.01	0.02	20	100
Dividend yield (%)	0.2	0.2	0.2	0.2	0.1	0.1		
PE range	12–22	14–20	10–18	12–19	16–26	12–29		

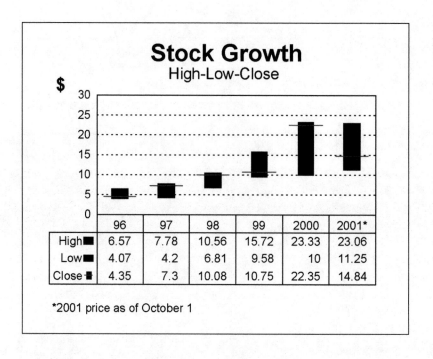

Stock Growth
High-Low-Close

$		96	97	98	99	2000	2001*
High■		6.57	7.78	10.56	15.72	23.33	23.06
Low■		4.07	4.2	6.81	9.58	10	11.25
Close■		4.35	7.3	10.08	10.75	22.35	14.84

*2001 price as of October 1

Abbott Laboratories

100 Abbott Park Road
Abbott Park, IL 60064-6400
847-937-6100
NYSE: ABT
www.abbott.com

Chairman and CEO: Miles D. White

Earnings Growth	★
Stock Growth	★ ★
Consistency	★ ★ ★ ★
Dividend	★ ★ ★
Total	**10 Points**

For well over a century, Abbott Laboratories has been developing drugs and diagnostic testing products for doctors and hospitals the world over. Founded in 1888, the Chicago operation is one of the world's leading makers of blood screening equipment, and was the first company to introduce an AIDS antibody test.

Abbott is also among the leaders in tests for hepatitis, sexually transmitted diseases, cancer, thyroid function, pregnancy, illicit drugs, and drug monitoring. With 30 consecutive years of increased sales and earnings, Abbott has been one of the nation's most consistent companies.

The company breaks its operations into five key segments, including:

- **Pharmaceuticals** (19 percent of total revenue). The firm produces a broad line of adult and pediatric pharmaceuticals, including treatments for epilepsy, migraine, bipolar disorder, benign prostatic hyperplasia, arthritis, hypertension, and HIV infection.

- **Diagnostics** (21 percent). Abbott's leading diagnostic products include test products for hepatitis, HIV antibodies and antigens, and other infectious diseases. It also makes tests for determining levels of abused drugs, physiological diagnostic tests, cancer monitoring tests, and fertility and pregnancy tests.
- **Hospital products** (19 percent). Leading products include critical care monitoring instruments, intravenous and irrigation fluids (and the equipment to administer them), drug delivery devices, and diagnostic imaging products.
- **Ross products** (15 percent). The company's Ross division offers a growing line of nutritional products, including Similac, Isomil, and Alimentum infant formulas, and Ensure, Jevity, Glucerna, PediaSure, and Pulmocare adult and pediatric nutritional formulas. Abbott is also the maker of Murine eye drops, Selsun Blue dandruff shampoo, and Tronolane hemorrhoid medication.
- **International** (24 percent). Abbott offers a broad line of hospital, pharmaceutical, and pediatric nutritional products that are made and marketed outside the United States. It has sales or operations in more than 130 countries.

The company has more than 130 research, manufacturing, and distribution facilities worldwide. Abbott Laboratories was founded in 1888 by Dr. Wallace C. Abbott, who began the business as a sideline venture in his small Chicago apartment, making pills from the alkaloid of plants.

Abbott has grown to about 60,000 employees and 107,000 shareholders. It has a market capitalization of about $75 billion.

EARNINGS PER SHARE GROWTH ★

Past 5 years: 71 percent (11.5 percent per year)
Past 10 years: 218 percent (12 percent per year)

STOCK GROWTH ★ ★

Past 10 years: 281 percent (14 percent per year)
Dollar growth: $10,000 over 10 years (including reinvested dividends) would have grown to about $43,000.
Average annual compounded rate of return (including reinvested dividends): 16 percent

CONSISTENCY   ★ ★ ★ ★

Increased earnings per share: 30 consecutive years (since 1971)
Increased sales: 30 consecutive years

DIVIDEND   ★ ★ ★

Dividend yield: 1.6 percent
Increased dividend: Every year since 1971
Past 5-year increase: 81 percent (13 percent per year)
Good dividend reinvestment and stock purchase plan; voluntary stock purchase plan allows contributions of $10 to $5,000 per quarter.

ABBOTT LABORATORIES AT A GLANCE

Fiscal year ended: Dec. 31
Revenue and net income in $millions

	1995	1996	1997	1998	1999	2000	5-Year Growth Avg. Annual (%)	5-Year Growth Total (%)
Revenue ($)	10	11	11.9	12.5	13.2	13.7	6.5	37
Net income ($)	1.68	1.87	2.08	2.33	2.44	2.79	11	66
Earnings/share ($)	1.04	1.18	1.32	1.50	1.57	1.78	11.5	71
Dividends/share ($)	0.42	0.48	0.54	0.60	0.68	0.76	13	81
Dividend yield (%)	1.9	1.9	1.6	1.2	1.9	1.6		
PE range	14–21	16–24	18–26	21–33	21–34	16–31		

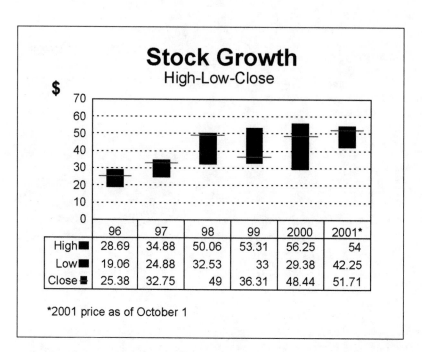

Stock Growth
High-Low-Close

	96	97	98	99	2000	2001*
High■	28.69	34.88	50.06	53.31	56.25	54
Low■	19.06	24.88	32.53	33	29.38	42.25
Close ▆	25.38	32.75	49	36.31	48.44	51.71

*2001 price as of October 1

Wells Fargo & Company

WELLS FARGO

420 Montgomery Street
San Francisco, CA 94163
800-411-4932
NYSE: WFC
www.wellsfargo.com

Chairman, President, and CEO: Richard M. Kovacevich

Earnings Growth	★
Stock Growth	★ ★ ★
Consistency	★ ★ ★
Dividend	★ ★ ★
Total	**10 Points**

Wells Fargo doesn't do business out of a stagecoach anymore. It has 5,500 shiny branch stores for its banking customers to use. The San Francisco–based operation is now the fourth-largest bank in America, thanks to its 1998 merger with Norwest Corp.

The company's biggest division is community banking, with 11 million customers in 23 states. Wells Fargo offers all the traditional consumer banking services, as well as investment brokerage and insurance. Community banking accounts for 69 percent of the company's business, including insurance and investments (15 percent) and specialized lending (12 percent).

In addition to community banking, the company has three other principal divisions:

- **Wholesale banking** (14 percent). The company has about 60,000 corporate and commercial customers. Wholesale banking services account for about 10 percent of the total, while commercial real estate lending makes up the other 4 percent.

- **Home mortgages** (11 percent). Wells Fargo is the nation's leading originator of home mortgages, with 4 million customers.
- **Consumer finance** (6 percent). The company has 4.5 million customers in 47 states and all 10 Canadian provinces.

The merger between Wells Fargo and Norwest is part of a long trend by the two banks. In all, the combined company has been involved in about 1,500 mergers and acquisitions over the past 150 years.

The merged company, based in San Francisco, has carried on part of the philosophy that was the key to Norwest's success prior to the merger. The company refers to its banking offices as "stores," and it approaches the business as a retailer rather than as a traditional bank. Its focus is on "cross-selling"—selling multiple services such as savings, checking, CDs, consumer loans, mortgages, credit cards, and investment services. A high percentage of Wells Fargo's customers uses several of its banking services.

Wells Fargo was founded in 1852 by Henry Wells and William G. Fargo and is most known in Old West folklore as a stagecoach operator. The company operated the westernmost leg of the Pony Express and ran stagecoach lines in the western United States. The banking business was separated from the express business in 1905.

Wells Fargo has about 113,000 employees and about 50,000 shareholders. The company has a market capitalization of about $83 billion.

EARNINGS PER SHARE GROWTH   ★

Past 5 years: 70 percent (11 percent per year)
Past 10 years: 242 percent (13 percent per year)

STOCK GROWTH   ★ ★ ★

Past 10 years: 585 percent (21 percent per year)
Dollar growth: $10,000 over 10 years (including reinvested dividends) would have grown to about $80,000.
Average annual compounded rate of return (including reinvested dividends): 23 percent

CONSISTENCY

Increased earnings per share: 9 of the past 10 years

DIVIDEND ★ ★ ★

Dividend yield: 1.7 percent

Increased dividend: 14 consecutive years

Past 5-year increase: 100 percent (15 percent per year)

Good dividend reinvestment and stock purchase plan; voluntary stock purchase plan allows contributions of $25 to $10,000 per month.

WELLS FARGO AT A GLANCE

Fiscal year ended: Dec. 31
Total assets and net income in $millions

	1995	1996	1997	1998	1999	2000	5-Year Growth Avg. Annual (%)	5-Year Growth Total (%)
Total assets ($)	72,134	80,175	88,540	202,475	218,102	272,426	31	278
Net income ($)	956	1,154	1,351	2,906	3,747	4,026	33	321
Earnings/share ($)	1.37	1.54	1.75	1.75	2.23	2.33	11	70
Dividends/share ($)	0.45	0.53	0.62	0.62	0.79	0.90	15	100
Dividend yield (%)	3.2	2.4	1.6	1.8	1.9	1.7		
PE range	7–13	11–17	14–26	21–34	14–21	13–24		

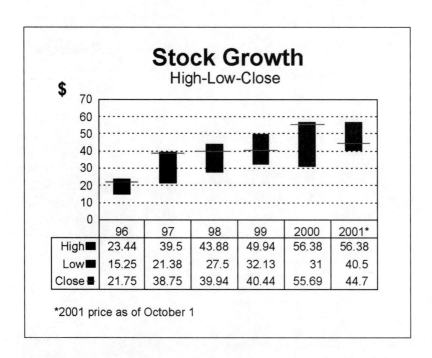

Stock Growth
High-Low-Close

	96	97	98	99	2000	2001*
High	23.44	39.5	43.88	49.94	56.38	56.38
Low	15.25	21.38	27.5	32.13	31	40.5
Close	21.75	38.75	39.94	40.44	55.69	44.7

*2001 price as of October 1

Tyco International, Ltd.

One Tyco Park
Exeter, NH 03833
603-778-9700
NYSE: TYC
www.tyco.com

Chairman, President, and CEO: L. Dennis Kozlowski

Earnings Growth	★ ★ ★ ★
Stock Growth	★ ★ ★ ★
Consistency	★ ★
Dividend	
Total	**10 Points**

Tyco International can help you get a better night's sleep—although bedding is not one of the many products Tyco manufactures. The company is a leading maker of fire detectors and security systems, so you'll sleep better once you're wired with Tyco.

The New Hampshire–based operation generates about 21 percent of its $29 billion in annual revenue from its fire and security services division. Tyco is the world's largest provider of electronic security systems and a leading manufacturer and installer of fire detection equipment and sprinkler systems. Tyco has operations in more than 100 countries around the world. Sales outside North America account for about 36 percent of total revenue.

The company makes fire extinguishers, fire hydrants, fire-fighting hoses, alarms, detection and fire suppression systems, sprinklers, and electronic security systems. It also installs, maintains, and monitors the electronic security systems it sells, which are used for both commercial and residential customers.

Tyco also operates divisions involved in a diverse mix of other areas, from pipes and plastics to electronics and medical supplies. Its other leading divisions include:

- **Health care and specialty products** (22 percent of revenue). The company makes minimally invasive surgical instruments; wound care, respiratory care, and pain medications; diagnostic imaging; and disposable medical supplies (including gauze, wound care products, and wound closure products). It also makes urological, incontinence, and anesthetic supplies; medical stress and resting electrode sensors; and medical and industrial chart paper. The division also makes polyethylene film; coated, laminated, and printed packaging materials; and garment hangers.
- **Flow control products** (14 percent). Tyco is the world's largest industrial valve and control manufacturer. It makes a full line of valves for industrial and process control systems for liquids, gases, and other substances. It also makes pipes, pipe fittings, meters, and pipe hangers.
- **Electronics** (34 percent). The company makes high-precision printed circuit boards and related products. It is the world's largest supplier of passive electronic components, including wireless, touch screen and fiber-optic components for cellular products, computers, appliances, instruments, and consumer electronics.

The other 9 percent of the company's revenue comes from TyCom, Ltd., an undersea fiber-optic telecommunications company that is 86 percent owned by Tyco.

Tyco has about 215,000 employees and 6,200 shareholders. It has a market capitalization of about $93 billion.

EARNINGS PER SHARE GROWTH ★ ★ ★ ★

Past 5 years: 432 percent (40 percent per year)
Past 10 years: 505 percent (20 percent per year)

STOCK GROWTH ★ ★ ★ ★

Past 10 years: 920 percent (26 percent per year)
Dollar growth: $10,000 over 10 years (including reinvested dividends) would have grown to about $110,000.
Average annual compounded rate of return (including reinvested dividends): 27 percent

CONSISTENCY ★ ★

Increased earnings per share: 8 of the past 10 years
Increased sales: 9 of the past 10 years

DIVIDEND

Dividend yield: 0.1 percent
Increased dividend: 1 of the past 10 years
Past 5-year increase: None
Tyco does not offer a dividend reinvestment and stock purchase plan.

TYCO INTERNATIONAL AT A GLANCE

Fiscal year ended: Sept. 30
Revenue and net income in $millions

	1995	1996	1997	1998	1999	2000	5-Year Growth Avg. Annual (%)	Total (%)
Revenue ($)	4,535	5,090	6,598	12,311	22,497	28,932	44	538
Net income ($)	125	248	310	419	1,177	2,562	110	1,950
Earnings/share ($)	0.41	0.51	0.65	1.01	1.53	2.18	40	432
Dividends/share ($)	0.05	0.05	0.05	0.05	0.05	0.05	—	—
Dividend yield (%)	0.8	0.6	0.4	0.2	0.1	0.1		
PE range	11–18	12–19	14–24	27–54	35–84	12–22		

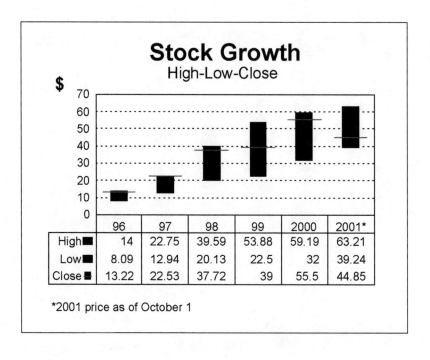

Stock Growth
High-Low-Close

	96	97	98	99	2000	2001*
High■	14	22.75	39.59	53.88	59.19	63.21
Low■	8.09	12.94	20.13	22.5	32	39.24
Close■	13.22	22.53	37.72	39	55.5	44.85

*2001 price as of October 1

64

Valspar Corporation

1101 Third Street South
Minneapolis, MN 55415
612-332-7371
NYSE: VAL
www.valspar.com

Chairman, President, and CEO: Richard M. Rompala

Earnings Growth	★ ★
Stock Growth	★
Consistency	★ ★ ★ ★
Dividend	★ ★ ★
Total	**10 Points**

Valspar makes red paint in many shades, but the company has been careful not to spill any on the corporate balance sheet. Paint it black, in fact, with 26 consecutive years of record earnings.

Valspar paints have been a mainstay of the American landscape for nearly 200 years. Recently, the company has been expanding globally as well. The Minneapolis-based manufacturer has operations and joint ventures throughout Europe and Asia, as well as in Australia, Mexico, and Brazil.

Valspar has 46 plants in North America, including three in Mexico and three in Canada.

The company's largest division is its consumer coatings group, which makes a full line of decorative paints, varnishes, and stains for sale to consumers by home centers, mass merchants, hardware wholesalers, and independent dealers. The consumer group accounts for about 34 percent of the company's $1.5 billion in total revenue.

Among its leading consumer brands are Colony, Valspar, Enterprise, Magicolor, McCloskey, BPS, and Masury.

Valspar's other divisions include:

- **Packaging coatings** (28 percent of revenue). Valspar is the world's largest supplier of coatings for the rigid packaging industry. Its leading segment is the production of coatings for food and beverage cans. It also produces coatings for aerosol cans, bottle crowns, closures for glass bottles, and coatings for flexible packaging—paper, film, and foil substrates.
- **Industrial coatings** (24 percent). The firm produces decorative and protective coatings for wood, metal, and plastics and is a major supplier to the furniture and wood paneling industry.
- **Special products** (14 percent). Valspar manufactures paints, coatings, and resins for marine applications, automotive and fleet refinish coatings, heavy-duty maintenance and high-performance floor finishing.

Valspar traces its origins to a Boston paint shop called Color and Paint, which opened in 1806. That business eventually became Valentine & Co., which introduced a line of Valspar quick-drying varnishes and stains in 1906. Valspar was touted as "the varnish that won't turn white." Its claim to fame was a boiling-water test that Valspar-varnished woods could endure with no apparent ill effects.

The company has 4,500 employees and about 1,900 shareholders. Valspar has a market capitalization of about $1.5 billion.

EARNINGS PER SHARE GROWTH   ★ ★

Past 5 years: 85 percent (13 percent per year)
Past 10 years: 260 percent (14 percent per year)

STOCK GROWTH   ★

Past 10 years: 160 percent (10 percent per year)
Dollar growth: $10,000 over 10 years (including reinvested dividends) would have grown to about $30,000.
Average annual compounded rate of return (including reinvested dividends): 11.5 percent

CONSISTENCY   ★ ★ ★ ★

Increased earnings per share: 26 consecutive years
Increased sales: 14 consecutive years

DIVIDEND

Dividend yield: 1.7 percent

Increased dividend: 23 consecutive years

Past 5-year increase: 73 percent (12 percent per year)

Good dividend reinvestment and stock purchase plan; voluntary stock purchase plan allows contributions of up to $10,000 per year. The company also offers a direct stock purchase plan with a minimum initial investment of $10,000.

VALSPAR AT A GLANCE

Fiscal year ended: Oct. 31
Revenue and net income in $millions

	1995	1996	1997	1998	1999	2000	5-Year Growth Avg. Annual (%)	Total (%)
Revenue ($)	790	860	1,017	1,155	1,388	1,483	13	88
Net income ($)	48	56	66	72	82	86	12	79
Earnings/share ($)	1.08	1.26	1.49	1.63	1.87	2.00	13	85
Dividends/share ($)	0.30	0.33	0.36	0.42	0.46	0.52	12	73
Dividend yield (%)	1.6	1.5	1.2	1.2	1.3	1.7		
PE range	10–24	12–24	15–26	16–25	12–27	11–18		

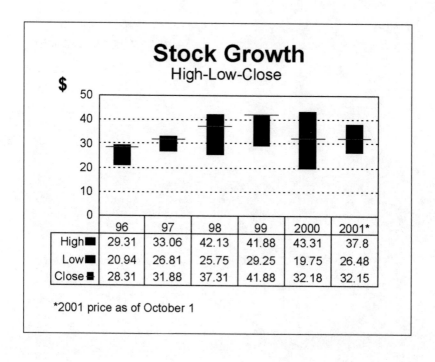

Stock Growth
High-Low-Close

	96	97	98	99	2000	2001*
High	29.31	33.06	42.13	41.88	43.31	37.8
Low	20.94	26.81	25.75	29.25	19.75	26.48
Close	28.31	31.88	37.31	41.88	32.18	32.15

*2001 price as of October 1

Best Buy Company, Inc.

7075 Flying Cloud Drive
Eden Prairie, MN 55344
952-947-2000
NYSE: BBY
www.bestbuy.com

Chairman and CEO: Richard Schulze

Earnings Growth	★ ★ ★ ★
Stock Growth	★ ★ ★ ★
Consistency	★ ★
Dividend	
Total	**10 Points**

For electronics junkies, Best Buy is the closest thing to heaven. The nation's largest retailer of consumer electronics, personal computers, entertainment software, and appliances operates more than 400 stores throughout the United States.

The Minneapolis retailer will soon be invading Canada as well, with 60 to 65 stores expected to open there in the next two to three years.

In addition to its Best Buy stores, the company also recently acquired Musicland, which operates about 1,300 stores under the names Musicland, On Cue, Media Play, Suncoast, and Sam Goody.

Musicland is one of the nation's largest retailers of music, videos, books, computer software, video games, and other entertainment-related products. Sam Goody and Suncoast are both mall-based music and video stores. On Cue is a rural-based music store, while Media Play operates metropolitan-based, large-format stores that feature music, videos, books, software, and related products.

But the heart of the business is the chain of Best Buy stores. The stores range in size from 30,000 square feet in the smaller markets to the 58,000-square-foot superstores in the larger markets. The stores stock a vast selection of music, software, videos, CD players, TV sets, computers and accessories, cameras, phones, video games, and major appliances.

The company has been successful by following several key strategies:

- It locates stores at sites that are easily accessible from major highways and thoroughfares.
- It builds enough stores in major markets to maximize leverage on fixed costs, such as advertising and operations management.
- The stores offer a format similar to a self-service discount store for many products with which customers are familiar and a higher level of customer service for more technically complex products.
- The stores offer customers the ability to subscribe to services such as Internet access, satellite TV, and wireless communication.
- It offers options not always available at competing stores, such as financing options, product delivery and installation, computer upgrades, and repair and warranty services.
- The company controls costs by centrally managing all buying, merchandising, and distribution.

Best Buy was founded in 1966 as an audio components retailer. The company has about 45,000 employees and 1,700 shareholders. It has a market capitalization of about $11 billion.

EARNINGS PER SHARE GROWTH   ★ ★ ★ ★

Past 5 years: 564 percent (46 percent per year)
Past 10 years: 3,620 percent (47 percent per year)

STOCK GROWTH   ★ ★ ★ ★

Past 10 years: 6,740 percent (92 percent per year)
Dollar growth: $10,000 over 10 years would have grown to $685,000.
Average annual compounded rate of return: 92 percent

CONSISTENCY   ★ ★

Increased earnings per share: 8 of the past 10 years
Increased sales: 10 consecutive years

DIVIDEND

Best Buy pays no dividend.

BEST BUY AT A GLANCE

Fiscal year ended: Dec. 31
Revenue and net income in $millions

	1995	1996	1997	1998	1999	2000	5-Year Growth Avg. Annual (%)	Total (%)
Revenue ($)	7,217	7,771	8,358	10,078	12,494	15,327	16	112
Net income ($)	48	1.7	94	224	347	396	53	725
Earnings/share ($)	0.28	0.01	0.52	1.07	1.63	1.86	46	564
Dividends/share ($)	—	—	—	—	—	—		
Dividend yield (%)	—	—	—	—	—	—		
PE range	16–35	11–27	200–650	4–29	14–46	25–49		

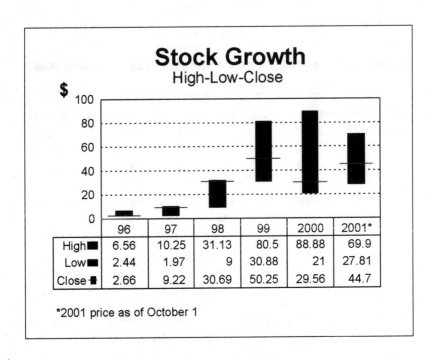

Stock Growth
High-Low-Close

	96	97	98	99	2000	2001*
High	6.56	10.25	31.13	80.5	88.88	69.9
Low	2.44	1.97	9	30.88	21	27.81
Close	2.66	9.22	30.69	50.25	29.56	44.7

*2001 price as of October 1

The Kroger Company

1014 Vine Street
Cincinnati, OH 45202
513-762-4000
NYSE: KR
www.kroger.com

Chairman and CEO: Joseph Pichler
President: David Dillon

Earnings Growth	★ ★
Stock Growth	★ ★ ★ ★
Consistency	★ ★ ★ ★
Dividend	
Total	**10 Points**

Founded in 1883, Kroger has become the nation's largest grocery store chain with more than 2,300 stores throughout the United States. But many of its stores are operated under different names. For instance, in addition to its Kroger groceries, the company operates Ralphs, King Soopers, City Market, Dillons, Smiths, Fry's, QFC, Kessel, Cala Bell, Owen's, JayC, Hilander, Gerges, and Pay Less grocery stores. It also operates Food4Less and Foods Co. warehouse grocery stores.

Although its grocery operations account for more than 90 percent of its total revenue, Kroger also operates a number of other types of stores, including the Fred Meyer multidepartment stores. It operates a total of about 800 convenience stores, including Tom Thumb, Turkey Hill, Kwik Shop, Loaf 'N Jug Mini Marts, and Quik Shop. Kroger also operates three jewelry store chains, including Fred Meyer Jewelers, Littman, and Barclay Jewelers. In all, the company has about 400 jewelry stores.

The company builds three different types of grocery stores, including combination food and drug stores, multidepartment stores, and low-price warehouse stores. Most of its stores are combination stores, which are large enough to offer the traditional grocery items as well as "whole health" foods, pharmacies, pet centers, and specialty perishable items, such as fresh seafood and organic produce.

One of Kroger's key strategic advantages is that it does much of its own product production. Kroger operates 42 manufacturing plants, including 15 dairies, 12 deli or bakery plants, 5 grocery product plants, 5 ice cream or beverage plants, 3 meat plants, and 2 cheese plants. In all, the company produces about 3,000 of its own private-label products. It also carries another 2,500 private-label items in its stores that are produced at outside plants to Kroger's specifications.

Kroger's stores are located throughout much of the United States. Its highest concentration is in its home state of Ohio, with about 190 stores, and in California, with about 440 stores. Other leading states include Texas, 174 stores; Georgia, 144 stores; Indiana, 121 stores; and Colorado, 115 stores.

Kroger has about 315,000 full-time and part-time employees and 55,000 shareholders. It has a market capitalization of about $20 billion.

EARNINGS PER SHARE GROWTH ★ ★

Past 5 years: 113 percent (16 percent per year)
Past 10 years: 538 percent (20 percent per year)

STOCK GROWTH ★ ★ ★ ★

Past 10 years: 658 percent (22 percent per year)
Dollar growth: $10,000 over 10 years would have grown to $75,000.
Average annual compounded rate of return: 22 percent

CONSISTENCY ★ ★ ★ ★

Increased earnings per share: 10 consecutive years
Increased sales: 10 consecutive years

DIVIDEND

Kroger has not paid a dividend since 1988.

KROGER AT A GLANCE

Fiscal year ended: Jan. 31
Revenue and net income in $millions

	1996	1997	1998	1999	2000	2001	5-Year Growth Avg. Annual (%)	Total (%)
Revenue ($)	23,938	25,171	26,567	28,203	45,352	49,000	15	105
Net income ($)	319	353	444	538	966	1,130	29	254
Earnings/share ($)	0.63	0.67	0.85	1.02	1.13	1.34	16	113
Dividends/share ($)	—	—	—	—	—	—		
Dividend yield (%)	—	—	—	—	—	—		
PE range	9–14	12–17	13–22	20–36	20–47	14–27		

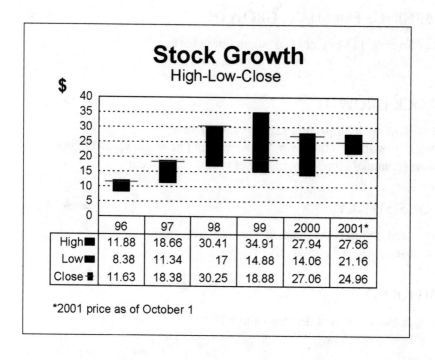

Stock Growth
High-Low-Close

	96	97	98	99	2000	2001*
High	11.88	18.66	30.41	34.91	27.94	27.66
Low	8.38	11.34	17	14.88	14.06	21.16
Close	11.63	18.38	30.25	18.88	27.06	24.96

*2001 price as of October 1

67

American International Group, Inc.

70 Pine Street
New York, NY 10270
212-770-7000
NYSE: AIG
www.aig.com

Chairman and CEO: Maurice R. Greenberg

Earnings Growth	★ ★
Stock Growth	★ ★ ★ ★
Consistency	★ ★ ★ ★
Dividend	
Total	**10 Points**

American International Group (AIG) offers insurance coverage that covers the world. Not only is the New York–based operation the leading underwriter of commercial and industrial insurance in the United States, it also provides insurance and financial services to customers in about 130 countries around the world.

AIG's global businesses include financial products and asset management, real estate investment management and retirement savings products, aircraft leasing, and trading and market making.

The company has been growing steadily in recent years, with 16 consecutive years of record earnings. That steady pace should continue as AIG aggressively pursues opportunities in the largely underinsured foreign markets.

Underlying AIG's financial success is its commitment to efficiency, which has resulted in one of the lowest expense ratios in the industry.

The company sells a wide range of insurance products, including property and casualty, life, commercial, and industrial policies. The company's general domestic operations account for about 29 percent of total income; foreign general operations account for 11 percent; domestic life insurance, 15 percent; foreign life, 25 percent; financial services, 15 percent; and asset management, 5 percent.

AIG was founded in China in 1919 by C.V. Starr, who opened a small insurance agency in Shanghai. At the time, Shanghai was the bustling commercial center of China and East Asia. But because of political unrest, Starr had to move his agency to New York in 1939, where it adopted its current name. As a sign of the times, AIG reestablished a presence in Shanghai in 1992. The same year, AIG opened an office in Moscow, the first American insurance company to do so. Foreign operations continue to be one of the company's greatest strengths.

Worldwide, the company has about 40,000 employees and about 10,000 shareholders. It has a market capitalization of about $190 billion.

EARNINGS PER SHARE GROWTH   ★ ★

Past 5 years: 106 percent (15.5 percent per year)
Past 10 years: 317 percent (15 percent per year)

STOCK GROWTH   ★ ★ ★ ★

Past 10 years: 756 percent (24 percent per year)
Dollar growth: $10,000 over 10 years (including reinvested dividends) would have grown to $88,000.
Average annual compounded rate of return (including reinvested dividends): 24.5 percent

CONSISTENCY   ★ ★ ★ ★

Increased earnings per share: 16 consecutive years
Increased sales: 10 consecutive years

DIVIDEND

Dividend yield: 0.2 percent
Increased dividend: Every year since 1993
Past 5-year increase: 75 percent (12 percent per year)
American International Group does not offer a dividend reinvestment plan.

AMERICAN INTERNATIONAL AT A GLANCE

Fiscal year ended: Dec. 31
Total assets and net income in $millions

	1995	1996	1997	1998	1999	2000	5-Year Growth Avg. Annual (%)	Total (%)
Total assets ($)	151,000	172,000	199,700	233,700	268,200	306,600	15	103
Net income ($)	2,704	3,171	3,711	4,282	5,055	5,636	16	108
Earnings/share ($)	1.17	1.37	1.60	1.84	2.15	2.41	15.5	106
Dividends/share ($)	0.08	0.09	0.10	0.11	0.13	0.14	12	75
Dividend yield (%)	0.4	0.3	0.3	0.3	0.2	0.1		
PE range	12–18	14–19	15–24	18–29	23–34	21–43		

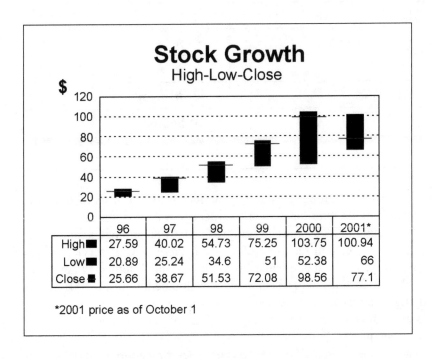

Stock Growth
High-Low-Close

	96	97	98	99	2000	2001*
High	27.59	40.02	54.73	75.25	103.75	100.94
Low	20.89	25.24	34.6	51	52.38	66
Close	25.66	38.67	51.53	72.08	98.56	77.1

*2001 price as of October 1

68

Pitney Bowes, Inc.

:::: Pitney Bowes

World Headquarters
1 Elmcroft Road
Stamford, CT 06926
203-356-5000
NYSE: PBI
www.pitneybowes.com

Chairman and CEO: Michael Critelli
President: Marc Breslawsky

Earnings Growth	★
Stock Growth	★ ★
Consistency	★ ★ ★
Dividend	★ ★ ★ ★
Total	**10 Points**

For a company that relies on mailing services for most of its income, the advent of e-mail could have been a critical blow. But Pitney Bowes has continued to build its business by embracing new technologies rather than running from them. In fact, one of the company's newest services is offering postage to client companies instantly over the Internet. Pitney spent most of its $125 million in research and development funds in 2001 on developing an advanced digital mailing system.

Pitney Bowes is the world's largest maker of postage meters and mailing equipment.

The company typically leases postage metering equipment to its customers and sells supplies. It also offers related services to its metering customers. In addition to postage meters, Pitney provides mailing machines, address hygiene software, letter and parcel scales, mail openers, mail room furniture, folders, and paper handling and shipping equipment. Postage meters and other mailing equipment account for 73 percent of the company's $3.8 billion in annual revenue.

The Stamford, Connecticut operation recently sold its mortgage serving business and was slated to spin off its office systems division in late 2001.

It continues to offer facilities management services, assisting companies with a variety of support functions, such as correspondence mail, copy centers, fax services, electronic printing, reprographics management, high-volume automated mail center management, and related activities. Target customers are large industrial companies, banking and financial institutions, and services organizations such as law firms and accounting firms. The company's enterprise solutions segment accounts for about 23 percent of total revenue.

Pitney has one other division, capital services, which provides financing for such large-ticket products as aircraft, over-the-road trucks and trailers, railcars, locomotives, commercial real estate, and high-tech equipment. Capital services accounts for about 4 percent of total revenue.

Pitney has about 29,000 employees and 31,000 shareholders. It has a market capitalization of about $10 billion.

EARNINGS PER SHARE GROWTH ★

Past 5 years: 81 percent (12.5 percent per year)
Past 10 years: 199 percent (12 percent per year)

STOCK GROWTH ★ ★

Past 10 years: 323 percent (15.5 percent per year)
Dollar growth: $10,000 over 10 years (including reinvested dividends) would have grown to about $52,000.
Average annual compounded rate of return (including reinvested dividends): 18 percent

CONSISTENCY ★ ★ ★

Increased earnings per share: 9 of the past 10 years
Increased sales: 9 of the past 10 years

DIVIDEND   ★ ★ ★ ★

Dividend yield: 2.7 percent
Increased dividend: 18 consecutive years
Past 5-year increase: 90 percent (14 percent per year)
Good dividend reinvestment and stock purchase plan; voluntary stock purchase plan allows contributions of $100 to $3,000 per quarter.

PITNEY BOWES AT A GLANCE

Fiscal year ended: Dec. 31
Revenue and net income in $millions

	1995	1996	1997	1998	1999	2000	5-Year Growth Avg. Annual (%)	Total (%)
Revenue ($)	3,555	3,859	4,100	4,220	4,433	3,881	1.5	9
Net income ($)	408	470	526	568	630	626	9	53
Earnings/share ($)	1.34	1.56	1.82	2.03	2.31	2.42	12.5	81
Dividends/share ($)	0.60	0.69	0.80	0.90	1.02	1.14	14	90
Dividend yield (%)	3.1	2.7	1.8	1.4	2.1	3.4		
PE range	11–18	13–20	15–26	26–41	19–35	11–24		

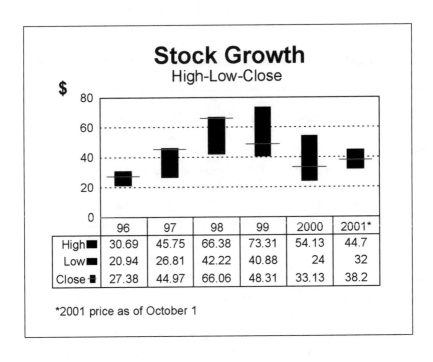

Stock Growth
High-Low-Close

	96	97	98	99	2000	2001*
High■	30.69	45.75	66.38	73.31	54.13	44.7
Low■	20.94	26.81	42.22	40.88	24	32
Close■	27.38	44.97	66.06	48.31	33.13	38.2

*2001 price as of October 1

ABM Industries

160 Pacific Avenue, Suite 222
San Francisco, CA 94111
415-733-4000
NYSE: ABM
www.abm.com

Chairman: Martinn H. Mandles
President and CEO: Henrik C. Slipsager

Earnings Growth	★ ★
Stock Growth	★ ★ ★
Consistency	★ ★ ★
Dividend	★ ★
Total	**10 Points**

ABM Industries does the dirty work of thousands of corporations and institutions across North America. The company is one of the largest facility services contractors in the country, with annual revenue of nearly $2 billion.

Building maintenance is ABM's biggest area, with 43,000 people providing janitorial and related services for companies in 40 states. The company offers a wide range of basic cleaning services for a variety of facilities and clients, including office buildings, department stores, theaters, warehouses, educational and medical institutions, and airport terminals.

The company also has several other key divisions, including:

- **Engineering services.** The firm provides on-site operating engineers, who control, monitor, and maintain all air-conditioning, electrical, energy, heating, mechanical, plumbing, and ventilation systems at commercial buildings, hotels, schools, factories, and warehouses.
- **Commercial security services.** ABM provides security professionals for highrise buildings, high-tech computer campuses and complexes, financial institutions, data center facilities, and commercial and indus-

trial sites. The security arm has over 5,000 employees and 30 branch offices across the country.

- **Parking.** ABM manages parking facilities that are either leased from or managed for third parties. Its Ampco System Parking subsidiary operates over 1,550 parking lots and garages in 25 states.
- **Elevator services.** Through its Amtech subsidiary, the company provides maintenance, repair, and modernization for all makes of elevators and escalators. The company has offices in 17 states and service in 21.
- **Lighting service.** The company provides bulb replacement, fixture cleaning, and lighting system maintenance, as well as the design, installation, and repair of outdoor signs.
- **Mechanical services.** ABM provides heating, ventilation, and air-conditioning maintenance for commercial and industrial facilities in California and Arizona.

ABM was founded in 1909 in San Francisco as a one-man window cleaning service. The company has about 60,000 employees and a market capitalization of about $800 million.

EARNINGS PER SHARE GROWTH ★ ★

Past 5 years: 99 percent (14.5 percent per year)
Past 10 years: 198 percent (11.5 percent per year)

STOCK GROWTH ★ ★ ★

Past 10 years: 367 percent (17 percent per year)
Dollar growth: $10,000 over 10 years (including reinvested dividends) would have grown to $57,000.
Average annual compounded rate of return (including reinvested dividends): 19 percent

CONSISTENCY ★ ★ ★

Increased earnings per share: 9 of the past 10 years
Increased sales: More than 10 consecutive years

DIVIDEND ★ ★

Dividend yield: 1.8 percent
Increased dividend: Every year since 1993
Past 5-year increase: 103 percent (15 percent per year)
ABM does not offer a dividend reinvestment and stock purchase plan.

ABM INDUSTRIES AT A GLANCE

Fiscal year ended: Oct. 31
Revenue and net income in $millions

	1995	1996	1997	1998	1999	2000	5-Year Growth Avg. Annual (%)	5-Year Growth Total (%)
Revenue ($)	956	1,067	1,252	1,502	1,630	1,808	13	89
Net income ($)	18	22	27	34	40	44	19	144
Earnings/share ($)	0.93	1.05	1.22	1.44	1.65	1.85	14.5	99
Dividends/share ($)	0.30	0.35	0.40	0.48	0.56	0.61	15	103
Dividend yield (%)	2.5	1.9	1.4	1.5	2.7	2.1		
PE range	10–15	12–19	14–25	17–25	12–20	10–17		

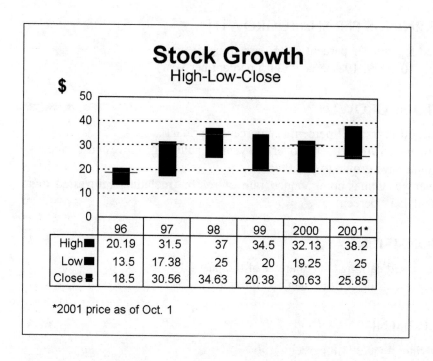

Stock Growth
High-Low-Close

	96	97	98	99	2000	2001*
High■	20.19	31.5	37	34.5	32.13	38.2
Low■	13.5	17.38	25	20	19.25	25
Close■	18.5	30.56	34.63	20.38	30.63	25.85

*2001 price as of Oct. 1

SunTrust Banks, Inc.

SUNTRUST

303 Peachtree Street, N.E.
Atlanta, GA 30308
404-588-7711
NYSE: STI
www.suntrust.com

Chairman, President, and CEO: L. Philip Humann

Earnings Growth	★
Stock Growth	★ ★
Consistency	★ ★ ★
Dividend	★ ★ ★ ★
Total	**10 Points**

SunTrust branches are spread far and wide across the sun-drenched cities of the southeastern United States. The Atlanta institution operates more than 1,100 branches in the southeastern United States and a network of nearly 2,000 ATM machines. Its highest concentration of branches is in Florida, Georgia, Tennessee, Virginia, Maryland, and Washington, D.C. In all, SunTrust has nearly four million customers.

The company provides a wide range of personal, corporate, and institutional banking services, trust and investment management, investment banking, factoring, mortgage banking, credit cards, discount brokerage, credit-related insurance, and data processing and information services.

Commercial loans account for about 43 percent of the company's outstanding loans, followed by mortgages, 28 percent; consumer loans, 14 percent; construction, 4 percent; and other real estate–related loans, 11 percent.

The company took on its present identity as SunTrust Banks in 1985 with the merger of Sun Banks of Florida and Trust Company of Georgia. It has grown rapidly through a series of acquisitions throughout its operating area.

The company can credit part of its strong recent growth to an investment it picked up in 1919 as the Trust Company of Georgia.

When the Coca-Cola Company went public in 1919, it gave 5,000 shares (worth $110,000) of its stock as part of the underwriting fee to the two underwriters, J. P. Morgan Bank and the Trust Company of Georgia (now SunTrust Banks). J. P. Morgan sold its stock, but Trust Company held on to its original shares.

After years of stock splits, that original $110,000 investment is now worth more than $3 billion. Even when the banking business is in a funk, SunTrust continues to ride high on the strength of its Coca-Cola stock.

SunTrust has about 30,000 employees and a market capitalization of about $18 billion.

EARNINGS PER SHARE GROWTH   ★

Past 5 years: 76 percent (12 percent per year)
Past 10 years: 215 percent (12 percent per year)

STOCK GROWTH   ★ ★

Past 10 years: 306 percent (15 percent per year)
Dollar growth: $10,000 over 10 years (including reinvested dividends) would have grown to about $48,000.
Average annual compounded rate of return (including reinvested dividends): 17 percent

CONSISTENCY   ★ ★ ★

Increased earnings per share: 9 of the past 10 years

DIVIDEND   ★ ★ ★ ★

Dividend yield: 2.6 percent
Increased dividend: 23 consecutive years
Past 5-year increase: 100 percent (15 percent per year)
Good dividend reinvestment and stock purchase plan; voluntary stock purchase plan allows contributions of $10 to $60,000 per year.

SUNTRUST BANKS AT A GLANCE

Fiscal year ended: Dec. 31
Total assets and net income in $millions

	1995	1996	1997	1998	1999	2000	5-Year Growth Avg. Annual (%)	Total (%)
Total assets ($)	46,471	52,468	57,983	93,170	95,390	103,496	18	123
Net income ($)	565	617	667	971	1,124	1,294	18	129
Earnings/share ($)	2.47	2.76	3.13	3.08	3.54	4.35	12	76
Dividends/share ($)	0.74	0.83	0.93	1.00	1.38	1.48	15	100
Dividend yield (%)	2.5	1.7	1.4	1.3	2.0	2.4		
PE range	10–15	12–20	14–24	17–28	17–22	9–15		

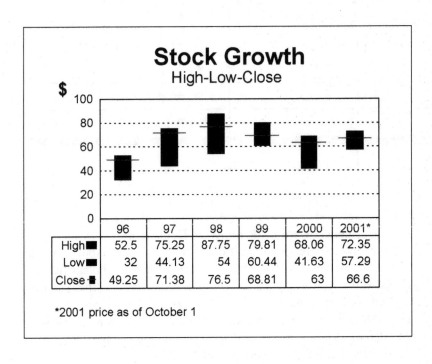

Stock Growth
High-Low-Close

$

	96	97	98	99	2000	2001*
High■	52.5	75.25	87.75	79.81	68.06	72.35
Low■	32	44.13	54	60.44	41.63	57.29
Close ■	49.25	71.38	76.5	68.81	63	66.6

*2001 price as of October 1

Avery Dennison Corporation

Miller Corporate Center
150 North Orange Grove Boulevard
Pasadena, CA 91103
626-304-2000
NYSE: AVY
www.averydennison.com

Chairman and CEO: Philip Neal
President: Dean Scarborough

Earnings Growth	★ ★
Stock Growth	★ ★
Consistency	★ ★ ★
Dividend	★ ★ ★
Total	**10 Points**

Somewhere out there is an Avery label with your name on it. And it's not that far away. Just look in the mail. Many of the address labels on your magazines and mailers were made by Avery Dennison.

In fact, even the letters that don't come with an Avery label may still have an Avery connection. The company helps the U.S. Postal Service produce its self-adhesive stamps and supplies adhesive coating, security printing, and converting technologies for postage stamp production.

Avery Dennison is one of the world's leading manufacturers of self-adhesive materials, labels, tapes, and specialty chemical adhesives.

The Pasadena, California operation has 200 manufacturing plants and sales offices in 42 countries around the world.

The company divides its operations into two key segments:

- **Pressure-sensitive adhesives and materials** (53 percent of revenue). The company makes pressure-sensitive base materials, specialty tapes, graphic films, reflective highway safety products, and chemicals. Avery sells pressure-sensitive coated papers, films, and foils to label printers for labeling, decorating, fastening, electronic data processing, and special applications. Its graphics products include a variety of films sold to the automotive, architectural, commercial sign, digital printing, and related markets.
- **Consumer and converted products** (47 percent). The company makes custom label products, high-performance specialty films and labels, and automotive applications and fasteners for the consumer sector. Its products are sold for use at home, school, and office, and include labels, notebooks, presentation dividers, three-ring binders, sheet protectors, and vinyl and heat-sealed products. The company also makes writing instruments, markers, notepads, and presentation products.

Avery also produces a wide variety of bar-coded tags and labels, and a line of machines for imprinting, dispensing, and attaching preprinted roll tags and labels. It also manufactures on-battery labels for battery makers, as well as specialty automotive film products for interior and exterior vehicle finishes, striping decoration, and identification.

Founded in 1946, the company has about 18,000 employees and a market capitalization of about $6 billion.

EARNINGS PER SHARE GROWTH ★ ★

Past 5 years: 112 percent (16 percent per year)
Past 10 years: 390 percent (17.5 percent per year)

STOCK GROWTH ★ ★

Past 10 years: 328 percent (15.5 percent per year)
Dollar growth: $10,000 over 10 years (including reinvested dividends) would have grown to $52,000.
Average annual compounded rate of return (including reinvested dividends): 18 percent

CONSISTENCY ★ ★ ★

Increased earnings per share: 9 of the past 10 years
Increased sales: 9 of the past 10 years

DIVIDEND

Dividend yield: 2.3 percent
Increased dividend: 9 of the past 10 years
Past 5-year increase: 98 percent (15 percent per year)
Good dividend reinvestment and stock purchase plan: an initial investment
of $500 is required for most plans; some options apply to regular contrib-
utors who choose to begin with less than $500.

AVERY DENNISON AT A GLANCE

Fiscal year ended: Dec. 31
Revenue and net income in $millions

	1995	1996	1997	1998	1999	2000	5-Year Growth Avg. Annual (%)	Total (%)
Revenue ($)	3,114	3,222	3,346	3,460	3,768	3,893	4	25
Net income ($)	142.7	175.9	204.8	223.3	257.8	283.5	15	99
Earnings/share ($)	1.34	1.63	1.93	2.15	2.54	2.84	16	112
Dividends/share ($)	0.56	0.62	0.72	0.87	1.13	1.11	15	98
Dividend yield (%)	2.3	1.7	1.6	1.7	2.0	1.7		
PE range	11–18	14–22	17–23	—	18–34	19–36		

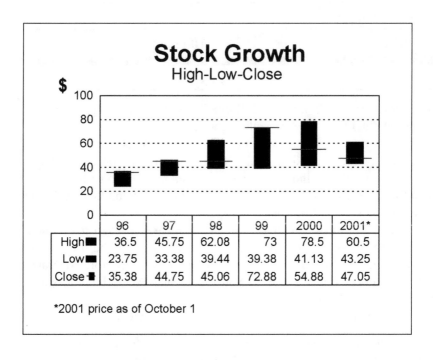

Stock Growth
High-Low-Close

	96	97	98	99	2000	2001*
High■	36.5	45.75	62.08	73	78.5	60.5
Low■	23.75	33.38	39.44	39.38	41.13	43.25
Close■	35.38	44.75	45.06	72.88	54.88	47.05

*2001 price as of October 1

Jones Apparel Group, Inc.

JONES APPAREL GROUP

250 Rittenhouse Circle
Bristol, PA 19007
215-785-4000
NYSE: JNY
www.jonesapparel.com

Chairman and CEO: Sidney Kimmel
President: Jackwyn Nemerov

Earnings Growth	★ ★ ★ ★
Stock Growth	★ ★ ★
Consistency	★ ★ ★
Dividend	
Total	**10 Points**

Jones Apparel not only makes a full line of women's clothing, but it also operates about 1,000 stores to sell its goods.

The company makes a long line of popular brands of shoes, accessories, and apparel, including Jones New York, Evan-Picone, Nine West, Easy Spirit, and Bandolino. It also produces and markets some lines under Ralph Lauren's licensed brands, including Lauren by Ralph Lauren, Ralph by Ralph Lauren, and Polo Jeans Company.

The company has marketed most of its apparel through department and clothing stores, but in recent years it has aggressively built up its retail presence. The company has about 500 retail specialty stores operated under the names Nine West, Easy Spirit, and Enzo Angiolini. Jones also operates about 500 outlet stores.

The company breaks its business into three segments:

- **Apparel** (53 percent of revenue). The company designs and markets apparel brands for several distinct groups of consumers. Its Jones New York and Rena Rowan brands are geared to young career professionals and baby boomers; its Polo Jeans are marketed to Generations X and Y; and its Nine West sportswear is marketed along with the company's shoes and handbags. The company also manufactures a number of private-label denim products for the mass merchant market.

- **Footwear and accessories** (23 percent). Its shoe brands include Nine West and Enzo Angiolini, which are both offered on the better department store floors, while its Easy Spirit line is sold in the moderate areas.
- **Retail** (24 percent). The company's 1,000 stores include both apparel and footwear outlets.

The vast majority of its revenues are generated in the United States, although much of the manufacturing is done in foreign factories.

Jones Apparel has about 19,000 employees and a market capitalization of about $5 billion.

EARNINGS PER SHARE GROWTH ★ ★ ★ ★

Past 5 years: 315 percent (33 percent per year)
Past 9 years: 611 percent (24 percent per year)

STOCK GROWTH ★ ★ ★

Past 9 years: 456 percent (21 percent per year)
Dollar growth: $10,000 over 10 years would have grown to about $55,000.
Average annual compounded rate of return: 21 percent

CONSISTENCY ★ ★ ★

Increased earnings per share: 9 consecutive years
Increased sales: 9 consecutive years

DIVIDEND

The Jones Apparel Group does not pay a dividend.

JONES APPAREL AT A GLANCE

Fiscal year ended: Dec. 31
Revenue and net income in $millions

	1995	1996	1997	1998	1999	2000	5-Year Growth Avg. Annual (%)	Total (%)
Revenue ($)	776	1,021	1,373	1,685	3,151	4,143	32	305
Net income ($)	64	81	122	155	238	303	36	373
Earnings/share ($)	0.60	0.75	1.13	1.47	2.02	2.49	33	315
Dividends/share ($)	—	—	—	—	—	—		
Dividend yield (%)	—	—	—	—	—	—		
PE range	10–15	11–24	14–25	10–25	13–22	8–14		

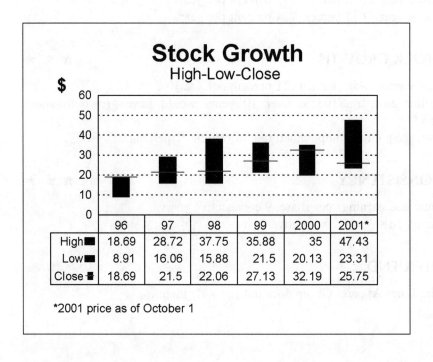

Stock Growth
High-Low-Close

$

	96	97	98	99	2000	2001*
High	18.69	28.72	37.75	35.88	35	47.43
Low	8.91	16.06	15.88	21.5	20.13	23.31
Close	18.69	21.5	22.06	27.13	32.19	25.75

*2001 price as of October 1

Eli Lilly & Company

Answers That Matter.

Lilly Corporate Center
Indianapolis, IN 46285
317-276-2000
NYSE: LLY
www.elililly.com

Chairman, President, and CEO: Sidney Taurel

Earnings Growth	★ ★ ★
Stock Growth	★ ★
Consistency	★ ★
Dividend	★ ★
Total	**9 Points**

Eli Lilly is well known for its breakthrough pharmaceuticals, such as Prozac and Ceclor, but the company's major focus is to become the pharmaceutical industry's "partner of choice." The Indianapolis operation is currently involved in more than 140 research and development collaborations with other companies and universities.

For instance, Lilly has helped Takeda Pharmaceuticals launch an oral diabetes drug in more than 70 countries; it works with Stanford University to search for cures for hepatitis; and it is involved in a collaboration with Ribozyme Pharmaceuticals to pursue treatments for hepatitis C.

Lilly produces medications for a variety of ailments, including:

- **Neuroscience products.** Lilly's largest-selling product group includes Prozac, which is used for the treatment of depression and, in many countries, for bulimia and obsessive-compulsive disorder; and Zyprexa, used for the treatment of schizophrenia and acute bipolar mania. Other leading medications include the Darvon line of analgesic products; Permax, a treatment for Parkinson's disease; and Sarafem, a treatment for premenstrual dysphoric disorder.

- **Endocrine products.** The company makes Humulin, a human insulin produced through recombinant DNA technology; Humalog, an injectable human insulin analog of recombinant DNA origin; and Iletin, an animal-source insulin. It also makes Evista for the treatment of osteoporosis and Humatrope, a human growth hormone produced by recombinant DNA technology.
- **Anti-infectives.** In addition to its oral antibiotics Ceclor, Dynabac, Keflex, Keftab, and Lorabid, Lilly also offers Vancocin HCl, an injectable antibiotic, and the injectable antibiotics Nebcin, Tazidime, Kefurox, and Kefzol, used to treat a wide range of bacterial infections in hospitals.

Lilly is also a leading producer of cardiovascular treatments and oncology medications. The company sells its products in about 160 countries. Foreign sales account for about 36 percent of total revenue.

The company was founded in 1876 by Colonel Eli Lilly, a chemist and a veteran of the Civil War who was frustrated by the poorly prepared and ineffective medicines of his day. He launched his business to upgrade the pharmaceutical industry and take it out of the hands of sideshow hucksters. He even hired a chemist in 1886 to serve as a full-time research scientist.

Lilly has about 36,000 employees and about 59,000 shareholders. It has a market capitalization of about $86 billion.

EARNINGS PER SHARE GROWTH   ★ ★ ★

Past 5 years: 130 percent (18 percent per year)
Past 10 years: 160 percent (10 percent per year)

STOCK GROWTH   ★ ★

Past 10 years: 306 percent (15 percent per year)
Dollar growth: $10,000 over 10 years (including reinvested dividends) would have grown to $50,000.
Average annual compounded rate of return (including reinvested dividends): 17.5 percent

CONSISTENCY   ★ ★

Increased earnings per share: 8 of the past 10 years
Increased sales: 9 of the past 10 years

DIVIDEND   ★ ★

Dividend yield: 1.4 percent
Increased dividend: More than 15 consecutive years
Past 5-year increase: 57 percent (9 percent per year)
Good dividend reinvestment and stock purchase plan; voluntary stock purchase plan requires a minimum initial investment of $1,000, with subsequent investments of at least $50 up to a maximum of $150,000 a year.

ELI LILLY AT A GLANCE

Fiscal year ended: Dec. 31
Revenue and net income in $millions

	1995	1996	1997	1998	1999	2000	5-Year Growth Avg. Annual (%)	Total (%)
Revenue ($)	6,764	7,347	8,518	9,237	10,003	10,862	10	60
Net income ($)	1,307	1,458	1,729	2,175	2,525	2,904	17	122
Earnings/share ($)	1.15	1.33	1.57	1.94	2.28	2.65	18	130
Dividends/share ($)	0.66	0.69	0.74	0.80	0.92	1.04	9	57
Dividend yield (%)	3.3	2.1	1.1	1.1	1.4	1.1		
PE range	12–21	17–27	19–39	30–48	26–42	19–39		

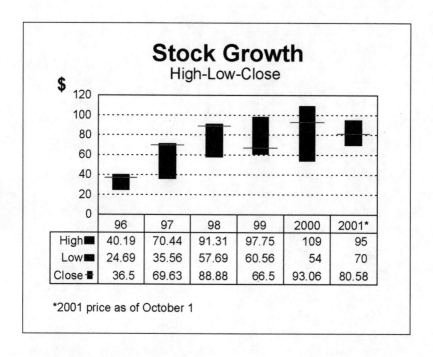

Stock Growth
High-Low-Close

$

	96	97	98	99	2000	2001*
High	40.19	70.44	91.31	97.75	109	95
Low	24.69	35.56	57.69	60.56	54	70
Close	36.5	69.63	88.88	66.5	93.06	80.58

*2001 price as of October 1

The Procter & Gamble Company

Procter&Gamble

One Procter & Gamble Plaza
Cincinnati, OH 45202
513-983-1100
NYSE: PG
www.pg.com

Chairman: John Pepper
President and CEO: Alan G. Lafley

Earnings Growth	
Stock Growth	★ ★
Consistency	★ ★ ★
Dividend	★ ★ ★ ★
Total	**9 Points**

If you're like millions of Americans, Procter & Gamble has invaded nearly every closet and cupboard of your house. From dish soaps and laundry detergents to coffee and cosmetics, the Cincinnati operation puts more than 300 product brands on the market.

But Americans aren't the only ones who use Tide, Cheer, Ivory, Bounce, and the long line of other P&G products. The company sells its soaps, foods, and beauty care products in more than 140 countries. About 49 percent of the company's $40 billion in revenue is generated outside of North America.

P&G's best-selling product is Tide laundry detergent. Introduced in 1946, Tide is the nation's number one detergent. The company also makes Cheer, Downy, Bold, Oxydol, Cascade, Era, Ivory, Zest, Coast, Joy, Ace Bleach, Ariel, Bounce, Dawn, and Mr. Clean. Laundry and cleaning products account for about 30 percent of total revenue.

In addition to cleaning products, the company produces leading products in several key categories, including:

- **Paper products** (29 percent of revenue). Leading brands include Bounty, Pampers, Puffs, Luvs, Tampax, Always, Charmin, Whisper, and Attends.
- **Beauty care** (19 percent). The company makes a wide range of beauty care products, including Cover Girl, Vidal Sassoon, Secret, Clearasil, Noxzema, Coast, Lava, Oil of Olay, Safeguard, Zest, Max Factor, Sure, Head & Shoulders, and Old Spice.
- **Food and beverages** (11 percent). Leading products include Crisco, Folgers, Hawaiian Punch, Jif, Olean, Pringles, and Sunny Delight Florida Citrus Punch.
- **Health care** (10 percent). The company makes Crest, Gleem, Scope, Metamucil, Vicks, Pepto Bismol, Nyquil, and a number of prescription and over-the-counter medications.

Founded in 1837 by William Procter and James Gamble, the company is the world's leading producer of soaps and cosmetics. P&G has managed to maintain its strong market position through a relentless advertising approach. For many years, the company has been TV's biggest advertiser.

P&G has 110,000 employees and about 275,000 shareholders. It has a market capitalization of about $84 billion.

EARNINGS PER SHARE GROWTH

Past 5 years: −6 percent (−1 percent per year)
Past 10 years: 64 percent (11 percent per year)

STOCK GROWTH ★ ★

Past 10 years: 288 percent (14.5 percent per year)
Dollar growth: $10,000 over 10 years (including reinvested dividends) would have grown to about $46,000.
Average annual compounded rate of return (including reinvested dividends): 16.5 percent

CONSISTENCY ★ ★ ★

Increased earnings per share: 9 of the past 10 years
Increased sales: 8 of the past 10 years

DIVIDEND   ★ ★ ★ ★

Dividend yield: 2.0 percent
Increased dividend: 45 consecutive years
Past 5-year increase: 75 percent (12 percent per year)
Good dividend reinvestment and stock purchase plan; voluntary stock purchase plan allows contributions of $100 to $120,000 annually.

PROCTER & GAMBLE AT A GLANCE

Fiscal year ended: June 30
Revenue and net income in $millions

	1996	1997	1998	1999	2000	2001	5-Year Growth Avg. Annual (%)	Total (%)
Revenue ($)	35,284	35,764	37,154	38,125	39,951	39,244	2	11
Net income ($)	3,046	3,415	3,780	4,148	4,230	NA	10	60
Earnings/share ($)	2.15	2.28	2.56	2.59	2.95	2.02	–1	–6
Dividends/share ($)	0.80	0.90	1.01	1.14	1.28	1.40	12	75
Dividend yield (%)	1.5	1.1	1.1	1.3	1.6	1.6		
PE range	19–27	22–36	25–37	31–44	26–58	20–40		

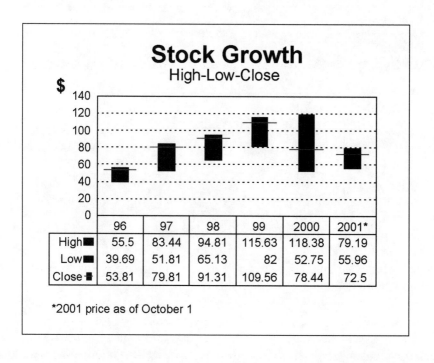

Stock Growth
High-Low-Close

$	96	97	98	99	2000	2001*
High■	55.5	83.44	94.81	115.63	118.38	79.19
Low■	39.69	51.81	65.13	82	52.75	55.96
Close■	53.81	79.81	91.31	109.56	78.44	72.5

*2001 price as of October 1

Sonic Corporation

America's Drive·In.

101 Park Avenue
Oklahoma City, OK 73102
405-280-7654
Nasdaq: SONC
www.sonicdrivein.com

Chairman and CEO: J. Clifford Hudson
President: Kenneth Keymer

Earnings Growth	★ ★ ★ ★
Stock Growth	★ ★
Consistency	★ ★ ★
Dividend	
Total	**9 Points**

There's a Sonic boom across the entire southern half of the United States. More than 2,000 Sonic restaurants have popped up across the warmer stretches of America, from California to southern Florida. The Oklahoma City fast-food operation is the largest drive-in restaurant chain in the nation.

Texas leads the Sonic blast with 622 restaurants, followed by Oklahoma with 214, Tennessee with 174, and Missouri with 157.

But if you live in New England or across the northern tier of the United States from Oregon to Michigan, you're out of luck. Sonic prefers to place its restaurants in locations where consumers are inclined to dine outdoors more than three months a year.

Besides, roller skates don't work well in the snow. Part of Sonic's unique appeal is that its carhops serve their customers on roller skates.

The company also offers a unique menu. In addition to the usual burgers, fries, and onion rings, Sonic also offers "Toaster" sandwiches—burgers or chicken served on thick Texas toast—mozzarella sticks, "Ched 'R' Peppers," and a wide range of fountain drinks, malts, shakes, and ice cream sundaes. As the company claims, "We're prepared to make nearly any fountain drink or frozen concoction you can dream up."

Most Sonic restaurants are owned and operated by franchisees. Franchise owners pay a fee of $15,000 to $30,000 to the company as well as a royalty on revenues of up to 5 percent, depending on sales volume.

The company provides special training for its franchisees, as well as management support, including advertising and marketing, financing assistance, and site selection assistance.

The company adds 150 to 200 new restaurants each year.

Founded in 1953, Sonic has about 250 corporate employees. Company-owned restaurants have about 950 full-time and 9,000 part-time employees. The company has a market capitalization of about $700 million.

EARNINGS PER SHARE GROWTH ★ ★ ★ ★

Past 5 years: 149 percent (20 percent per year)
Past 9 years: 588 percent (21 percent per year)

STOCK GROWTH ★ ★

Past 10 years: 353 percent (16 percent per year)
Dollar growth: $10,000 over 10 years would have grown to about $44,000.
Average annual compounded rate of return: 16 percent

CONSISTENCY ★ ★ ★

Increased earnings per share: 8 of the past 9 years (since Sonic went public in 1991)
Increased sales: 9 consecutive years

DIVIDEND

Sonic pays no dividend.

SONIC AT A GLANCE

Fiscal year ended: August 31
Revenue and net income in $millions

	1995	1996	1997	1998	1999	2000	5-Year Growth Avg. Annual (%)	Total (%)
Revenue ($)	124	151	184	219	257	280	18	126
Net income ($)	12.5	1	19	22	27	33	21.5	164
Earnings/share ($)	0.47	0.55	0.63	0.75	0.94	1.17	20	149
Dividends/share ($)	—	—	—	—	—	—		
Dividend yield (%)	—	—	—	—	—	—		
PE range	10–19	17–31	8–21	10–24	15–24	13–23		

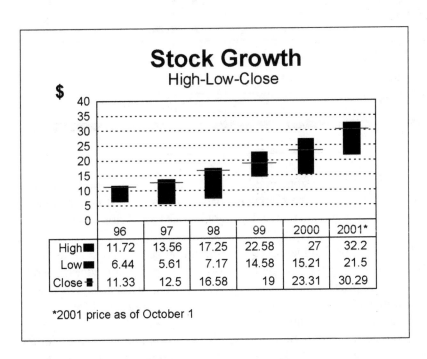

Stock Growth
High-Low-Close

	96	97	98	99	2000	2001*
High■	11.72	13.56	17.25	22.58	27	32.2
Low■	6.44	5.61	7.17	14.58	15.21	21.5
Close■	11.33	12.5	16.58	19	23.31	30.29

*2001 price as of October 1

56 East Bell Drive
Warsaw, IN 46582
219-267-6639
Nasdaq: BMET
www.biomet.com

Chairman: Niles L. Noblitt
President and CEO: Dane A. Miller

Earnings Growth	★ ★
Stock Growth	★ ★ ★
Consistency	★ ★ ★ ★
Dividend	
Total	**9 Points**

Hip on the blink, knee gone numb, shoulder in shambles? Biomet has the fix for what ails you. The company specializes in reconstructive devices used to replace joints that have degenerated due to arthritis, osteoporosis, or injury.

The company also manufactures a broad range of related items, such as electrical bone growth stimulators, orthopedic support devices, operating room supplies, general surgical instruments, arthroscopy products, spinal implants, bone cements, bone substitutes, craniomaxillofacial implants, and dental implants.

About 63 percent of Biomet's nearly $1 billion in annual sales comes from its reconstructive devices segment. The company has developed—or in some cases acquired—several models of knee replacement devices that can be surgically implanted. It also manufactures several hip and shoulder replacement systems and replacement products for elbows and ankles.

The Warsaw, Indiana operation generates about 20 percent of its revenue through fixation and related products, such as special screws, nuts, nails, plates, pins, wires, and other products used by surgeons to set and stabilize fractures. It also makes drills and saws used for cranial and small bone surgery. Biomet has developed electrical stimulation devices used for the treatment of recalcitrant bone fractures that have not healed through conventional surgical and nonsurgical methods.

Biomet's other primary segment is its spinal products division, which accounts for 6 percent of revenue. The company makes a spinal fusion stimulation system used in conjunction with bone grafting to increase the probability of successful fusion. It also makes spinal fixation systems, including a modular titanium link and a polydirectional screw that enable the surgeon to tailor the spinal segmental construction to the patient's anatomy.

Biomet also manufactures operating room supplies, such as filters, glove liners and drapes, casting materials and splints, arthroscopy products, and orthopedic support devices, such as braces, knee immobilizers, and elbow, wrist, abdominal, thigh, and ankle supports. Those products account for about 11 percent of total revenue.

Biomet products are sold in more than 100 countries. Foreign sales account for about 34 percent of total revenue.

Incorporated in 1977, Biomet has about 4,000 employees and 7,000 shareholders. It has a market capitalization of about $8 billion.

EARNINGS PER SHARE GROWTH ★ ★

Past 5 years: 102 percent (15 percent per year)
Past 10 years: 360 percent (16.5 percent per year)

STOCK GROWTH

Past 10 years: 464 percent (19 percent per year)
Dollar growth: $10,000 over 10 years (including reinvested dividends) would have grown to $58,000.
Average annual compounded rate of return (including reinvested dividends): 19.5 percent

CONSISTENCY

Increased earnings per share: 23 consecutive years
Increased sales: 23 consecutive years

DIVIDEND

Dividend yield: 0.3 percent
Increased dividend: 4 consecutive years
Past 4-year increase: 59 percent (10 percent per year)
Biomet does not offer a dividend reinvestment and stock purchase plan.

BIOMET AT A GLANCE

Fiscal year ended: May 31
Revenue and net income in $millions

	1996	1997	1998	1999	2000	2001	5-Year Growth Avg. Annual (%)	Total (%)
Revenue ($)	535	580	651	757	921	1,030	14	92
Net income ($)	94	106	125	149	174	204	17	117
Earnings/share ($)	0.36	0.41	0.48	0.58	0.65	0.73	15	102
Dividends/share ($)	—	0.044	0.047	0.053	0.06	0.07	10*	59*
Dividend yield (%)	—	0.6	0.4	0.3	0.4	0.2		
PE range	23–36	22–38	31–58	31–63	20–47	19–43		

* Dividend percentages based on 4-year growth.

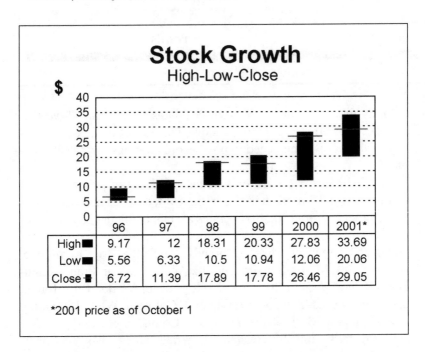

Stock Growth
High-Low-Close

$

	96	97	98	99	2000	2001*
High ■	9.17	12	18.31	20.33	27.83	33.69
Low ■	5.56	6.33	10.5	10.94	12.06	20.06
Close ■	6.72	11.39	17.89	17.78	26.46	29.05

*2001 price as of October 1

Sherwin-Williams Company

101 Prospect Avenue N.W.
Cleveland, OH 44115
216-566-2000
NYSE: SHW
www.sherwin.com

Chairman and CEO: Christopher M. Connor

Earnings Growth	★
Stock Growth	★
Consistency	★ ★ ★ ★
Dividend	★ ★ ★
Total	**9 Points**

Known for its all-weather paints, Sherwin-Williams has been an all-weather kind of company. Earnings growth has slowed recently, but the Cleveland-based operation has still managed to post record earnings for 23 consecutive years.

Sherwin-Williams is the nation's largest producer of paints and varnishes. It has about 2,300 paint stores in the United States and operations in about 30 other countries. It also operates a chain of about 135 auto coatings stores.

Among the company's leading brands are Dutch Boy, Kem-Tone, Sherwin-Williams, Martin-Senour, Curinol, Acme, ProMar, Pratt & Lambert, Perma-Clad, Western, Standox, Krylon, Color Works, Rust Tough, Rubberset, Excelo, Lazzuril, Marson, Globo, Colorgin, White Lightning, Red Devil, Sprayon, Moly-White, and Dupli-Color.

The company's paint store business generates about 61 percent of its $5 billion in total annual revenue.

Sherwin-Williams stores offer paints, wall coverings, floor coverings, window treatments, spray equipment, brushes, scrapers, rollers, and related products. The company also sells custom and industrial aerosol paints, paint applicators, retail and wholesale consumer aerosols, and cleaning products. Company stores are geared to the do-it-yourself customer, professional painters, industrial and commercial maintenance customers, and small to midsize manufacturers.

The greatest concentration of Sherwin-Williams stores are in the Midwest, with about 160 stores in its home state of Ohio, 80 in Illinois, 110 in Pennsylvania, 78 in Michigan, 57 in Indiana, and 55 in Missouri. The company has 90 stores in California, 196 in Texas, and 110 in New York. It also operates about 70 stores in Mexico, 26 in Canada, and 20 in Puerto Rico.

The company's other major segment is consumer products (23 percent of revenues), which includes paints sold both through the stores and through other retailers and professional building centers.

The firm's automotive coatings centers account for about 9 percent of revenue, while its international sales make up about 5 percent.

Sherwin-Williams paints first adorned homes and barns in northern Ohio shortly after the Civil War in 1866. Sherwin-Williams has about 26,000 employees and 12,000 shareholders. It has a market capitalization of about $4 billion.

EARNINGS PER SHARE GROWTH   ★

Past 5 years: 62 percent (10 percent per year)
Past 10 years: 168 percent (10.5 percent per year)

STOCK GROWTH   ★

Past 10 years: 155 percent (10 percent per year)
Dollar growth: $10,000 over 10 years (including reinvested dividends) would have grown to about $29,000.
Average annual compounded rate of return (including reinvested dividends): 11.5 percent

CONSISTENCY   ★ ★ ★ ★

Increased earnings per share: 23 consecutive years
Increased sales: 23 consecutive years

DIVIDEND

Dividend yield: 2.5 percent
Increased dividend: 23 consecutive years
Past 5-year increase: 69 percent (11 percent per year)
Good dividend reinvestment and stock purchase plan; voluntary stock purchase plan allows contributions of $10 to $2,000 per month.

SHERWIN-WILLIAMS AT A GLANCE

Fiscal year ended: Dec. 31
Revenue and net income in $millions

	1995	1996	1997	1998	1999	2000	5-Year Growth Avg. Annual (%)	Total (%)
Revenue ($)	3,274	4,133	4,881	4,934	5,004	5,212	10	59
Net income ($)	201	229	261	273	304	310	9	54
Earnings/share ($)	1.17	1.33	1.50	1.57	1.80	1.90	10	62
Dividends/share ($)	0.32	0.35	0.40	0.45	0.48	0.54	11	69
Dividend yield (%)	1.8	1.3	1.4	1.5	2.3	2.1		
PE range	11–19	14–21	16–22	12–24	10–18	172–279		

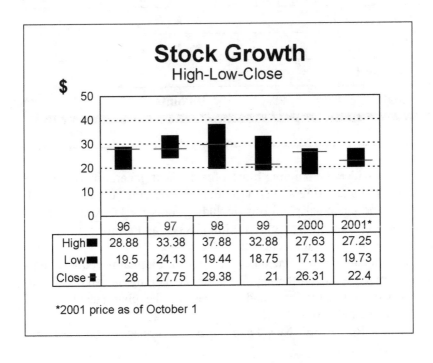

Stock Growth
High-Low-Close

$						
	96	97	98	99	2000	2001*
High	28.88	33.38	37.88	32.88	27.63	27.25
Low	19.5	24.13	19.44	18.75	17.13	19.73
Close	28	27.75	29.38	21	26.31	22.4

*2001 price as of October 1

Cambrex Corporation

CAMBREX

One Meadowlands Plaza
East Rutherford, NJ 07073
201-804-3000
NYSE: CBM
www.cambrex.com

Chairman and CEO: James A. Mack
President: Claes Glassell

Earnings Growth	★ ★
Stock Growth	★ ★ ★ ★
Consistency	★ ★ ★
Dividend	
Total	**9 Points**

Cambrex provides the building blocks for the next generation of miracle drugs. The company offers pharmaceutical outsourcing services for both biological and chemical platforms, including tools for DNA and protein separation and sequencing, cell-based bioassays, and a broad line of human cells, including adult stem cells.

The company has become a key supplier for biopharmaceutical companies involved with cell therapy. Cambrex is also the industry leader in endotoxin detection products and services for the pharmaceutical and medical device industries.

The East Rutherford, New Jersey operation breaks its business into four key segments:

- **Human health** (47 percent of total revenue). The company supplies more than 100 active pharmaceutical ingredients and 130 advanced intermediates used in the synthesis of pharmaceutical ingredients. Its products are used by the pharmaceutical, nutritional, personal care, and medical device industries. Cambrex also provides a variety of services, including contract research, process optimization, and analytical services.
- **Biosciences** (20 percent). The company provides cell and molecular biology products, endotoxin detection products, bioassay products, and custom manufacturing services. Its leading products include discovery cell systems, stem cell systems, cell culture media, Sera and growth factors, and molecular and cell biology reagents. In all, the company sells 1,800 products to more than 14,000 customers worldwide.
- **Animal health and agriculture** (11 percent). Cambrex produces feed additives and intermediates used in animal health and agricultural products.
- **Specialty and fire chemicals** (22 percent). The company manufactures performance-enhancing chemicals and polymer systems used in complex urethanes, plastics, and coatings.

Cambrex sells its products worldwide. Foreign sales account for about 48 percent of the company's total revenue.

The company has been aggressively acquiring other related companies, including about nine acquisitions between 1997 and 2001.

Founded in 1981, Cambrex has about 2,000 employees and 4,400 shareholders. It has a market capitalization of about $1.5 billion.

EARNINGS PER SHARE GROWTH   ★ ★

Past 5 years: 94 percent (14 percent per year)
Past 10 years: 955 percent (27 percent per year)

STOCK GROWTH   ★ ★ ★ ★

Past 10 years: 1,471 percent (32 percent per year)
Dollar growth: $10,000 over 10 years (including reinvested dividends) would have grown to $160,000.
Average annual compounded rate of return (including reinvested dividends): 32 percent

CONSISTENCY

Increased earnings per share: 9 of the past 10 years
Increased sales: 11 consecutive years

DIVIDEND

Dividend yield: 0.2 percent
Increased dividend: 5 of the past 10 years
Past 5-year increase: 71 percent (11.5 percent per year)
Cambrex does not offer a dividend reinvestment and stock purchase plan.

CAMBREX AT A GLANCE

Fiscal year ended: Dec. 31
Revenue and net income in $millions

	1995	1996	1997	1998	1999	2000	5-Year Growth Avg. Annual (%)	Total (%)
Revenue ($)	357	369	374	457	481	484	6	36
Net income ($)	20	28	18	39	38	50	20	150
Earnings/share ($)	0.98	1.19	1.30	1.59	1.72	1.90	14	94
Dividends/share ($)	0.07	0.08	0.10	0.11	0.12	0.12	11.5	71
Dividend yield (%)	0.6	0.5	0.5	0.4	0.4	0.3		
PE range	8–14	10–14	21–36	12–19	13–24	15–27		

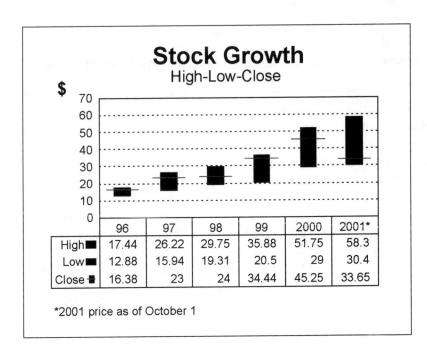

Stock Growth
High-Low-Close

$

	96	97	98	99	2000	2001*
High■	17.44	26.22	29.75	35.88	51.75	58.3
Low■	12.88	15.94	19.31	20.5	29	30.4
Close■	16.38	23	24	34.44	45.25	33.65

*2001 price as of October 1

Biogen, Inc.

14 Cambridge Center
Cambridge, MA 02142
617-679-2000
Nasdaq: BGEN
www.biogen.com

Chairman: James L. Vincent
President and CEO: James C. Mullen

Earnings Growth	★ ★ ★ ★
Stock Growth	★ ★ ★ ★
Consistency	★
Dividend	
Total	**9 Points**

A single product accounts for the vast majority of Biogen's $926 million in total revenue, but the Cambridge, Massachusetts operation is trying hard to develop its next winner. The company currently has 20 research products under way in the areas of immunology, cancer, neuroscience, and fibrosis.

Founded in 1978, Biogen is one of the nation's oldest biotech companies. Its main product is Avonex, which is the world's leading multiple sclerosis treatment. Worldwide, about 100,000 patients use Avonex. The drug was introduced in the United States in 1996 and in Europe in 1997. It is now sold in more than 50 countries.

Avonex accounts for about 82 percent of Biogen's total annual revenue. The rest comes from the worldwide sales by licensees of a number of other products, including diagnostic products and alpha interferon and hepatitis B vaccines.

Much of the company's new research and development efforts are focused on finding new uses for Avonex, as well as on other new products to treat inflammatory and autoimmune diseases, neurological diseases, cancer, fibrosis, and congestive heart failure.

Biogen also maintains active clinical research programs in protein therapeutics, small molecules, genomics, and gene therapy. The company's real expertise is in molecular biology, cell biology, immunology, and protein chemistry. Biogen's leading research projects include:

- **Amevive.** The company is focusing on using the drug Amevive to inhibit specific cellular interaction critical to the inflammation process, thereby reducing the harmful side effects inflammation can have on the body's tissue.
- **Antegren.** Biogen is working with Elan Corp. to develop and market Antegren, which is a humanized monoclonal antibody designed to reduce inflammation by blocking cell adhesion to blood vessel walls and subsequent migration of white blood cells into tissue.
- **Adenosine A1 receptor antagonists.** The company is developing small molecule adenosine A1 receptor antagonists as a potential treatment for congestive heart failure.

Biogen sells its products worldwide. Foreign sales account for about 27 percent of the company's total revenue.

Biogen has about 1,500 employees and a market capitalization of about $9 billion.

EARNINGS PER SHARE GROWTH ★ ★ ★ ★

Past 5 years: 5,300 percent (158 percent per year)
Past 10 years: 10,700 percent (60 percent per year)

STOCK GROWTH ★ ★ ★ ★

Past 10 years: 999 percent (27 percent per year)
Dollar growth: $10,000 over 10 years would have grown to $109,000.

CONSISTENCY ★

Increased earnings per share: 7 of the past 10 years
Increased sales: 8 of the past 10 consecutive years

DIVIDEND

Biogen does not pay a dividend.

BIOGEN AT A GLANCE

Fiscal year ended: Dec. 31
Revenue and net income in $millions

	1995	1996	1997	1998	1999	2000	5-Year Growth Avg. Annual (%)	5-Year Growth Total (%)
Revenue ($)	135	260	411	558	794	926	47	586
Net income ($)	6	41	89	139	220	333	159	5,450
Earnings/share ($)	0.04	0.28	0.58	0.90	1.40	2.16	158	5,300
Dividends/share ($)	—	—	—	—	—	—		
Dividend yield (%)	—	—	—	—	—	—		
PE range	—	46–78	24–45	18–48	27–64	21–59		

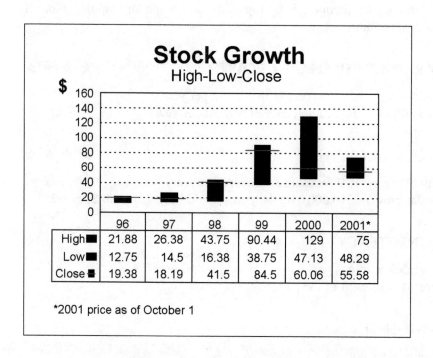

Stock Growth
High-Low-Close

	96	97	98	99	2000	2001*
High■	21.88	26.38	43.75	90.44	129	75
Low■	12.75	14.5	16.38	38.75	47.13	48.29
Close■	19.38	18.19	41.5	84.5	60.06	55.58

*2001 price as of October 1

80

Bemis Company

222 South Ninth Street, Suite 2300
Minneapolis, MN 55402-4099
612-376-3003
NYSE: BMS
www.bemis.com

Chairman: John Roe
President and CEO: Jeffrey Curler

Earnings Growth	★
Stock Growth	★
Consistency	★ ★ ★ ★
Dividend	★ ★ ★
Total	**9 Points**

Whether they wrap it, sack it, box it, or bag it, Bemis makes the packaging for hundreds of foods, candies, medical products, and household goods. The 143-year-old Minneapolis operation is North America's largest manufacturer of flexible packaging.

The company's flexible packaging includes plastic, polyethylene, and paper packaging used for a wide variety of foods and other products.

Flexible packaging accounts for about 76 percent of the company's $2.2 billion in total annual revenue. Its flexible packaging includes:

- **Coated and laminated film packaging (plastics).** The company does resin manufacturing, extruding, coating, laminating, metallizing, printing, and converting for packaging meats, cheese, coffee, condiments, potato chips, candy, and medical products.
- **Polyethylene packaging products.** Bemis makes preformed bags, extruded products, and printed roll packaging for items such as bread, bakery goods, seeds, lawn and garden products, ice, and fresh and frozen vegetables.

- **Industrial and consumer paper bags.** The firm makes multiwall and small paper bags, balers, printed paper roll stock, and bag closing materials for industrial and consumer packaging products such as pet foods, chemicals, dairy products, fertilizers, feed, minerals, flour, and sugar.

Bemis also manufactures packaging systems that provide automated bag handling, weighing, filling, closing, and sealing.

The company's other leading segment is its pressure-sensitive materials, which account for about 24 percent of total sales. Products include industrial adhesives for mounting and bonding, quality roll label and sheet print stock for packaging labels, and a line of specialized laminates for graphics and photography.

Founded in 1858 as a grain bag manufacturer, Bemis has sales offices and plants throughout the United States, Canada, Great Britain, Europe, Scandinavia, Australia, and South and Central America. Foreign operations account for about 16 percent of total revenue.

Bemis has about 11,000 employees and 6,000 shareholders. It has a market capitalization of about $2 billion.

EARNINGS PER SHARE GROWTH ★

Past 5 years: 50 percent (8 percent per year)
Past 10 years: 146 percent (9 percent per year)

STOCK GROWTH ★

Past 10 years: 174 percent (10 percent per year)
Dollar growth: $10,000 over 10 years (including reinvested dividends) would have grown to $310,000.
Average annual compounded rate of return (including reinvested dividends): 12 percent

CONSISTENCY ★ ★ ★ ★

Increased earnings per share: 16 consecutive years
Increased sales: 9 of the past 10 years

DIVIDEND   ★ ★ ★

Dividend yield: 2.3 percent
Increased dividend: 16 consecutive years
Past 5-year increase: 50 percent (8 percent per year)
Good dividend reinvestment and stock purchase plan; voluntary stock purchase plan allows contributions of $25 to $10,000 per quarter.

BEMIS AT A GLANCE

Fiscal year ended: Dec. 31
Revenue and net income in $millions

	1995	1996	1997	1998	1999	2000	5-Year Growth Avg. Annual (%)	Total (%)
Revenue ($)	1,523	1,690	1,918	1,889	1,963	2,165	7	42
Net income ($)	85	103	101	101	115	131	9	54
Earnings/share ($)	1.63	1.93	1.88	1.90	2.18	2.44	8	50
Dividends/share ($)	0.64	0.72	0.80	0.88	0.92	0.96	8	50
Dividend yield (%)	2.4	1.95	1.82	2.32	2.64	2.86		
PE range	14–18	13–19	17–25	17–24	13–18	16–33		

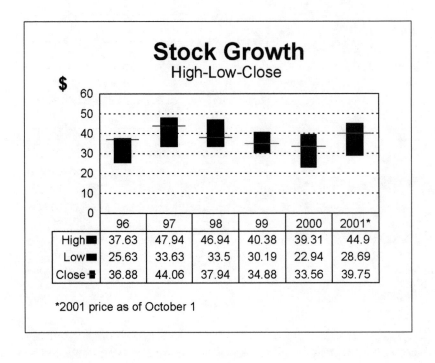

Stock Growth
High-Low-Close

$	96	97	98	99	2000	2001*
High■	37.63	47.94	46.94	40.38	39.31	44.9
Low■	25.63	33.63	33.5	30.19	22.94	28.69
Close■	36.88	44.06	37.94	34.88	33.56	39.75

*2001 price as of October 1

81

Emerson Electric Company

8000 West Florissant Avenue
P.O. Box 4100
St. Louis, MO 63136
314-533-2000
NYSE: EMR
www.emersonelectric.com

Chairman: Charles F. Knight
CEO: David N. Farr
President: James G. Berges

Earnings Growth	★
Stock Growth	★ ★
Consistency	★ ★ ★
Dividend	★ ★ ★
Total	**9 Points**

After 43 consecutive years of record earnings, Emerson Electric Company's streak finally ended in fiscal 2001. But sales revenue continues to climb, and the company is still making solid profits on its vast line of electrical and electronic products and systems for the industrial and commercial markets.

The 111-year-old operation manufactures a wide range of motors for industrial and heavy commercial applications, industrial automation equipment, gear drives, power distribution equipment, and temperature and environmental control systems.

Emerson divides its operations into five key segments:

- **Process controls** (19 percent of annual revenue). The company manufactures measurement and analytical instruments, valves, control systems, and factory automation software.

- **Industrial automation** (22 percent). The company makes industrial motors and drives, industrial machinery, fluid control systems, and heating and lighting equipment.
- **Electronics and telecommunications** (21 percent). Emerson manufactures power supplies, power conditioning equipment, environmental control systems, site monitoring systems, and electrical switching equipment.
- **Heating, ventilation, and air-conditioning** (16 percent). The firm makes compressors, hermetic terminals, thermostats, and valves.
- **Appliances and tools** (22 percent). The company makes hand tools, plumbing and bench power tools, disposals, motors, and controls.

Much of the company's success can be traced to its ability to continue to fill the product pipeline with innovative new offerings. About one-third of its revenue comes from products introduced in the previous five years, and the company introduces about 500 products each year.

The St. Louis–based operation sells its products worldwide, with operations in more than 150 countries. About 38 percent of its revenue comes from foreign sales.

The company was founded in 1890 by John Wesley Emerson, shortly after Thomas A. Edison installed his first electrical generators. In his small St. Louis shop, Emerson manufactured room fans, ceiling fans, and electrical motors.

Emerson has about 123,000 employees and 35,000 shareholders. The company has a market capitalization of about $23 billion.

EARNINGS PER SHARE GROWTH   ★

Past 5 years: 63 percent (10 percent per year)
Past 10 years: 139 percent (9 percent per year)

STOCK GROWTH

Past 10 years: 184 percent (11 percent per year)
Dollar growth: $10,000 over 10 years (including reinvested dividends) would have grown to $36,000.
Average annual compounded rate of return (including reinvested dividends): 13.5 percent

CONSISTENCY

Increased earnings per share: 9 of 10 years through fiscal 2001
Increased sales: 9 of the past 10 years

DIVIDEND

Dividend yield: 2.8 percent
Increased dividend: 16 consecutive years
Past 5-year increase: 61 percent (10 percent per year)
Good dividend reinvestment and stock purchase plan; voluntary stock purchase plan allows contributions of $10 to $60,000 per year.

EMERSON ELECTRIC AT A GLANCE

Fiscal year ended: Sept. 30
Revenue and net income in $millions

	1995	1996	1997	1998	1999	2000	5-Year Growth Avg. Annual (%)	Total (%)
Revenue ($)	10,013	11,150	12,299	13,447	14,270	15,545	9	55
Net income ($)	908	1,018	1,122	1,229	1,314	1,422	9	57
Earnings/share ($)	2.03	2.28	2.52	2.77	3.00	3.30	10	63
Dividends/share ($)	0.89	0.98	1.08	1.18	1.30	1.43	10	61
Dividend yield (%)	2.7	2.4	1.1	1.0	1.5	1.3		
PE range	15–20	17–33	21–29	22–33	13–25	11–21		

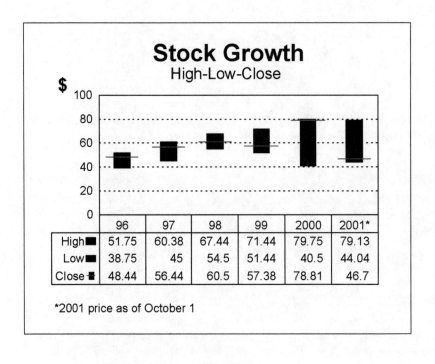

Stock Growth
High-Low-Close

$		96	97	98	99	2000	2001*
	High■	51.75	60.38	67.44	71.44	79.75	79.13
	Low■	38.75	45	54.5	51.44	40.5	44.04
	Close■	48.44	56.44	60.5	57.38	78.81	46.7

*2001 price as of October 1

Altera Corporation

101 Innovation Drive
San Jose, CA 95134
408-544-7000
Nasdaq: ALTR
www.altera.com

President and CEO: John Daane
Chairman: Rodney Smith

Earnings Growth	★ ★ ★ ★
Stock Growth	★ ★ ★ ★
Consistency	★
Dividend	
Total	**9 Points**

Altera specializes in the production of microchips that can be programmed by engineers quickly and easily with software that runs on personal computers or engineering workstations. Altera's leading product is the "programmable logic chip," which is used to set up many of the standard functions in computers, telephones, data communications equipment, and industrial applications.

Altera also offers a line of software tools for logic development. The company's primary markets include communications equipment (67 percent of sales), electronic data processing (17 percent), industrial equipment (11 percent), consumer products (2 percent), and other applications such as military and aerospace systems (3 percent).

Altera chips are used in the electronic systems of high-speed trains, high-definition television sets, professional video recording systems, complex medical equipment, traffic lights, printers, and a wide variety of other high-end, high-tech products.

In all, the company has more than 13,000 corporate customers around the world. International sales account for about 43 percent of total revenue. The company sells more than 500 different products and product combinations.

The first logic chip, introduced by Altera in 1984, boasted a density of 300 gates (a unit of measurement for logic). Now, the densities reach as high as 1.5 million gates on a single chip, allowing dramatically faster and more complex programmable performance.

Altera also produces specialized software packages for engineering functions and provides application assistance, design services, and customer training.

The programmable chip market has been growing rapidly in recent years—although even that market was hurt by the recent decline in the tech sector. But the convenience of programmable chips makes them a popular choice for electronics manufacturers. Altera's programmable chips can be purchased "off the shelf" and configured by customers to their specific requirements.

Founded in 1983, Altera has about 2,000 employees and a market capitalization of about $9 billion.

EARNINGS PER SHARE GROWTH   ★ ★ ★ ★

Past 5 years: 300 percent (33 percent per year)
Past 10 years: 2,300 percent (38 percent per year)

STOCK GROWTH   ★ ★ ★ ★

Past 10 years: 4,175 percent (46 percent per year)
Dollar growth: $10,000 over 10 years would have grown to $420,000.

CONSISTENCY   ★

Increased earnings per share: 7 of the past 10 years
Increased sales: 9 of the past 10 years

DIVIDEND

Altera pays no dividend.

ALTERA AT A GLANCE

Fiscal year ended: Dec. 31
Revenue and net income in $millions

	1995	1996	1997	1998	1999	2000	5-Year Growth Avg. Annual (%)	5-Year Growth Total (%)
Revenue ($)	402	497	631	654	837	1,377	28	242
Net income ($)	87	109	152	154	218	399	36	358
Earnings/share ($)	0.24	0.29	0.39	0.39	0.53	0.96	33	300
Dividends/share ($)	—	—	—	—	—	—		
Dividend yield (%)	—	—	—	—	—	—		
PE range	19–27	11–34	19–42	18–39	22–63	16–56		

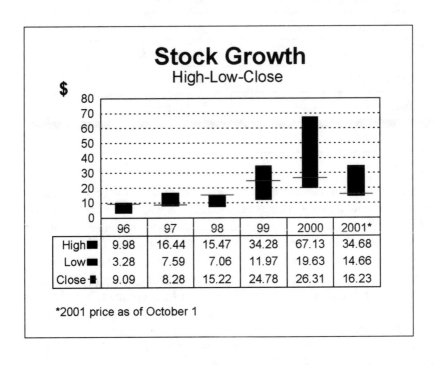

Stock Growth
High-Low-Close

$

	96	97	98	99	2000	2001*
High■	9.98	16.44	15.47	34.28	67.13	34.68
Low■	3.28	7.59	7.06	11.97	19.63	14.66
Close■	9.09	8.28	15.22	24.78	26.31	16.23

*2001 price as of October 1

83

Sara Lee Corporation

Three First National Plaza, Suite 4600
Chicago, IL 60602
312-726-2600
NYSE: SLE
www.saralee.com

Chairman: John H. Bryan
President and CEO: C. Steven McMillan

Earnings Growth	★
Stock Growth	★
Consistency	★ ★ ★ ★
Dividend	★ ★ ★
Total	**9 Points**

Sara Lee made its name in frozen desserts, but it is making its fortune in bras and intimate apparel. This is no Victoria's Secret, but Sara Lee is the world leader in the sale of women's intimate clothing. It is also among the leading makers of men's and boys' underwear and printed T-shirts.

Despite Sara Lee's dominant position in packaged meats and frozen desserts, its leading product segment in terms of total revenue is branded apparel, which accounts for about 43 percent of the company's $17.5 billion in annual revenue. Among its leading brands are Hanes, Playtex, L'eggs, Isotoner, Sheer Energy, Wonderbra, and Champion.

In addition to its intimates and underwear division, the Chicago-based operation breaks its operations into three other primary categories, including:

- **Foods** (28 percent of revenue). The company sells a broad range of foods and consumer products. It is the nation's leading marketer of packaged meats, including Ball Park Franks, Best's Kosher, Hillshire Farms, Mr. Turkey, State Fair, Argal, Hygrade, Imperial, and Jimmy Dean. It is also the leader in frozen desserts, including cheesecake, pound cake, pies, and other desserts.
- **Household products** (12 percent). Sara Lee's household products division generates 90 percent of its sales revenue outside the United States. The company makes shoe care products (Kiwi, Esquire, and Meltonian shoe polish), toiletries, over-the-counter medications, specialty detergents, and insecticides.
- **Beverages** (17 percent). Sara Lee holds leading positions in coffee sales in several Scandinavian countries. It also acquired Chock full o' Nuts and Nestlé's MJB, Hills Bros., and Chase & Sanborn brands in 2000. In the foreign market, its leading brands include Chat Noir, Douwe Egbert, Maison du Cafe, and Merrild.

Sara Lee has operations in more than 40 countries and sales in about 140 countries. Foreign sales account for about 43 percent of total revenue.

The company was founded in 1939 when Nathan Cummings acquired the C. D. Kenny Company, a small Baltimore sugar, tea, and coffee distributor. The company changed its name to Consolidated Grocers Corp. in 1945—a name that stuck until 1985 when the firm changed names again, this time to Sara Lee.

Sara Lee has about 155,000 employees and 85,000 shareholders. It has a market capitalization of about $16 billion.

EARNINGS PER SHARE GROWTH ★

Past 5 years: 49 percent (8 percent per year)
Past 10 years: 146 percent (9 percent per year)

STOCK GROWTH ★

Past 10 years: 213 percent (12 percent per year)
Dollar growth: $10,000 over 10 years (including reinvested dividends) would have grown to about $37,000.
Average annual compounded rate of return (including reinvested dividends): 14 percent

CONSISTENCY   ★ ★ ★ ★

Increased earnings per share: 26 consecutive years
Increased sales: 10 consecutive years

DIVIDEND   ★ ★ ★

Dividend yield: 2.5 percent
Increased dividend: 24 consecutive years
Past 5-year increase: 54 percent (9 percent per year)
Good dividend reinvestment and stock purchase plan; voluntary stock purchase plan allows contributions of $10 to $5,000 per quarter.

SARA LEE AT A GLANCE

Fiscal year ended: June 30
Revenue and net income in $millions

	1996	1997	1998	1999	2000	2001	5-Year Growth Avg. Annual (%)	5-Year Growth Total (%)
Revenue ($)	16,424	17,361	17,426	17,270	17,511	17,747	2	8
Net income ($)	916	1,009	1,102	1,147	1,158	1,136	4	24
Earnings/share ($)	0.89	0.99	1.11	1.21	1.27	1.33	8	49
Dividends/share ($)	0.37	0.41	0.45	0.49	0.53	0.57	9	54
Dividend yield (%)	2.1	2.5	1.7	2.2	2.2	2.6		
PE range	16–22	18–29	17–19	17–24	7–13	11–24		

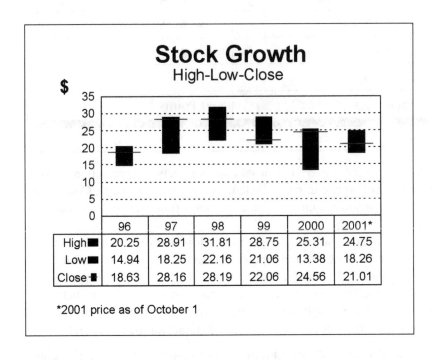

Stock Growth
High-Low-Close

	96	97	98	99	2000	2001*
High	20.25	28.91	31.81	28.75	25.31	24.75
Low	14.94	18.25	22.16	21.06	13.38	18.26
Close	18.63	28.16	28.19	22.06	24.56	21.01

*2001 price as of October 1

Veritas Software Corporation

VERITAS™

350 Ellis Street
Mountain View, CA 94043
650-335-8000
Nasdaq: VRTS
www.veritas.com

Chairman: Mark Leslie
President and CEO: Gary Bloom

Earnings Growth	★ ★ ★ ★
Stock Growth	★ ★ ★
Consistency	★ ★
Dividend	
Total	**9 Points**

There is no such thing as a fail-proof computer network protection system, but Veritas Software can make systems as secure as possible. Companies use Veritas software to ensure that their data is protected and accessible at all times.

The company's software protects data loss and file corruption, allows rapid recovery after disk or computer system failure, and enables information technology (IT) managers to work efficiently with large numbers of files. It also makes it possible to manage data distributed on large networks of computer systems without harming productivity or interrupting users.

Veritas offers software for several key applications, including:

- **File and volume management.** The company's software helps companies improve the manageability and performance of business-critical data. Its volume manager software protects against data loss due to hardware failure and accelerates system performance by allowing files to be spread across multiple disks. It also lets IT managers reconfigure data locations without interrupting users. Its file system software enables fast system recovery, generally within seconds, from operating system failure or disruption.

- **Data protection.** This software is used to back up and restore data.
- **Clustering and replication.** The company provides software that improves the availability of key applications in complex computing environments.
- **Desktop and mobile.** This software is used to protect data on a wide range of devices in the home, small office, and mobile business environments.

The company markets its software to original equipment manufacturers and indirect sales channels such as resellers, value-added resellers, hardware distributors, application software vendors, and systems integrators.

Among its leading customers are Dell, EMC, Amazon.com, American Airlines, AT&T, IBM, Yahoo!, Ford, GTE, Oracle, Sun Microsystems, Microsoft, and eBay.

Veritas has about 5,000 employees and a market capitalization of about $12 billion.

EARNINGS PER SHARE GROWTH ★ ★ ★ ★

Past 5 years: 900 percent (59 percent per year)
Past 10 years: Earnings only go back to 1993.

STOCK GROWTH ★ ★ ★

Past 5 years: 242 percent (28 percent per year)
Dollar growth: $10,000 over 5 years would have grown to $34,000.
Average annual compounded rate of return: 28 percent

CONSISTENCY ★ ★

Increased earnings per share: 7 consecutive years (since its IPO in 1993)
Increased sales: 7 consecutive years

DIVIDEND

Veritas pays no dividend.

VERITAS SOFTWARE AT A GLANCE

Fiscal year ended: Dec. 31
Revenue and net income in $millions

	1995	1996	1997	1998	1999	2000	5-Year Growth Avg. Annual (%)	Total (%)
Revenue ($)	24	73	121	211	596	1,207	157	4,929
Net income ($)	8.2	12	31	52	147	263	100	3,107
Earnings/share ($)	0.06	0.08	0.14	0.23	0.35	0.60	59	900
Dividends/share ($)	—	—	—	—	—	—		
Dividend yield (%)	—	—	—	—	—	—		
PE range	18–27	16–23	18–22	15–25	15–22	9–21		

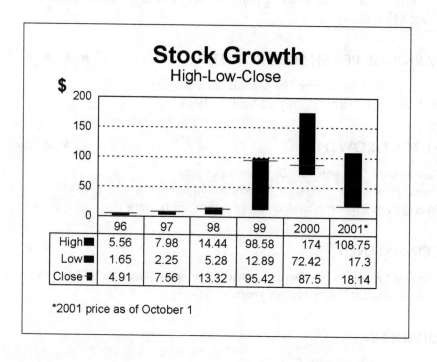

Stock Growth
High-Low-Close

	96	97	98	99	2000	2001*
High	5.56	7.98	14.44	98.58	174	108.75
Low	1.65	2.25	5.28	12.89	72.42	17.3
Close	4.91	7.56	13.32	95.42	87.5	18.14

*2001 price as of October 1

AOL Time Warner, Inc.

AOL Time Warner

---

75 Rockefeller Plaza
New York, NY 10019
212-484-8000
NYSE: AOL
www.timewarner.com

Chairman and CEO: Stephen M. Case
President: Bob Pitman

Earnings Growth	★ ★ ★ ★
Stock Growth	★ ★ ★ ★
Consistency	
Dividend	
Total	**8 Points**

Never before has a single company dominated so many media channels. With its acquisition of Time Warner, America Online became the world's leading media conglomerate. In addition to its own online presence, AOL Time Warner now commands a diversified array of magazines, television stations, and other media assets.

AOL is the world's leading Internet portal with more than 30 million subscribers.

Time Warner operates the world's largest media empire, including such popular magazines as *Time, Sports Illustrated, People,* and *Fortune.* It also operates some leading cable television networks, such as CNN, TBS, and TNT, and two of the world's leading music recording operations, Warner Music Group and EMI Group.

AOL operates two Internet services, America Online and Compu-Serve (which has nearly three million subscribers). The company also owns Netscape, which is one of the leading Internet browsers.

AOL was launched in 1989 as an outgrowth of a much smaller service called Q-Link, which was started in 1985. Shortly after the name change, the company began aggressively marketing to computer users throughout the United States.

AOL members pay a monthly fee ranging from $10 to $22 (depending on the hourly package) that provides them with a wide range of online information and services, including breaking news, business and financial news, stock quotes, investment research, sports, e-mail, and Internet access. Other features include electronic magazines and newspapers, travel features and weather reports, online classes and conferences, an online encyclopedia, and a variety of children's games and information features. The company also offers online shopping through its site, a service that is growing rapidly.

AOL is expanding worldwide, with similar services in Europe and Asia. It also owns about a 25 percent share of Hong Kong–based China.com.

AOL went public with its initial stock offering in 1992. With the Time Warner acquisition, AOL jumps from about 15,000 employees to about 90,000. The company has a market capitalization of about $165 billion.

EARNINGS PER SHARE GROWTH   ★ ★ ★ ★

Past 5 years: 9,300 percent (208 percent per year)
Past 10 years: 197,700 percent

STOCK GROWTH   ★ ★ ★ ★

Past 8 years: 25,313 percent (99 percent per year)
Dollar growth: $10,000 over 8 years would have grown to $2,541,000.

CONSISTENCY

Increased earnings per share: 6 of the past 10 years
Increased sales: 10 consecutive years

DIVIDEND

AOL Time Warner pays no dividend.

AOL TIME WARNER AT A GLANCE

Fiscal year ended: Dec. 31
Revenue and net income in $millions

	1995	1996	1997	1998	1999	2000	5-Year Growth Avg. Annual (%)	Total (%)
Revenue ($)	394	1,093	1,685	2,600	4,777	36,213	202	9,091
Net income ($)	19	30	−72	133	486	425	36	2,137
Earnings/share ($)	0.01	0.02	−0.05	0.07	0.20	0.94	208	9,300
Dividends/share ($)	—	—	—	—	—	—		
Dividend yield (%)	—	—	—	—	—	—		
PE range	42–78	82–261	—	—	37–321	68–175		

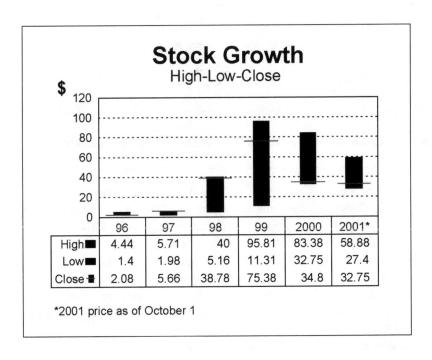

Stock Growth
High-Low-Close

	96	97	98	99	2000	2001*
High	4.44	5.71	40	95.81	83.38	58.88
Low	1.4	1.98	5.16	11.31	32.75	27.4
Close	2.08	5.66	38.78	75.38	34.8	32.75

*2001 price as of October 1

86
United Technologies Corporation

United Technologies Building
One Financial Plaza
Hartford, CT 06101
860-728-7000
NYSE: UTX
www.utc.com

Chairman and CEO: George David
President: Karl Krapek

Earnings Growth	★ ★ ★ ★
Stock Growth	★ ★ ★
Consistency	★
Dividend	
Total	**8 Points**

United Technologies is not what you'd call a new economy technology company. It doesn't make semiconductors or software. Its products are strictly "old school" technology—Carrier air conditioners, Otis elevators, Sikorsky helicopters, and Pratt & Whitney aircraft engines.

The company focuses on most of the aerospace and building industries with a broad range of products and support services. In 2001, *Fortune* magazine ranked United Technologies as the "most admired" company in the aerospace industry, placing it ahead of such rivals as Boeing and Lockheed Martin.

The company's principal subsidiaries are:

- **Otis Elevator.** The world's largest elevator company does 77 percent of its business outside of the United States. As goes the commercial construction market, so goes Otis. Construction in the United States and other international markets has been steady, although U.S. commercial construction has been slowing since its 1998 peak.

- **Carrier.** This is the world's largest manufacturer of commercial and residential heating, ventilation, and air-conditioning (HVAC) systems and equipment. Carrier also makes refrigeration equipment for trucks and the big rigs that rumble down the highways. The Carrier unit provides aftermarket service and components for the HVAC and trucking markets.
- **Pratt & Whitney.** A major supplier of commercial, general aviation, and military aircraft engines for both domestic and international aircraft manufacturers, Pratt & Whitney produces engines that have been selected for the Air Force's F-22 fighter aircraft. They have also been picked for the demonstration aircraft of the Joint Strike fighter program that plans to develop a single fighter for several branches of the U.S. military and the United Kingdom's Royal Navy.
- **The Flight Systems.** This division produces commercial and military helicopters. Sikorsky supplies the U.S. military with the Blackhawk helicopter and is developing with Boeing the Comanche helicopter for the U.S. Army. The Hamilton Sunstrand unit provides aerospace and industrial products and aftermarket services for a broad range of industries.

The company has operations around the world. International sales account for about 39 percent of revenue.

Founded in 1934, United Technologies has about 150,000 employees and a market capitalization of about $35 billion.

EARNINGS PER SHARE GROWTH ★ ★ ★ ★

Past 5 years: 148 percent (20 percent per year)
Past 10 years: 157 percent (10 percent per year)

STOCK GROWTH ★ ★ ★

Past 10 years: 450 percent (19 percent per year)
Dollar growth: $10,000 over 10 years (including reinvested dividends) would have grown to about $67,000.
Average annual compounded rate of return (including reinvested dividends): 21 percent

CONSISTENCY ★

Increased earnings per share: 7 of the past 10 years
Increased sales: 7 of the past 10 years

DIVIDEND

Dividend yield: 1.3 percent
Increased dividend: 7 consecutive years
Past 5-year increase: 63 percent (10 percent per year)
United Technologies does not offer a dividend reinvestment and stock purchase plan.

UNITED TECHNOLOGIES AT A GLANCE

Fiscal year ended: Dec. 31
Revenue and net income in $millions

	1995	1996	1997	1998	1999	2000	5-Year Growth Avg. Annual (%)	Total (%)
Revenue ($)	22,802	23,512	24,713	25,715	24,127	26,583	2	16
Net income ($)	750	906	1,072	1,255	841	1,808	19	141
Earnings/share ($)	1.43	1.73	2.11	2.53	1.65	3.55	20	148
Dividends/share ($)	0.51	0.55	0.62	0.70	0.76	0.83	10	63
Dividend yield (%)	2.6	1.7	1.7	1.3	1.2	1.1		
PE range	11–17	13–20	17–23	13–24	31–46	13–22		

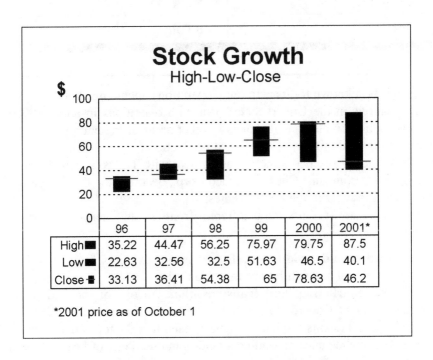

Stock Growth
High-Low-Close

	96	97	98	99	2000	2001*
High	35.22	44.47	56.25	75.97	79.75	87.5
Low	22.63	32.56	32.5	51.63	46.5	40.1
Close	33.13	36.41	54.38	65	78.63	46.2

*2001 price as of October 1

87

Chevron Corporation

575 Market Street
San Francisco, CA 94105
415-894-7700
NYSE: CHV
www.chevron.com

Chairman and CEO: David J. O'Reilly

Earnings Growth	★ ★ ★ ★
Stock Growth	
Consistency	★
Dividend	★ ★ ★
Total	**8 Points**

Chevron is best known for its petroleum operations, including about 8,000 service stations in the United States. But with operations in about 100 countries, Chevron also has its hands in other areas of the energy industry, including coal mining and chemical production.

The company reached a merger agreement with Texaco in late 2001. The combined company, ChevronTexaco Corp., becomes the third largest oil and gas producer in the United States.

Chevron operates on several different fronts in the energy industry, including:

- **Exploration and production.** The company explores for and produces crude oil and natural gas in 25 countries.
- **Refining, marketing, and transportation.** As one of the nation's largest refiners, Chevron turns crude oil into gasoline, diesel and aviation fuels, lubricants, asphalt, and chemicals. It is the top seller of asphalt nationwide and the leading single-brand marketer of heavy-duty and industrial oils in North America. In Canada, the company is the

leading marketer of transportation fuels with 200 outlets in British Columbia. Chevron is also a 50 percent owner of Caltex, which is involved in refining and the distribution of fuel in 60 countries.

- **Chemicals.** Chevron produces plastics and petrochemicals, including styrene and additives for fuel and lubricants. It has plants in the United States and four other countries, and sales in more than 80 countries.
- **Shipping.** The company operates one of the world's largest tanker fleets, including 34 of its own tankers and about 35 more that it leases. The tankers are used to ship crude oil and refined products around the world.

Chevron traces its roots to the Pacific Coast Oil Company opened in Los Angeles in 1879. The company was acquired by John D. Rockefeller's Standard Oil Trust in 1900, and then spun off into Standard Oil Company of California in 1911 as part of the breakup of Rockefeller's operation. The company changed its name to Chevron in 1984.

The company has about 31,000 employees and 136,000 shareholders. It has a market capitalization of about $60 billion. Including Texaco, the company will have about 55,000 employees and a market capitalization of nearly $100 billion.

EARNINGS PER SHARE GROWTH

Past 5 years: 165 percent (21 percent per year)
Past 10 years: 164 percent (10 percent per year)

STOCK GROWTH

Past 10 years: 150 percent (9 percent per year)
Dollar growth: $10,000 over 10 years (including reinvested dividends) would have grown to about $34,000.
Average annual compounded rate of return (including reinvested dividends): 13 percent

CONSISTENCY

Increased earnings per share: 7 of the past 10 years
Increased sales: 5 of the past 10 years

DIVIDEND   ★ ★ ★

Dividend yield: 2.8 percent
Increased dividend: 10 consecutive years
Past 5-year increase: 35 percent (6 percent per year)
Chevron has a good dividend reinvestment and stock purchase plan.

CHEVRON AT A GLANCE

Fiscal year ended: Dec. 31
Revenue and net income in $millions

	1995	1996	1997	1998	1999	2000	5-Year Growth Avg. Annual (%)	Total (%)
Revenue ($)	31,322	36,874	35,009	30,557	36,586	51,996	11	66
Net income ($)	1,962	2,651	3,180	1,339	2,070	5,185	21	164
Earnings/share ($)	3.01	4.06	4.85	2.04	3.14	7.97	21	165
Dividends/share ($)	1.93	2.08	2.28	2.44	2.48	2.60	6	35
Dividend yield (%)	4.0	3.5	3.0	3.0	2.8	3.1		
PE range	12–19	12–17	12–18	33–44	23–33	8–11		

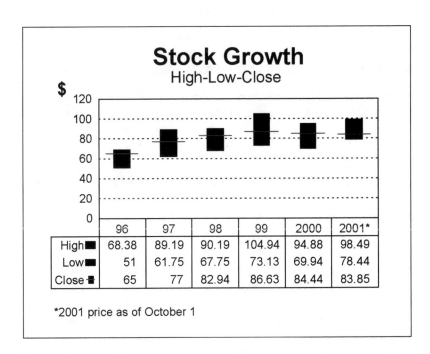

Stock Growth
High-Low-Close

	96	97	98	99	2000	2001*
High	68.38	89.19	90.19	104.94	94.88	98.49
Low	51	61.75	67.75	73.13	69.94	78.44
Close	65	77	82.94	86.63	84.44	83.85

*2001 price as of October 1

William Wrigley, Jr. & Company

410 North Michigan Avenue
Chicago, IL 60611
312-644-2121
NYSE: WWY
www.wrigley.com

President and CEO: William Wrigley, Jr.

Earnings Growth	
Stock Growth	★ ★
Consistency	★ ★ ★ ★
Dividend	★ ★
Total	**8 Points**

Wrigley has turned chewing gum into a $2 billion business. From its humble beginnings 110 years ago, the Chicago chewing gum giant has spread its Juicy Fruit, Doublemint, Spearmint, and other brands to more than 140 countries around the world.

Wrigley may never make it into Singapore—where it's a federal offense to chew gum in public—but its gums are popping up all through Asia. Even in China, Wrigley gum consumption has been growing at nearly 50 percent per year since 1993 when the company opened a manufacturing facility in the Guangdong province. China is now Wrigley's third largest foreign market behind Australia and Canada. Other leading markets include France, Germany, the Philippines, Poland, Russia, Taiwan, and the United Kingdom.

International sales account for about 58 percent of the company's $2.1 billion in total annual sales. For Wrigley, which has seen its U.S. sales growth stagnate in recent years, the increasing international sales have helped the company extend its string of record sales and earnings to 18 consecutive years.

Not only is Wrigley the leading gum producer in the United States—with about a 50 percent share of the total gum market—it is the leading producer in the world.

Brand extension has paid big dividends for Wrigley. The company has added about 15 new brands in recent years. Wrigley's top-grossing brands continue to be Spearmint, Doublemint, Juicy Fruit, Big Red, and Winterfresh. Its Extra sugarfree gum (available in several flavors and as bubble gum) is the nation's top-selling sugarfree brand. The sugarfree line is also beginning to sell well in European markets. Other Wrigley brands include Freedent, Orbit, Eclipse, Hubba Bubba, and Sugarfree Hubba Bubba.

Wrigley also owns Amurol Products, which manufactures children's novelty bubble gum and other confectionery products, including Big League Chew, Bubble Tape gum, BubbleJug, SqueezePop, OUCH!, and Bubble Beeper.

Wrigley was founded in 1891 by William Wrigley, Jr., the late great-grandfather of current President and CEO William Wrigley, Jr., 38. The original William Wrigley, Jr., was a baking soda salesman who first offered gum as a premium to customers who bought his baking soda. The gum quickly became more in demand than the baking soda, so Wrigley did what any smart marketer would do—he switched products. In 1893, he introduced his first flavors of Wrigley's gum, Spearmint and Juicy Fruit, and an American institution was born.

As Will Rogers once put it, "All Wrigley had was an idea. He was the first man to discover that American jaws must wag, so why not give them something to wag against." Now jaws all over the world are wagging with Wrigley's.

The Wrigley Company has 9,800 employees and 37,000 shareholders. It has a market capitalization of $11 billion.

EARNINGS PER SHARE GROWTH

Past 5 years: 49 percent (8 percent per year)
Past 10 years: 190 percent (11 percent per year)

STOCK GROWTH

Past 10 years: 345 percent (16 percent per year)
Dollar growth: $10,000 over 10 years (including reinvested dividends) would have grown to about $52,000.
Average annual compounded rate of return (including reinvested dividends): 18 percent

CONSISTENCY   ★ ★ ★ ★

Increased earnings per share: 18 consecutive years
Increased sales: 18 consecutive years

DIVIDEND   ★ ★

Dividend yield: 1.8 percent
Increased dividend: 19 consecutive years
Past 5-year increase: 46 percent (8 percent per year)
Good dividend reinvestment and stock purchase plan; voluntary stock
purchase plan allows contributions of $50 to $5,000 per month.

WRIGLEY AT A GLANCE

Fiscal year ended: Dec. 31
Revenue and net income in $millions

	1995	1996	1997	1998	1999	2000	5-Year Growth Avg. Annual (%)	Total (%)
Revenue ($)	1,755	1,836	1,937	2,005	2,061	2,146	4	22
Net income ($)	224	230	272	304	308	329	8	47
Earnings/share ($)	0.97	1.05	1.18	1.29	1.33	1.45	8	49
Dividends/share ($)	0.48	0.51	0.59	0.65	0.67	0.70	8	46
Dividend yield (%)	2.1	1.8	1.5	1.5	1.6	1.8		
PE range	18–25	24–31	23–35	27–39	25–37	20–33		

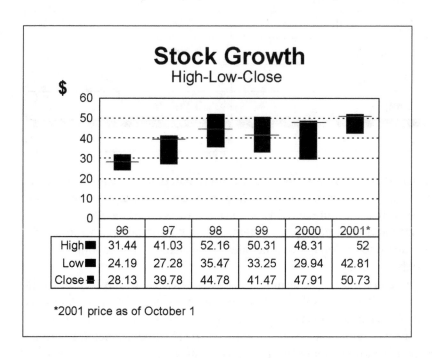

Stock Growth
High-Low-Close

	96	97	98	99	2000	2001*
High■	31.44	41.03	52.16	50.31	48.31	52
Low■	24.19	27.28	35.47	33.25	29.94	42.81
Close■	28.13	39.78	44.78	41.47	47.91	50.73

*2001 price as of October 1

⚫HermanMiller

855 East Main Avenue
P.O. Box 302
Zeeland, MI 49464
616-654-3000
Nasdaq: MLHR
www.hermanmiller.com

President and CEO: Michael A. Volkema

Earnings Growth	★ ★ ★ ★
Stock Growth	★ ★
Consistency	★ ★
Dividend	
Total	**8 Points**

Herman Miller is not just an office furniture company. It designs entire office furniture "systems." One of its newest offerings is the Resolve system, an open office furniture and divider system that is based on 120 degree angles around a steel pole. The system, which can be tailored to fit nearly any office size or shape, even includes fabric screens and canopies for office definition.

The company has won numerous awards for its office furniture and systems. Before its Resolve system, the company drew rave reviews for its Action Office and Ethospace systems. But more important, it has also won the respect of corporate buyers around the world who have helped Herman Miller ratchet up annual sales to nearly $2 billion.

The Zeeland, Michigan operation sells its products in about 40 countries through a network of subsidiaries, licensees, and sales offices. Foreign sales account for about 15 percent of total revenue.

In addition to its innovative office systems, the company has developed some of the most highly respected office furniture in the business. It introduced the Ergon chair in 1976, which drew praise for its ergonomic design. In 1984, it introduced the Equa chair, which was also designed for comfort and ergonomic support. And in 1994, Herman Miller introduced a chair that would become almost legendary in Silicon Valley—the Aeron chair. Despite its retail cost of about $1,500, the Aeron still became the chair of choice for many of the cash-rich Internet and technology startups, as well as for other established companies.

Herman Miller expanded to the residential furniture market in 1994 with the introduction of historical-style pieces designed by Charles and Ray Eames and George Nelson. The company also began introducing home office furniture systems in 1994.

D. J. DePree founded the company in 1923 when he and his father-in-law, Herman Miller, and several others purchased a small furniture maker in Michigan.

Herman Miller has about 10,000 employees and 26,000 shareholders. It has a market capitalization of $2 billion.

EARNINGS PER SHARE GROWTH   ★ ★ ★ ★

Past 5 years: 223 percent (26 percent per year)
Past 10 years: 402 percent (17.5 percent per year)

STOCK GROWTH   ★ ★

Past 10 years: 328 percent (16 percent per year)
Dollar growth: $10,000 over 10 years (including reinvested dividends) would have grown to $52,000.
Average annual compounded rate of return (including reinvested dividends): 18 percent

CONSISTENCY   ★ ★

Increased earnings per share: 8 of the past 10 years
Increased sales: 8 of the past 10 years

DIVIDEND

Dividend yield: 0.6 percent
Increased dividend: 2 of the past 10 years
Past 5-year increase: 15 percent (3 percent per year)
Herman Miller does not offer a dividend reinvestment plan.

HERMAN MILLER AT A GLANCE

Fiscal year ended: May 31
Revenue and net income in $millions

	1996	1997	1998	1999	2000	2001	5-Year Growth Avg. Annual (%)	Total (%)
Revenue ($)	1,284	1,450	1,719	1,766	1,938	2,236	12	74
Net income ($)	57	74	128	142	140	144	20	152
Earnings/share ($)	0.56	0.88	1.39	1.62	1.74	1.81	26	223
Dividends/share ($)	0.13	0.14	0.15	0.15	0.15	0.15	3	15
Dividend yield (%)	0.1	1.1	0.6	0.6	0.5	0.5		
PE range	14–30	17–37	13–26	9–16	10–19	10–20		

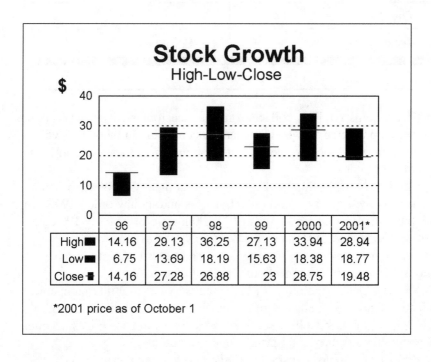

Stock Growth
High-Low-Close

	96	97	98	99	2000	2001*
High■	14.16	29.13	36.25	27.13	33.94	28.94
Low■	6.75	13.69	18.19	15.63	18.38	18.77
Close-■	14.16	27.28	26.88	23	28.75	19.48

*2001 price as of October 1

First Data Corporation

6200 South Quebec Street
Greenwood, CO 80111
303-488-8000
NYSE: FDC
www.firstdata.com

Chairman and CEO: Henry C. Duques
President: Charles F. Tote

Earnings Growth	★ ★
Stock Growth	★ ★ ★
Consistency	★ ★ ★
Dividend	
Total	**8 Points**

First Data helps retailers collect from their customers. It is the leading electronic commerce and payment services company in the world, with a customer base that includes nearly 3 million merchant locations and 1,400 credit card issuers.

The Denver operation is also the parent company of Western Union, which is the world leader in money transfers and money orders. Western Union has money transfer agents in 109,000 locations in nearly 190 countries and territories. Customers use Western Union to send or receive cash quickly to meet emergency situations, to send funds to family in other locations, or to pay bills or meet other obligations.

Western Union also offers bill payment services to utility companies, collection agencies, finance companies, and other institutions through its Easy Pay and Quick Collect services. Western Union's services account for about 40 percent of First Data's total revenue.

First Data also does business in several other key areas:

- **Merchant services** (32 percent of revenue). The company enables merchants to accept any type of electronic payment, including credit, debit, stored-value, and smart cards. It processes and settles more than 7 billion credit and debit card transactions valued at more than $425 billion for nearly 2.6 million merchant locations. First Data also provides payment-processing services for about 120,000 Internet merchants. Through its TeleCheck subsidiary, First Data authorizes more than 3.2 billion check transactions totaling $160 billion for more than 270,000 retail, financial institution, and other industry clients.
- **Card issuing services** (26 percent). First Data is the leading third-party processor of bankcard transactions, serving about 1,400 credit card issuers worldwide. The company has nearly 300 million domestic and international card accounts on file. It provides a full range of services, including adding new accounts, activating cards, driving usage, keeping profitable cardholders, building loyalty, and managing risk. Its cardholder services include personalizing and issuing plastic cards, activating the cards, ongoing correspondence with cardholders, authorizations, fraud and risk management, and producing and mailing statements.
- **Emerging payment technologies.** The company formed eONE Global in 2000 to pursue Internet and wireless payment products.
- **Other services** (2 percent). The company also operates some small ventures, including TeleServices, Call Interactive, and International Banking Technologies.

The company traces its roots to the founding of Western Union in 1851. First Data has about 25,000 employees and a market capitalization of about $26 billion.

EARNINGS PER SHARE GROWTH ★ ★

Past 5 years: 110 percent (16 percent per year)
Past 8 years: 229 percent (16 percent per year)

STOCK GROWTH ★ ★ ★

Past 8 years: 367 percent (21 percent per year)
Dollar growth: $10,000 over 10 years (including reinvested dividends) would have grown to $47,000.
Average annual compounded rate of return (including reinvested dividends): 21 percent

CONSISTENCY   ★ ★ ★

Increased earnings per share: 8 consecutive years
Increased sales: 7 of the past 9 years

DIVIDEND

Dividend yield: 0.1 percent
Increased dividend: 3 of the past 8 years
Past 5-year increase: 33 percent (6 percent per year)
First Data does not offer a dividend reinvestment and stock purchase plan.

FIRST DATA AT A GLANCE

Fiscal year ended: Dec. 31
Revenue and net income in $millions

	1995	1996	1997	1998	1999	2000	5-Year Growth Avg. Annual (%)	Total (%)
Revenue ($)	4,081	4,938	5,234	5,118	5,520	5,705	7	40
Net income ($)	456	636	691	697	770	884	14	94
Earnings/share ($)	1.02	1.37	1.51	1.56	1.77	2.14	16	110
Dividends/share ($)	0.06	0.07	0.08	0.08	0.08	0.08	6	33
Dividend yield (%)	0.2	0.2	0.2	0.3	0.2	0.2		
PE range	22–34	22–32	31–58	18–34	11–18	16–25		

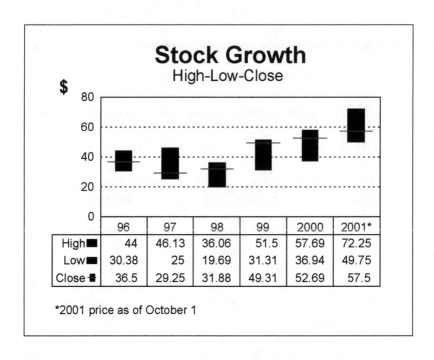

Stock Growth
High-Low-Close

	96	97	98	99	2000	2001*
High■	44	46.13	36.06	51.5	57.69	72.25
Low■	30.38	25	19.69	31.31	36.94	49.75
Close■	36.5	29.25	31.88	49.31	52.69	57.5

*2001 price as of October 1

ConAgra Foods, Inc.

One ConAgra Drive
Omaha, NE 68102
402-595-4707
NYSE: CAG
www.conagra.com

Chairman, President, and CEO: Bruce Rohde

Earnings Growth	
Stock Growth	★
Consistency	★ ★ ★
Dividend	★ ★ ★ ★
Total	**8 Points**

ConAgra serves up a vast platter of foods and meats. It is North America's largest supplier of food service products, and the second largest supplier of retail foods.

The Omaha operation is the second-largest food supplier in the world, with annual sales of about $27 billion.

From feeds and fertilizer to Banquet chickens and Peter Pan peanut butter, ConAgra covers nearly every furrow and fowl of the agricultural industry. The company is involved in a wide range of ventures, including grain merchandising, crop inputs (fertilizers, seeds, insecticides, and other crop protection chemicals), and commodity services.

But ConAgra's bread and butter is its grocery and refrigerated foods divisions. Among the company's most recognized brands are Hunt's tomato products, Healthy Choice, Banquet meals, Armour meats, Bumble Bee tuna, Louis Kemp seafood, La Choy, Chun King, Lunch Makers, Wesson. Other leading brands include Country Pride, Blue Bonnet, Parkay, Reddi Wip, Act II and Orville Redenbacher's popcorn, Slim Jim, Decker, Chef Boyardee, PAM Cooking Spray, Snack Pack puddings, Van Camp's, and Peter Pan.

The company also produces frozen potato products, delicatessen and food service products, and pet accessories.

Packaged foods account for about 29 percent of the company's annual revenue, refrigerated foods make up 50 percent, and agricultural products account for 21 percent.

ConAgra operates a North American network of grain merchandising offices and more than 90 grain elevators, river loading facilities, export elevators, and barges.

It also operates about 25 flour mills in 14 states, and a commodity trading business with offices in 15 nations that trades agricultural commodities and foodstuffs on the world market.

The 81-year-old company has operations in 35 countries. International sales account for about 6 percent of ConAgra's pretax income.

ConAgra has 85,000 employees and about 165,000 shareholders. The company has a market capitalization of $12 billion.

EARNINGS PER SHARE GROWTH

Past 5 years: 13 percent (2 percent per year)
Past 10 years: 87 percent (6 percent per year)

STOCK GROWTH ★

Past 10 years: 127 percent (8.5 percent per year)
Dollar growth: $10,000 over 10 years (including reinvested dividends) would have grown to $28,000.
Average annual compounded rate of return (including reinvested dividends): 11 percent

CONSISTENCY

Increased earnings per share: 9 of the past 10 years
Increased sales: 8 of the past 10 years

DIVIDEND

Dividend yield: 3.8 percent
Increased dividend: 25 consecutive years
Past 5-year increase: 91 percent (14 percent per year)
Good dividend reinvestment and stock purchase plan; voluntary stock purchase plan allows contributions of $50 to $50,000 per year.

CONAGRA AT A GLANCE

Fiscal year ended: May 31
Revenue and net income in $millions

	1996	1997	1998	1999	2000	2001	5-Year Growth Avg. Annual (%)	5-Year Growth Total (%)
Revenue ($)	24,321	24,408	24,545	24,844	25,535	27,194	2	11
Net income ($)	545	631	618	696	801	683	5	25
Earnings/share ($)	1.17	1.34	1.36	1.46	1.67	1.33	2	13
Dividends/share ($)	0.46	0.53	0.61	0.69	0.79	0.88	14	91
Dividend yield (%)	1.85	1.6	1.92	3.05	3.03	3.5		
PE range	47–69	18–28	16–24	27–45	18–32	17–26		

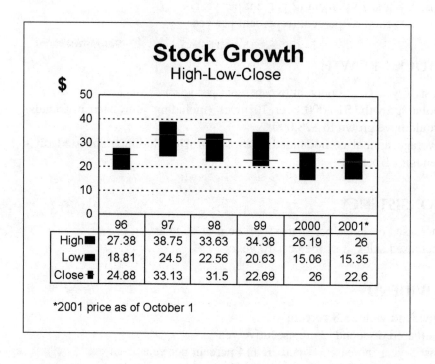

Stock Growth
High-Low-Close

$	96	97	98	99	2000	2001*
High■	27.38	38.75	33.63	34.38	26.19	26
Low■	18.81	24.5	22.56	20.63	15.06	15.35
Close■	24.88	33.13	31.5	22.69	26	22.6

*2001 price as of October 1

McDonald's Corporation

McDonald's Plaza
Oak Brook, IL 60523
630-623-3000
NYSE: MCD
www.mcdonalds.com

Chairman and CEO: Jack M. Greenberg

Earnings Growth	★
Stock Growth	★
Consistency	★ ★ ★ ★
Dividend	★
Total	**7 Points**

No matter where you go in the world, it's hard to escape the shadow of the golden arches. Even American Samoa and French Guyana opened new McDonald's restaurants recently, bringing to 120 the total number of countries around the world that offer McDonald's fare.

The company operates more than 6,000 restaurants in the Asia-Pacific region, another 6,000 in Europe, and nearly 2,000 in Latin America. In all, about half of the company's 30,000 restaurants are located outside the United States. Foreign operations account for about 45 percent of total sales and 52 percent of operating profit.

The Chicago-based operation adds about 1,600 new restaurants a year.

The company also operates a handful of smaller chains, including Aroma Café, Chipotle Mexican Grill, and Donatos Pizza. It acquired the 800-store chain of Boston Market restaurants in 2000.

In addition to its foreign expansion, McDonald's has also tried to keep its earnings growing by introducing a continuing line of new selections, such as ice cream, chicken, salads, breakfast products, and other specialties. McDonald's also maintains its marketing edge by keeping prices as low as any restaurant in the fast-food business.

The company is very careful to shape its foreign offerings to the tastes of the local culture. In Norway, McDonald's serves a grilled salmon sandwich with dill sauce; in Japan, it serves Chicken Tatsuta, a fried chicken sandwich spiced with soy sauce and ginger; in Germany, the restaurants serve frankfurters, beer, and a cold four-course meal; and in India, where the cow is sacred, McDonald's features chicken and fish sandwiches along with some special veggie nuggets and a veggie burger. No beef is served.

Most McDonald's restaurants are owned by independent businesspeople, who operate them through a franchise agreement. Typically, the company tries to recruit investors who will be active, on-premises owners rather than outside investors. The conventional franchise arrangement is for a term of 20 years and requires an investment of about $600,000, 60 percent of which may be financed. Each outlet is also subject to franchise fees based on a percentage of sales. With few exceptions, McDonald's does not supply food, paper, or equipment to any restaurants but approves suppliers from which those items can be purchased.

Restaurant managers receive training at the company's Hamburger University at the McDonald's corporate headquarters in Oak Brook, Illinois. Outside the United States, there are Hamburger University training centers in Germany, England, Japan, Brazil, and Australia.

The typical new restaurant generates revenues of about $1.5 million the first year. About 58 percent of McDonald's restaurants are owned by franchisees, 27 percent by the company, and 15 percent by affiliates.

McDonald's was founded in 1955 by the late Ray Kroc. Now, more than 45 million customers a day—and 17 billion a year—dine beneath the golden arches.

McDonald's has 413,000 employees and 954,000 shareholders. The company has a market capitalization of about $40 billion.

EARNINGS PER SHARE GROWTH   ★

Past 5 years: 51 percent (9 percent per year)
Past 10 years: 165 percent (10 percent per year)

STOCK GROWTH

Past 10 years: 240 percent (13 percent per year)
Dollar growth: $10,000 over 10 years (including reinvested dividends) would have grown to $37,000.
Average annual compounded rate of return (including reinvested dividends): 14 percent

CONSISTENCY   ★ ★ ★ ★

Increased earnings per share: 34 consecutive years
Increased sales: 34 consecutive years

DIVIDEND   ★

Dividend yield: 0.7 percent
Increased dividend: 35 consecutive years
Past 5-year increase: 69 percent (11 percent per year)
Good dividend reinvestment and stock purchase plan; McDonald's MC-Direct shares program allows contributions of $50 or more following an initial investment of $500.

MCDONALD'S AT A GLANCE

Fiscal year ended: Dec. 31
Revenue and net income in $millions

	1995	1996	1997	1998	1999	2000	5-Year Growth Avg. Annual (%)	Total (%)
Revenue ($)	9,794	10,687	11,409	12,421	13,259	14,243	8	45
Net income ($)	1,427	1,573	1,642	1,770	1,948	1,977	7	38
Earnings/share ($)	0.97	1.11	1.15	1.26	1.39	1.46	9	51
Dividends/share ($)	0.13	0.15	0.16	0.18	0.20	0.22	11	69
Dividend yield (%)	0.7	0.6	0.7	0.6	0.5	0.7		
PE range	17–21	19–25	18–23	20–36	25–35	18–29		

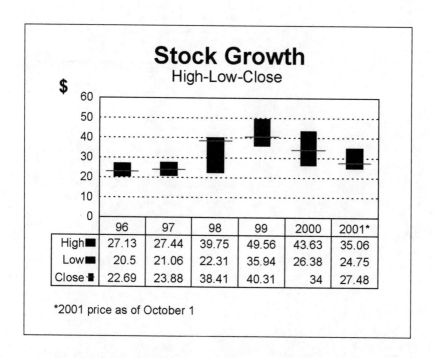

Stock Growth
High-Low-Close

$						
	96	97	98	99	2000	2001*
High■	27.13	27.44	39.75	49.56	43.63	35.06
Low■	20.5	21.06	22.31	35.94	26.38	24.75
Close■	22.69	23.88	38.41	40.31	34	27.48

*2001 price as of October 1

Cisco Systems

170 West Tasman Drive
San Jose, CA 95134
408-526-4100
Nasdaq: CSCO
www.cisco.com

Chairman: John Morgridge
CEO: John T. Chambers

Earnings Growth	
Stock Growth	★ ★ ★ ★
Consistency	★ ★ ★
Dividend	
Total	**7 Points**

Cisco Systems helps hold the World Wide Web together through its array of routers, switches, and access servers. The company supplies more than 80 percent of all routers used on the Internet backbone.

Cisco is also the world's leading supplier of networking products for corporate intranets, in addition to the global Internet. The San Jose, California operation markets its products to four types of buyers:

- Large organizations with complex networking needs, such as corporations, government agencies, and universities
- Major network operators, such as telecommunications carriers, cable companies, and Internet service providers (ISPs)
- Volume markets, such as small businesses and home office users
- Other suppliers who license features of Cisco software for inclusion in their products or services

Under Cisco's corporate growth strategy, dubbed "technical agnosticism," the company adopts competing technologies instead of fighting them. It pursues this strategy mostly by acquiring the most promising start-up technology companies (about a half-dozen each year). This keeps Cisco at the cutting edge of technology and prevents the management team from growing inbred and stale.

One of Cisco's most notable strengths is its product architecture. Its entire product line runs the company's IOS operating system, which is perhaps second only to Microsoft Windows in importance. Customers like the fact that its technicians need learn only a single computing environment to do almost any task—which helps lock in Cisco's market position.

After a decade of unrivaled success, Cisco hit choppy waters in the great technology meltdown. As a result, the company restructured its operations into 11 key business groups, including access, aggregation, IOS Technologies, Internet switching and services, Ethernet access, network management services, core routing, optical storage, voice, and wireless.

Cisco sells its products through a direct sales force of about 15,000 representatives and technical support personnel. Internationally, the company sells its products in 115 countries through about 120 distributors. Foreign sales account for about 40 percent of the revenue.

Cisco was founded in 1984 by a husband-wife team working at Stanford University who set out to develop a way to tie the world's local networks together. The company brought its first product to market in 1986, and sales have been soaring ever since.

The company has about 34,000 employees and a market capitalization of about $120 billion.

EARNINGS PER SHARE GROWTH

Past 5 years: The company had a loss in the most recent fiscal year.

STOCK GROWTH   ★ ★ ★ ★

Past 10 years: 10,633 percent (58 percent per year)
Dollar growth: $10,000 over 10 years would have grown to $1.02 million.
Average annual compounded rate of return: 58 percent

CONSISTENCY   ★ ★ ★

Increased earnings per share: 9 of the past 10 years
Increased sales: 13 consecutive years

DIVIDEND

Cisco pays no dividend.

CISCO SYSTEMS AT A GLANCE

Fiscal year ended: July 31
Revenue and net income in $millions

	1996	1997	1998	1999	2000	2001	5-Year Growth Avg. Annual (%)	5-Year Growth Total (%)
Revenue ($)	4,101	6,452	8,489	12,173	18,928	22,293	42	443
Net income ($)	915	1,047	1,331	2,023	2,668	–1,014	—	—
Earnings/share ($)	0.15	0.17	0.21	0.30	0.39	–0.14	—	—
Dividends/share ($)	—	—	—	—	—	—		
Dividend yield (%)	—	—	—	—	—	—		
PE range	23–50	29–60	42–122	78–186	97–228			

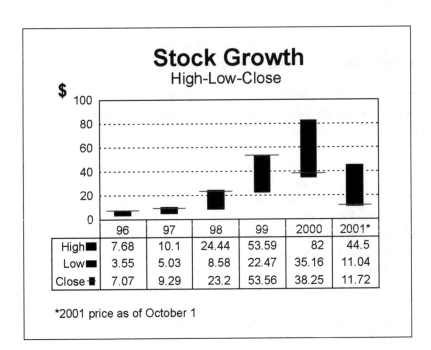

Stock Growth
High-Low-Close

	96	97	98	99	2000	2001*
High	7.68	10.1	24.44	53.59	82	44.5
Low	3.55	5.03	8.58	22.47	35.16	11.04
Close	7.07	9.29	23.2	53.56	38.25	11.72

*2001 price as of October 1

94

Hershey Foods Company

100 Crystal A Drive
Hershey, PA 17033
717-534-6799
NYSE: HSY
www.hersheys.com

Chairman and CEO: Kenneth L. Wolfe
President: Richard H. Lenny

Earnings Growth	
Stock Growth	★ ★
Consistency	★ ★ ★
Dividend	★ ★
Total	**7 Points**

In this country, Hershey has become almost synonymous with chocolate. But Hershey candies come in a lot more flavors than just chocolate. In all, the company offers more than 50 brands of candies. It is the nation's leading confectionery producer, with about a 35 percent share of the nation's $11 billion sweet tooth market.

Through brand extension and a series of acquisitions, Hershey has assembled a long line of popular candies. Its top brands include Reese's, Kit Kat, Hershey's chocolate bar, and Hershey's Kisses. Other popular brands include Milk Duds, Peter Paul Almond Joy, Mounds Bars, Caramello, Cadbury's chocolate bars and Creme Eggs, Hershey's Big Block, Special Dark, Golden Almond, Golden Almond Nuggets, Krackel, and Rolo caramels.

Hershey is also the maker of Skor, Mr. Goodbar, Reese's Pieces, 5th Avenue, Bar None, York Peppermint Pattie, Whoppers, Whatchamacallit, Reese's NutRageous, ReeseSticks, and Symphony.

The company also produces a wide selection of nonchocolate candies, such as PayDay, Twizzlers, Jolly Ranchers, Good & Plenty, Good & Fruity, Amazin' Fruit gummy bears, Chuckles, Heide jujubes, Hershey's caramels and Jelly Beans, Sour Dudes, Nibs, Rain-Blo gumballs, Wunder-beans, Zagnut, and Zero candy bars. The company also produces Luden's cough drops.

In addition to its candies, Hershey offers a line of chocolate mixes, including Hershey's cocoa, chocolate milk mix, baking chocolate, chocolate syrup, fudge topping, chocolate chips and premium chunks, and chocolate flavor puddings. It also makes Reese's baking chips, Reese's peanut butter, and Mounds coconut flakes.

Hershey products are sold in more than 90 countries worldwide, although its international operations account for slightly less than 10 percent of its $4.2 billion in annual revenue.

Founded by Milton Hershey in 1893, the Hershey, Pennsylvania operation has about 14,000 employees and 44,000 shareholders. The company has a market capitalization of about $8 billion.

EARNINGS PER SHARE GROWTH

Past 5 years: 41 percent (7 percent per year)
Past 10 years: 119 percent (8 percent per year)

STOCK GROWTH   ★ ★

Past 10 years: 283 percent (14 percent per year)
Dollar growth: $10,000 over 10 years (including reinvested dividends) would have grown to $44,000.
Average annual compounded rate of return (including reinvested dividends): 16 percent

CONSISTENCY   ★ ★ ★

Increased earnings per share: 9 of the past 10 years
Increased sales: 9 of the past 10 years

DIVIDEND   ★ ★

Dividend yield: 1.8 percent
Increased dividend: 26 consecutive years
Past 5-year increase: 56 percent (9 percent per year)
Good dividend reinvestment and stock purchase plan; voluntary stock purchase plan allows contributions of $100 to $10,000 per month following an initial $500 investment.

HERSHEY FOODS AT A GLANCE

Fiscal year ended: Dec. 31
Revenue and net income in $millions

	1995	1996	1997	1998	1999	2000	5-Year Growth Avg. Annual (%)	5-Year Growth Total (%)
Revenue ($)	3,691	3,989	4,302	4,436	3,971	4,221	3	14
Net income ($)	280	308	336	333	295	330	3	18
Earnings/share ($)	1.69	2.00	2.23	2.29	2.09	2.39	7	41
Dividends/share ($)	0.69	0.76	0.84	0.92	1.00	1.08	9	56
Dividend yield (%)	2.3	1.9	1.7	1.5	1.8	2.2		
PE range	13–19	18–29	18–28	25–32	14–19	15–27		

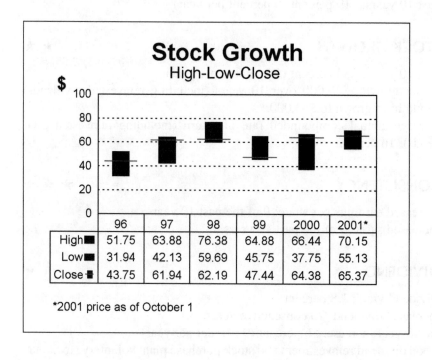

Stock Growth
High-Low-Close

	96	97	98	99	2000	2001*
High	51.75	63.88	76.38	64.88	66.44	70.15
Low	31.94	42.13	59.69	45.75	37.75	55.13
Close	43.75	61.94	62.19	47.44	64.38	65.37

*2001 price as of October 1

Dionex Corporation

1228 Titan Way
P.O. Box 3603
Sunnyvale, CA 94086
408-737-0700
Nasdaq: DNEX
www.dionex.com

President and CEO: A. Blaine Bowman

Earnings Growth	★
Stock Growth	★ ★ ★
Consistency	★ ★ ★
Dividend	
Total	**7 Points**

As the requirements of advanced scientific research become increasingly complex, the sophistication of research equipment must also keep pace. Dionex makes a growing line of scientific research and analysis equipment, including instruments that can separate and quantify the individual components of complex chemical mixtures.

The company's equipment gives researchers the ability to analyze product ingredients, monitor pollutants and impurities, and identify the molecular components of a wide range of solutions and materials. For instance, Dionex equipment can measure the tartar control impact of the toothpaste you use, the level of nitrates in the hot dogs you eat, the trace amounts of zinc or iron in the beer you drink, or the measure of phosphates in your rainwater.

The Sunnyvale, California operation manufactures chromatography systems, sample preparation devices, and related products used by many of the largest industrial companies in the world, as well as government agencies, researchers, and universities.

The advanced technology has helped Dionex grow rapidly, posting record revenues for 20 consecutive years and record earnings per share for 19 of the past 20 years (earnings dropped slightly in fiscal 2001).

The company's top-selling product is the Dionex Ion Chromatography system, which separates and analyzes charged (ionic) molecules in water-based solutions. The systems are used for such applications as environmental monitoring, corrosion monitoring, evaluation of raw materials, quality control of industrial processes and pharmaceutical and industrial products, research and development, and regulation of the chemical composition of foods, beverages, and cosmetics.

The Ion Chromatography systems are used by environmental testing laboratories, food companies, chemical and petrochemical firms, power-generating facilities, electronics manufacturers, government agencies, and academic institutions.

The company has also developed more advanced liquid chromatography systems used to separate and identify molecules such as proteins, carbohydrates, amino acids, pharmaceuticals, and chemicals.

Dionex markets its instruments worldwide. It has sales offices in the United States, Canada, Japan, and throughout Europe. About 58 percent of the company's $187 million in annual sales comes from customers outside of North America.

Dionex has about 800 employees and 1,600 shareholders. It has a market capitalization of about $650 million.

EARNINGS PER SHARE GROWTH   ★

Past 5 years: 60 percent (10 percent per year)
Past 10 years: 233 percent (9 percent per year)

STOCK GROWTH   ★ ★ ★

Past 10 years: 454 percent (18.5 percent per year)
Dollar growth: $10,000 over 10 years would have grown to $54,000.
Average annual compounded rate of return: 18.5 percent

CONSISTENCY   ★ ★ ★

Increased earnings per share: 9 of the past 10 consecutive years
Increased sales: 20 consecutive years

DIVIDEND

Dionex pays no dividend.

DIONEX AT A GLANCE

Fiscal year ended: June 30
Revenue and net income in $millions

	1996	1997	1998	1999	2000	2001	5-Year Growth Avg. Annual (%)	Total (%)
Revenue ($)	133	142	151	173	180	187	7	40
Net income ($)	24	26.2	28.6	28.5	34	31.8	6	32
Earnings/share ($)	0.87	1.03	1.18	1.20	1.46	1.40	10	60
Dividends/share ($)	—	—	—	—	—	—		
Dividend yield (%)	—	—	—	—	—	—		
PE range	15–23	16–26	15–33	26–42	14–29	23–38		

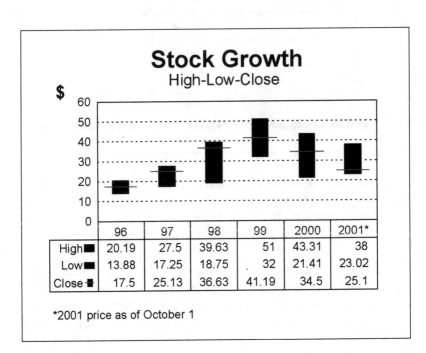

Stock Growth
High-Low-Close

$	96	97	98	99	2000	2001*
High	20.19	27.5	39.63	51	43.31	38
Low	13.88	17.25	18.75	32	21.41	23.02
Close	17.5	25.13	36.63	41.19	34.5	25.1

*2001 price as of October 1

Equifax, Inc.

EQUIFAX

15500 Peachtree Street, N.W.
Atlanta, GA 30309
404-885-8000
NYSE: EFX
www.equifax.com

Chairman and CEO: Thomas Chapman
President: Lee Kennedy

Earnings Growth	★
Stock Growth	★ ★
Consistency	★ ★ ★
Dividend	★
Total	**7 Points**

Equifax makes your business *its* business. The Atlanta-based operation is the nation's largest credit reporting operation, providing consumer credit reports for banks, retailers, financial institutions, utilities, oil companies, credit card companies, automobile finance and leasing firms, and mortgage lenders.

The Atlanta-based operation also offers a broad range of related services, such as debt collection, fraud detection and prevention, credit card marketing, database marketing and database management systems, mortgage loan origination information, mapping tools, and modeling and analytical services.

The company has operations worldwide, generating about half of its annual revenue outside of North America. Equifax operates several key business segments, including:

- **North American information services.** The company offers consumer credit information, credit card marketing services, fraud detection and prevention, mortgage loan analysis, account acquisition services, notification services, mortgage information, and consumer direct products. Customers include banks, financial institutions, retailers, credit card issuers, utility companies, health care administration firms, and insurance companies.
- **Consumer information services.** Equifax provides consumer, demographic, and lifestyle information and directories of residents and businesses. Customers include credit services users, insurers, catalogers, publishers, technology companies, and travel and manufacturing clients.
- **Card solutions.** The company offers credit card issuer services that enable banks, credit unions, retailers, and others to issue credit cards, and it provides merchant processing services.
- **Check solutions.** Equifax provides check risk management and processing services for retailers, hotels, auto dealers, and telecommunications companies.

The company also has operations in Europe and Latin America that provide consumer and commercial credit information and marketing services, credit scoring, check guarantee services, and auto lien information.

Equifax was founded in 1899 as a credit reporting agency under the name Retail Credit Company. It changed its name to Equifax in 1975.

The company has about 12,000 employees and 11,000 shareholders. It has a market capitalization of $5 billion.

EARNINGS PER SHARE GROWTH ★

Past 5 years: 71 percent (11 percent per year)
Past 10 years: 226 percent (13 percent per year)

STOCK GROWTH ★ ★

Past 10 years: 183 percent (11 percent per year)
Dollar growth: $10,000 over 10 years (including reinvested dividends) would have grown to $34,000.
Average annual compounded rate of return (including reinvested dividends): 13 percent

CONSISTENCY   ★ ★ ★

Increased earnings per share: 9 of the past 10 years
Increased sales: 9 of the past 10 years

DIVIDEND   ★

Dividend yield: 1.1 percent
Increased dividend: 9 of the past 10 years
Past 5-year increase: 16 percent (3 percent per year)
Equifax has a somewhat restricted dividend reinvestment and stock purchase plan; voluntary stock purchase plan allows contributions of up to $10,000 per month.

EQUIFAX AT A GLANCE

Fiscal year ended: Dec. 31
Revenue and net income in $millions

	1995	1996	1997	1998	1999	2000	5-Year Growth Avg. Annual (%)	Total (%)
Revenue ($)	1,623	1,811	1,366	1,621	1,773	1,966	4	21
Net income ($)	148	178	186	193	216	228	9	54
Earnings/share ($)	0.98	1.22	1.26	1.34	1.55	1.68	11	71
Dividends/share ($)	0.32	0.33	0.35	0.35	0.36	0.37	3	16
Dividend yield (%)	1.8	1.3	1.1	0.9	1.1	1.4		
PE range	14–25	17–33	21–29	22–33	13–25	11–21		

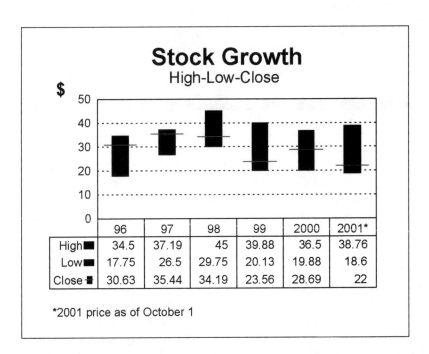

Stock Growth
High-Low-Close

	96	97	98	99	2000	2001*
High	34.5	37.19	45	39.88	36.5	38.76
Low	17.75	26.5	29.75	20.13	19.88	18.6
Close	30.63	35.44	34.19	23.56	28.69	22

*2001 price as of October 1

Coca-Cola Company

The Coca-Cola Company

One Coca-Cola Plaza
Atlanta, GA 30313
404-676-2121
NYSE: KO
www.cocacola.com

Chairman and CEO: Douglas N. Daft

Earnings Growth	
Stock Growth	★ ★
Consistency	★ ★
Dividend	★ ★
Total	**6 Points**

Coke may still be the "Real Thing," but it has 238 other siblings. In all, Coca-Cola puts out 239 different beverages, including soft drinks, sports drinks, juice, bottled water, teas, and coffees. The company supplies 19 percent of all nonalcoholic, ready-to-drink beverages sold around the world.

The original Coke still leads the way among all of the company's drinks—and all nonalcoholic drinks available on the market. Nationwide, Americans drink an average of about 425 8-oz. servings of Coca-Cola Company beverages each year. The company controls a 45 percent share of the U.S. soft drink market, compared with PepsiCo's 31 percent share.

In addition to Coke and Diet Coke, the company produces Cherry Coke, Fanta, Sprite, Diet Sprite, Mr. Pibb, Mellow Yello, TAB, Fresca, Barq's Root Beer, Surge, POWERaDE, Fruitopia, and other products developed for specific countries.

Through Coke's Minute Maid division, the company produces a variety of Minute Maid juices and soft drinks, Five Alive, Bright & Early, Bacardi brand tropical fruit mixers, and Hi-C fruit drinks. It is the world's largest distributor of juices and juice products.

Coke is by far the company's leading brand, accounting for about 62 percent of all beverage sales. Coca-Cola is the world's most recognized trademark.

The company quenches thirsts in nearly 200 countries around the globe. North American sales account for about 39 percent of Coke's $20 billion a year in revenue. Other regions where Coke beverages are sold include Europe, 21 percent of revenue; Asia-Pacific, 25 percent; Africa and the Middle East, 4 percent; and Latin America, 11 percent.

Mexicans drink the most Coke products, with a per capita consumption rate of 459 servings per year. Other leading markets include Chile, 346 servings per year; Australia, 292; Spain, 255; Argentina, 224; and Germany, 204. The company is focusing more effort on China, where per capita consumption is just 8 servings per year. But with 1.5 billion people, the Chinese market could become extremely lucrative if Coke could push consumption rates up to levels similar to Europe and South America.

Founded in 1886, Coca-Cola has about 37,000 employees and 366,000 shareholders. The company has a market capitalization of about $110 billion.

EARNINGS PER SHARE GROWTH

Past 5 years: 26 percent (5 percent per year)
Past 10 years: 190 percent (24 percent per year)

STOCK GROWTH   ★ ★

Past 10 years: 377 percent (17 percent per year)
Dollar growth: $10,000 over 10 years (including reinvested dividends) would have grown to $52,000.
Average annual compounded rate of return (including reinvested dividends): 18 percent

CONSISTENCY   ★ ★

Increased earnings per share: 8 of the past 10 years
Increased sales: 9 of the past 10 years

DIVIDEND

Dividend yield: 1.4 percent
Increased dividend: 39 consecutive years
Past 5-year increase: 54 percent (9 percent per year)
Good dividend reinvestment and stock purchase plan; voluntary stock purchase plan allows contributions of $10 to $125,000 per year.

COCA-COLA AT A GLANCE

Fiscal year ended: Dec. 31
Revenue and net income in $millions

	1995	1996	1997	1998	1999	2000	5-Year Growth Avg. Annual (%)	Total (%)
Revenue ($)	18,127	18,673	18,868	18,813	19,805	20,458	2	13
Net income ($)	2,986	3,492	4,129	3,533	2,431	2,177	—	–27
Earnings/share ($)	1.17	1.38	1.64	1.42	1.30	1.48	5	26
Dividends/share ($)	0.44	0.50	0.56	0.60	0.64	0.68	9	54
Dividend yield (%)	1.4	0.95	0.84	0.9	1.1	1.12		
PE range	21–34	26–39	30–44	37–62	48–72	49–76		

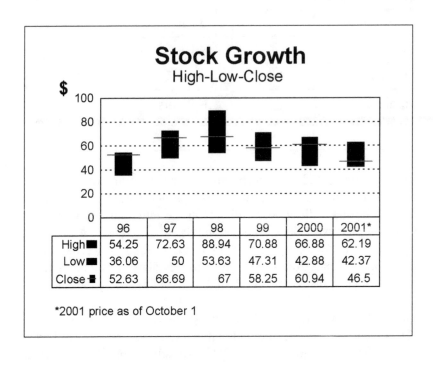

Stock Growth
High-Low-Close

	96	97	98	99	2000	2001*
High■	54.25	72.63	88.94	70.88	66.88	62.19
Low■	36.06	50	53.63	47.31	42.88	42.37
Close■	52.63	66.69	67	58.25	60.94	46.5

*2001 price as of October 1

PepsiCo, Inc.

700 Anderson Hill Road
Purchase, NY 10577
914-253-2000
NYSE: PEP
www.pepsico.com

Chairman and CEO: Steven Reinemund
President: Indra Nooyi

Earnings Growth	
Stock Growth	★ ★
Consistency	★ ★
Dividend	★ ★
Total	**6 Points**

Through good times and bad, Americans never lose their love for snack food. With its line of soft drinks, Frito-Lay chips, and Tropicana beverages, PepsiCo has been a willing coconspirator in the fattening of America—while fattening its own balance sheet along the way.

PepsiCo has about a 32 percent share of the U.S. soft drink market—ranking second to Coca-Cola—while its Frito-Lay division is far and away the market leader in snack chips both in the United States and around the world.

Frito-Lay controls about a 58 percent share of the U.S. chip market and a 28 percent share of the international market. It is the maker of Lay's potato chips, Fritos, Doritos, Cheetos, Ruffles, Tostitos, Sun Chips, Cracker Jack, and other snack chips. The snack food division accounts for about 64 percent of the company's $20 billion in annual revenue.

The company's soft drink division accounts for about 25 percent of total revenue, while its Tropicana division makes up the other 11 percent.

The Purchase, New York operation's flagship Pepsi-Cola brand accounts for 45 percent of PepsiCo's beverage sales in North America, followed by Mountain Dew (21 percent), diet colas (18 percent), and Lipton teas (4 percent). Other carbonated drinks make up 6 percent, other non-carbonated drinks account for 3 percent, and Aquafina water makes up the other 3 percent.

PepsiCo recently added to its arsenal of brand-name snacks and beverages by acquiring the Quaker Oats Company. Quaker's leading products include Gatorade, Quaker granola bars, rice cakes, and fruit and oatmeal bars, and such cereals as Oatmeal, Life, and Cap'n Crunch.

PepsiCo sells its products in about 200 countries around the world. About 30 percent of its sales come from outside the United States.

PepsiCo spun off its massive chain of fast-food franchises (Taco Bell, Pizza Hut, and Kentucky Fried Chicken) in 1997, and sold a majority stake of its Pepsi-Cola bottling subsidiary in 1999. It also bought Tropicana from Seagram in 1998.

Pepsi-Cola was first introduced in 1919, but the present-day company was formed in 1965 through the merger of Pepsi-Cola and Frito-Lay. The company has about 118,000 employees and 207,000 shareholders. It has a market capitalization of about $65 billion.

EARNINGS PER SHARE GROWTH

Past 5 years: 19 percent (3 percent per year)
Past 10 years: 124 percent (8.5 percent per year)

STOCK GROWTH   ★ ★

Past 10 years: 307 percent (15 percent per year)
Dollar growth: $10,000 over 10 years (including reinvested dividends) would have grown to $46,000.
Average annual compounded rate of return (including reinvested dividends): 16.5 percent

CONSISTENCY

Increased earnings per share: 8 of the past 10 years
Increased sales: 8 of the past 10 years

DIVIDEND   ★ ★

Dividend yield: 1.2 percent
Increased dividend: More than 25 consecutive years
Past 5-year increase: 43 percent (7.5 percent per year)
Good dividend reinvestment and stock purchase plan; voluntary stock purchase plan allows contributions of $25 to $5,000 per month.

PEPSICO AT A GLANCE

Fiscal year ended: Dec. 31
Revenue and net income in $millions

	1995	1996	1997	1998	1999	2000	5-Year Growth Avg. Annual (%)	5-Year Growth Total (%)
Revenue ($)	30,421	31,645	20,917	22,348	20,367	20,438	—	–33
Net income ($)	1,990	1,865	1,730	1,760	1,845	2,183	2	10
Earnings/share ($)	1.24	1.17	1.10	1.16	1.23	1.48	3	19
Dividends/share ($)	0.39	0.45	0.49	0.52	0.54	0.56	7.5	43
Dividend yield (%)	1.7	1.5	1.4	1.3	1.5	1.4		
PE range	14–23	46–61	30–43	21–34	21–31	20–33		

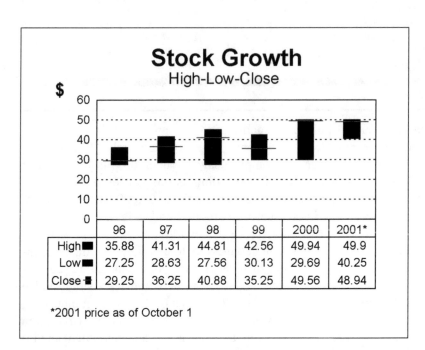

Stock Growth
High-Low-Close

	96	97	98	99	2000	2001*
High■	35.88	41.31	44.81	42.56	49.94	49.9
Low■	27.25	28.63	27.56	30.13	29.69	40.25
Close-■	29.25	36.25	40.88	35.25	49.56	48.94

*2001 price as of October 1

Molex, Inc.

2222 Wellington Court
Lisle, IL 60532
630-969-4550
Nasdaq: MOLX
www.molex.com

Co-Chairman: John H. Krehbiel
Co-Chairman: Frederick A. Krehbiel
President and CEO: J. Joseph King

Earnings Growth	
Stock Growth	★ ★ ★
Consistency	★ ★
Dividend	★
Total	**6 Points**

With its vast line of electronic and electrical connectors, Molex was able to ride the recent technology boom to unexpected highs. When boom turned to bust, however, the company saw a sudden drop in fortune. But Molex is still profitable and still expanding its line of offerings.

In all, the company manufactures more than 100,000 electronic, electrical, and fiber-optic interconnection products and switches. It is the second largest connector manufacturer in the world.

Molex markets its wires and connectors to a variety of industries, including computer (33 percent of revenue); telecommunications (26 percent); automotive (16 percent); consumer, including televisions, video games, Internet applications, and related products (15 percent); industrial, including factory robotics, power equipment, controls, and transportation equipment (6 percent); and other areas, such as medical equipment and instrumentation (4 percent).

The Chicago-based operation is global in scope, with 52 plants in 19 countries and sales in more than 50 countries around the world. Foreign sales account for about 61 percent of the company's $2.2 billion annual revenue.

Molex was founded in 1938 in Brookfield, Illinois, as a manufacturer of a plastic molding material developed by company founder, Frederick Krehbiel. Trademarked "Molex," the material was used for a variety of products, including toy guns and clock castings.

A few years later, the company discovered that its Molex plastic had excellent electrical insulating properties and began using it for a variety of electrical connection applications. Today, the company's selection of more than 100,000 products includes electric terminals, connectors, planer cables, cable assemblies, backplanes, and mechanical and electric switches. The firm also manufactures crimping machines and terminal inserting equipment.

Molex sells its goods almost entirely to original manufacturers for use in other products rather than to consumers or retailers.

Molex has about 18,000 employees and 12,000 shareholders. It has a market capitalization of about $7 billion.

EARNINGS PER SHARE GROWTH

Past 5 years: 39 percent (7 percent per year)
Past 10 years: 202 percent (12 percent per year)

STOCK GROWTH ★ ★ ★

Past 10 years: 445 percent (18.5 percent per year)
Dollar growth: $10,000 over 10 years (including reinvested dividends) would have grown to $55,000.
Average annual compounded rate of return (including reinvested dividends): 18.5 percent

CONSISTENCY ★ ★

Increased earnings per share: 8 of the past 10 years
Increased sales: 11 consecutive years

DIVIDEND ★

Dividend yield: 0.3 percent
Increased dividend: 22 consecutive years
Past 5-year increase: 233 percent (27 percent per year)
Molex does not offer a dividend reinvestment and stock purchase plan.

MOLEX AT A GLANCE

Fiscal year ended: June 30
Revenue and net income in $millions

	1996	1997	1998	1999	2000	2001	5-Year Growth Avg. Annual (%)	Total (%)
Revenue ($)	1,383	1,540	1,623	1,712	2,217	2,366	11	71
Net income ($)	145	167	182	178	222	204	7	41
Earnings/share ($)	0.74	0.85	0.93	0.92	1.12	1.03	7	39
Dividends/share ($)	0.03	0.04	0.05	0.05	0.09	0.10	27	233
Dividend yield (%)	0.2	0.2	0.2	0.2	0.3	0.3		
PE range	19–27	20–36	19–33	22–50	30–56	25–50		

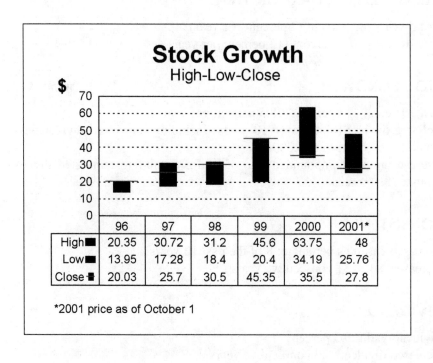

Stock Growth
High-Low-Close

$						
	96	97	98	99	2000	2001*
High	20.35	30.72	31.2	45.6	63.75	48
Low	13.95	17.28	18.4	20.4	34.19	25.76
Close	20.03	25.7	30.5	45.35	35.5	27.8

*2001 price as of October 1

100

Sigma-Aldrich Corporation

3050 Spruce Street
St. Louis, MO 63103
314-771-5765
Nasdaq: SIAL
www.sigma-aldrich.com

Chairman, President, and CEO: David R. Harvey

Earnings Growth	
Stock Growth	★
Consistency	★ ★
Dividend	★
Total	**4 Points**

Sigma-Aldrich keeps the world's research laboratories well stocked with biochemical and organic chemical products. The company supplies more than 80,000 chemicals used in scientific and genomic research, biotechnology, pharmaceutical development, chemical manufacturing, and medical diagnosis.

The St. Louis operation is the world's leading supplier of research chemicals and products used in life science and high-tech applications, with about a 13 percent share of the worldwide market. The company has distribution centers in 15 countries and sales in 160 countries. Foreign sales account for about 55 percent of total revenue.

The company also sends out 3.5 million catalogs and operates a Web site. Its scientific research unit accounts for about 55 percent of the company's $1.1 billion annual revenue.

The company also supplies chemicals and related products through three other business units, including:

- **Biotechnology** (20 percent of revenue). The company provides biochemicals and kits for biotechnology and human genome life science research. It is a key supplier in the areas of immunochemistry, cell culture, molecular biology, and chromatography, with a 9 percent share of the biotechnology chemicals industry. It is also a major manufacturer of synthetic DNA. The company is building a $55 million Life Science and Technology Center in St. Louis.
- **Fine chemicals** (17 percent). The firm supplies large-scale organic chemicals and biochemicals used in pharmaceutical, biotechnology, and high-technology industrial applications. It operates manufacturing facilities in five countries and has a global sourcing and procurement service with a database of 240,000 compounds.
- **Diagnostics** (6 percent). Sigma-Aldrich is a niche supplier of reagents and instruments used in medical diagnosis.

Of the roughly 85,000 chemicals and related products listed in the Sigma-Aldrich catalog, the company manufactures about half and purchases the other half from a variety of sources.

Sigma-Aldrich has about 6,100 employees and a market capitalization of about $3.2 billion.

EARNINGS PER SHARE GROWTH

Past 5 years: 31 percent (6 percent per year)
Past 10 years: 140 percent (9 percent per year)

STOCK GROWTH   ★

Past 10 years: 208 percent (12 percent per year)
Dollar growth: $10,000 over 10 years (including reinvested dividends) would have grown to about $34,000.
Average annual compounded rate of return (including reinvested dividends): 13 percent

CONSISTENCY

Increased earnings per share: 8 of the past 10 years
Increased sales: 9 of the past 10 years

DIVIDEND ★

Dividend yield: 1.0 percent
Increased dividend: 26 consecutive years
Past 5-year increase: 63 percent (10 percent per year)

SIGMA-ALDRICH AT A GLANCE

Fiscal year ended: Dec. 31
Revenue and net income in $millions

	1995	1996	1997	1998	1999	2000	5-Year Growth Avg. Annual (%)	Total (%)
Revenue ($)	960	1,035	1,127	1,194	1,038	1,096	2	14
Net income ($)	132	148	166	166	149	139	1	5
Earnings/share ($)	1.32	1.48	1.66	1.65	1.47	1.73	6	31
Dividends/share ($)	0.19	0.23	0.26	0.28	0.29	0.31	10	63
Dividend yield (%)	0.9	0.8	0.8	0.9	1.0	1.0		
PE range	14–20	16–22	19–29	17–29	16–23	12–24		

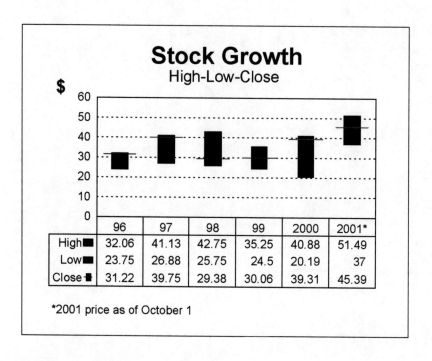

Stock Growth
High-Low-Close

	96	97	98	99	2000	2001*
High■	32.06	41.13	42.75	35.25	40.88	51.49
Low■	23.75	26.88	25.75	24.5	20.19	37
Close-■	31.22	39.75	29.38	30.06	39.31	45.39

*2001 price as of October 1

The 100 Best Stocks by Industry

Industry	Ranking
ALCOHOLIC BEVERAGES	
Anheuser-Busch Companies, Inc.	52
APPAREL	
Jones Apparel Group, Inc.	72
AUTOMOTIVE	
Harley-Davidson, Inc.	13
BANKING AND LENDING	
BB&T Corp.	25
Fannie Mae	10
Fifth Third Bancorp	4
Freddie Mac	12
Household International, Inc.	23
MBNA Corp.	20
M&T Bank Corp.	24
SouthTrust Corp.	7
SunTrust Banks, Inc.	70
Synovus Financial Corp.	17
U.S. Bancorp	3
Wells Fargo & Co.	62
CHEMICALS, COATINGS, AND CLEANSERS	
Cambrex Corp.	78
Ecolab, Inc.	43
Sherwin-Williams Co.	77
Sigma-Aldrich Corp.	100
Valspar Corp.	64
COMPUTERS AND RELATED TECHNOLOGY	
Altera Corp.	82
Cisco Systems	93
Dell Computer Corp.	57

Industry	Ranking
COMPUTERS AND RELATED TECHNOLOGY, continued	
EMC Corp.	59
Intel Corp.	41
Linear Technology Corp.	48
Maxim Integrated Products	54
Microsoft Corp.	31
Oracle Corp.	37
Veritas Software Corp.	84
CONSTRUCTION	
Toll Brothers, Inc.	51
CONSUMER PRODUCTS	
Colgate-Palmolive Co.	39
The Procter & Gamble Co.	74
CORPORATE SERVICES	
ABM Industries	69
Automatic Data Processing, Inc.	46
Cintas Corp.	21
Concord EFS, Inc.	32
Equifax, Inc.	96
First Data Corp.	90
Fiserv, Inc.	29
Interpublic Group of Companies	47
Omnicom Group, Inc.	18
Paychex, Inc.	2
ELECTRONICS	
Emerson Electric Co.	81
General Electric Co.	11
Molex, Inc.	99
ENERGY	
Chevron Corp.	87
FOOD AND BEVERAGE PRODUCTION	
Coca-Cola Co.	97
ConAgra Foods, Inc.	91

Industry	**Ranking**

FOOD AND BEVERAGE PRODUCTION, continued

Hershey Foods Co.	94
PepsiCo, Inc.	98
Sara Lee Corp.	83
Sysco Corp.	27
William Wrigley, Jr. & Co.	88

FOOD AND DRUG RETAIL

The Kroger Co.	66
Safeway, Inc.	56
Walgreen Co.	14

HEALTH CARE AND MEDICAL

Abbott Laboratories	61
Amgen, Inc.	50
Biogen, Inc.	79
Biomet, Inc.	76
Bristol-Myers Squibb Co.	38
Cardinal Health	30
Johnson & Johnson	15
Eli Lilly & Co.	73
Medtronic, Inc.	8
Merck & Company, Inc.	9
Pfizer, Inc.	5
Schering-Plough Corp.	22
Stryker Corp.	36
Universal Health Services, Inc.	55

INDUSTRIAL EQUIPMENT AND SUPPLIES

Danaher Corp.	49
Dionex Corp.	95
Donaldson Company, Inc.	44
Fastenal Co.	34
Tyco International, Ltd.	63
United Technologies Corp.	86

INSURANCE

AFLAC, Inc.	40
American International Group, Inc.	67

Industry	Ranking
INSURANCE, continued	
Jefferson-Pilot Corp.	42
UnitedHealth Group, Inc.	58
INVESTING AND FINANCIAL	
Alliance Capital Management Holding LP	1
AOL Time Warner, Inc.	85
Franklin Resources, Inc.	45
Legg Mason, Inc.	35
State Street Corp.	16
T. Rowe Price Group, Inc.	6
OFFICE EQUIPMENT AND SUPPLIES	
Avery Dennison Corp.	71
Herman Miller	89
Pitney Bowes, Inc.	68
PACKAGING	
Bemis Co.	80
RESTAURANTS	
McDonald's Corp.	92
Sonic Corp.	75
Starbucks Corp.	53
RETAIL	
Bed Bath & Beyond, Inc.	33
Best Buy Co., Inc.	65
Home Depot, Inc.	19
Kohl's Corp.	26
Wal-Mart Stores, Inc.	28
TRANSPORTATION	
Southwest Airlines Co.	60

The 100 Best Stocks by State

State	Ranking
ALABAMA	
SouthTrust Corp. (Birmingham)	7
ARKANSAS	
Wal-Mart Stores, Inc. (Bentonville)	28
CALIFORNIA	
ABM Industries (San Francisco)	69
Altera Corp. (San Jose)	82
Amgen, Inc. (Thousand Oaks)	50
Avery Dennison Corp. (Pasadena)	71
Chevron Corp. (San Francisco)	87
Cisco Systems (San Jose)	93
Dionex Corp. (Sunnyvale)	95
Franklin Resources, Inc. (San Mateo)	45
Intel Corp. (Santa Clara)	41
Linear Technology Corp. (Milpitas)	48
Maxim Integrated Products (Sunnyvale)	54
Oracle Corp. (Redwood Shores)	37
Safeway, Inc. (Pleasanton)	56
Veritas Software Corp. (Mountain View)	84
Wells Fargo & Co. (San Francisco)	62
COLORADO	
First Data Corp. (Greenwood)	90
CONNECTICUT	
General Electric Co. (Fairfield)	11
Pitney Bowes, Inc. (Stamford)	68
United Technologies Corp. (New Hampshire)	86
DELAWARE	
MBNA Corp. (Wilmington)	20

State	Ranking
DISTRICT OF COLUMBIA	
Danaher Corp. (Washington)	49
Fannie Mae (Washington)	10
GEORGIA	
AFLAC, Inc. (Columbus)	40
Coca-Cola Co. (Atlanta)	97
Equifax, Inc. (Atlanta)	96
Home Depot, Inc. (Atlanta)	19
SunTrust Banks, Inc. (Atlanta)	70
Synovus Financial Corp. (Columbus)	17
ILLINOIS	
Abbott Laboratories (Abbott Park)	61
Household International, Inc. (Prospect Heights)	23
McDonald's Corp. (Oak Brook)	92
Molex, Inc. (Lisle)	99
Sara Lee Corp. (Chicago)	83
Walgreen Co. (Deerfield)	14
William Wrigley, Jr. & Co. (Chicago)	88
INDIANA	
Biomet, Inc. (Warsaw)	76
Eli Lilly & Co. (Indianapolis)	73
MARYLAND	
Legg Mason, Inc. (Baltimore)	35
T. Rowe Price Group, Inc. (Baltimore)	6
MASSACHUSETTS	
Biogen, Inc. (Cambridge)	79
EMC Corp. (Hopkinton)	59
State Street Corp. (Boston)	16
MICHIGAN	
Herman Miller (Zeeland)	89
Stryker Corp. (Kalamazoo)	36

State	Ranking

MINNESOTA

Bemis Co. (Minneapolis)	80
Best Buy Co., Inc. (Eden Prairie)	65
Donaldson Co., Inc. (Minneapolis)	44
Ecolab, Inc. (St. Paul)	43
Fastenal Co. (Winona)	34
Medtronic, Inc. (Minneapolis)	8
UnitedHealth Group, Inc. (Minnetonka)	58
U.S. Bancorp (Minneapolis)	3
Valspar Corp. (Minneapolis)	64

MISSOURI

Anheuser-Busch Companies, Inc. (St. Louis)	52
Emerson Electric Co. (St. Louis)	81
Sigma-Aldrich Corp. (St. Louis)	100

NEBRASKA

ConAgra Foods, Inc. (Omaha)	91

NEW HAMPSHIRE

Tyco International, Ltd. (Exeter)	63

NEW JERSEY

Automatic Data Processing, Inc. (Roseland)	46
Bed Bath & Beyond, Inc. (Union)	33
Cambrex Corp. (East Rutherford)	78
Johnson & Johnson (New Brunswick)	15
Merck & Co. Inc. (Whitehouse Station)	9
Schering-Plough Corp. (Kenilworth)	22

NEW YORK

Alliance Capital Management Holding LP (New York)	1
American International Group, Inc. (New York)	67
AOL Time Warner, Inc. (New York)	85
Bristol-Myers Squibb Co. (New York)	38
Colgate-Palmolive Co. (New York)	39
Interpublic Group of Companies (New York)	47
M&T Bank Corp. (Buffalo)	24

State	Ranking

NEW YORK, continued

Omnicom Group, Inc. (New York)	18
Paychex, Inc. (Rochester)	2
PepsiCo, Inc. (Purchase)	98
Pfizer, Inc. (New York)	5

NORTH CAROLINA

BB&T Corp. (Winston-Salem)	25
Jefferson-Pilot Corp. (Greensboro)	42

OHIO

Cardinal Health (Dublin)	30
Cintas Corp. (Cincinnati)	21
Fifth Third Bancorp (Cincinnati)	4
The Kroger Co. (Cincinnati)	66
The Procter & Gamble Co. (Cincinnati)	74
Sherwin-Williams Co. (Cleveland)	77

OKLAHOMA

Sonic Corp. (Oklahoma City)	75

PENNSYLVANIA

Hersey Foods Co. (Hershey)	94
Jones Apparel Group, Inc. (Bristol)	72
Toll Brothers, Inc. (Huntingdon Valley)	51
Universal Health Services, Inc. (King of Prussia)	55

TENNESSEE

Concord EFS, Inc. (Memphis)	32

TEXAS

Dell Computer Corp. (Round Rock)	57
Southwest Airlines Co. (Dallas)	60
Sysco Corp. (Houston)	27

VIRGINIA

Freddie Mac (McLean)	12

State	Ranking

WASHINGTON

Microsoft Corp. (Redmond)	31
Starbucks Corp. (Seattle)	53

WISCONSIN

Fiserv, Inc. (Brookfield)	29
Harley-Davidson, Inc. (Milwaukee)	13
Kohl's Corp. (Menomonee Falls)	26

Index

FREE ONLINE RESEARCH
at
AllstarStocks.com

Follow many of the *100 Best Stocks* and take advantage of a broad range of investment information and links to valuable research tools at Gene Walden's Web site, <www.allstarstocks.com>.

AllstarStocks.com, which is currently free, includes occasional articles by Gene Walden and other research information designed to help investors track and analyze stocks and mutual funds.